"I have a pretty short attention _____ ɔook down. *The Rabbi and the CEO* is carefully researched and ɯ ᴕ read, and it's one of those extremely rare books that give mere mortals real access to great management. If you lead anything, do yourself a favor: Get this book. It offers a kind of leadership power that is all too often missing in boardrooms and that you simply won't find elsewhere."

—ALI VELSHI
CNN Senior Business Correspondent and host of *Your $$$$$*

"*The Rabbi and the CEO* provides an insightful "lighthouse" to navigate the dynamic world of leadership and management in the 21st century. More than ever in today's challenging environment, authentic leadership and a strong moral compass are paramount, and this book provides strong insight and tools into these critical areas for success."

—DR. MARTIN CROSS
CEO, Novartis-Australia

"As the CEO of UJA-Federation, I find myself speaking to audiences all over the Jewish community about leadership, values and the "vision deficit" in our organizations and communities. All our institutions can benefit from better management and leadership. *The Rabbi and the CEO* is engaging, packed with insights, rich in perspectives, and yes, wisdom. The writing keeps the reader (or at least this reader) absorbed. I recommend this volume to all those, both in the Jewish community and far beyond, who must lead today. Kol ha'kavod."

—DR. JOHN RUSKAY
Executive Vice President and CEO, UJA

"In an age where anything goes, and unfortunately almost anything does, it's refreshing to rediscover a familiar anchor. The leadership wisdom contained here is timeless, powerful and actionable—just what you'd expect when you combine a Rabbi and a CEO!"

—SCOTT A. SNOOK
Professor of Organizational Behavior, Harvard Business School

"In my 30 years as the leader of The Hunger Project, I have faced all the challenges any 21st-century leader will ever face, from mobilizing a truly global movement to fostering alignment on a nearly impossible vision, from empowering leaders at all levels of society to keeping the organization true to its mission under intensely adverse circumstances. I am pleased that today's and tomorrow's leaders will have *The Rabbi and the CEO* as a guide at their side. This compelling work of scholarship and humanity helps leaders tackle seemingly insurmountable challenges. Above all, it is a manual for that most elusive of leadership skills: unleashing the human spirit."

—JOAN HOLMES
Founding President, The Hunger Project;
Member, UN Millenium Project Hunger Task Force

"It has been said that you can tell the worth of a person's religion not by how he acts in synagogue on Saturday or in church on Sunday, but by what he does in business Monday through Friday. In *The Rabbi and the CEO*, a highly creative application of the Ten Commandments, Dr. Zweifel and Rabbi Raskin have a great deal to teach us and each other about living both a godly life and, in every way, a successful one."

—RABBI JOSEPH TELUSHKIN
Author of *Jewish Literacy* and *A Code of Jewish Ethics*

"As leaders in business and in life, we need breakthroughs in how we think and act for the uncharted territory of our future. This book provokes and inspires us to build this leadership capacity in ourselves and others. Act now."

—ANNE GRISWOLD
Director Organizational Effectiveness,
LifeScan, a Johnson & Johnson company

"An invaluable moral compass for today's turbulent times. Buy this book; sell your kidneys if you have to."

—RABBI SIMCHA WEINSTEIN
Author of *Up, Up and Oy Vey* and *Shtick Shift*

"This is powerful stuff. In turbulent times, more and more managers, in Japan and elsewhere, draw inspiration from the Bible. I have built my company on these principles and tools, from checking my own blind spots and letting go of control, to effective communication with my people and global citizenship, to turning breakdowns into breakthroughs. *The Rabbi and the CEO* makes the difference between a good company and a great company."

—MIKIO UEKUSA
Chairman, Akebono Corporation, Japan

"Do we have any true leaders today, or are we all followers? In response to our current crisis of leadership, Dr. Thomas D. Zweifel and Rabbi Aaron L. Raskin, in a fascinating collaboration, have created an important and uplifting book—a profound and practical guide for both active and aspiring leaders. Based on the timeless Ten Commandments, *The Rabbi and the CEO* offers a timely model for leaders of the 21st Century."

—SIMON JACOBSON
Author of *Toward a Meaningful Life*

"This book has the merits of relevance and reverence. It offers relevant, pragmatic and sound business guidelines inspired and informed by profound reverence for the primary spiritual sources of the Jewish faith. I recommend it to all who care about the ethical values of our 'globalized' business world."

—RABBI DR. TZVI HERSH WEINREB
Executive Vice President, Union of Orthodox Jewish
Congregations of America

"The CEO and the Rabbi advise simple changes that have traction and generate results. It is an awesome project, it hits home, and I can apply it. Imperative reading for every CEO."

—LAWRENCE OBSTFELD
CEO, Image Navigation Ltd.

"Authors Raskin and Zweifel have provided us with a sorely needed exposition of the new leadership model based on the template of creation, the Torah—the Jewish wisdom teachings. Its core principles and central pillars provide a powerful light at the end of the darkened tunnel of the twenty-first century. The authors' prowess as social commentators is matched by scholarly underpinnings allowing their words to ring true.

Leadership holds the key to the 'new world.' But leadership is no longer the domain of those in positions of power. Today, in a world where view and opinion has been democratized through the Internet, leadership devolves on each and every one of us. Each one of us holds the key to the global future. The authors have done us a great service in putting that key into our hands. Dare we unlock the door that Torah provides to create a much better way? If we continue on the current path of egoism and insecurity, 'that way madness lies.'"

—RABBI LAIBL WOLF
Australia; Author of *Practical Kabbalah*

"*The Rabbi and the CEO* couldn't be more timely. As the financial industry is being rocked by a tsunami, this book provides an anchor in the rough seas of volatile global markets and corruption scandals. More personally, the financial and career successes I have enjoyed have all come from living the lessons in this book. Just read it. It's the highest-leverage investment you could make in your future."

—MICHAEL S. BROMBERG
Senior Vice President, Global Wealth Management

"Judaism's ideal is to join wisdom and wealth. A dynamic CEO and a dynamite Rabbi join to teach timeless principles to advance your career, cultivate your soul, and succeed spiritually and materially."

—MAGGID YITZHAK BUXBAUM
Author of *The Light and Fire of the Baal Shem Tov*

"Zweifel and Raskin take the Ten Commandments off the synagogue wall and put them where they belong—in the marketplace. There are valuable lessons here for today's leaders and decision makers."

—Professor Ari L. Goldman
Columbia University Graduate School of Journalism;
Author of *The Search for God at Harvard*

"Dr. Zweifel and Rabbi Raskin have provided a workable roadmap to understanding one of our greatest needs and mysteries—what is the meaning and impact of true leadership and how is it achieved? In my field of venture capital, they provide great vision and direction. 'Venture,5' in its broadest sense, is a new, freer way—the innovative changes that free all of us to enjoy new ways of living. 'Capital,' in its truest sense, is our inner resources. *The Rabbi and the CEO* demonstrates that the greatest source of capital comes not from our bank accounts, stock portfolios or corner offices, but from within each of us. After reading and rereading the book, I've learned so much, and I can't wait to impart it to venturers of every type."

—George Weiss
Founder and CEO, Beechtree Capital

"The inherited wisdom of Jewish tradition offers us guidance that is at once spiritual and practical. *The Rabbi and the CEO* offers the gift of this direction to 21st century leaders of all stripes. The book speaks to managers who want access to the principles and practices that have served leaders ever since Moses. It also provides state-of-the-art executive management tools for contemporary American religious leaders. Read it and you will gain the influence that comes from profound insight."

—Rabbi Tsvi Blanchard, Ph.D.
Director of Organizational Development, CLAL

"Moral values are the basis for the human race to prevail, and ethics are the fundamentals for leadership in business or any other activity. It's only natural to find a common denominator that links leaders in history and in business life. *The Rabbi and the CEO* is a very interesting effort to reflect the meaning of the Ten Commandments in the economic content of today. Exciting reading."

—DOV TADMOR
Chairman, Aviv Venture Capital

"Seamlessly bringing together ancient wisdom and 21st-century case studies, *The Rabbi and the CEO*'s impressive scope of inquiry and fresh ideas offers valuable insights for anyone interested in leadership. In the face of the leadership crisis in almost every walk of modern life, the book charts a road map to leadership at once effective and ethical, through a process looking both inward and outward. This book makes you stop and think, and then offers you tools to move forward."

—OREN GROSS
Irving Younger Professor of Law and Director, Institute for International Legal & Security Studies, University of Minnesota

"In Jewish prayer, the Torah is referred to as 'instructions for living.' For every dimension of life, the Torah contains timeless—and priceless—wisdom. This book brings the light of Jewish wisdom to people who carry particularly great responsibility in life: leaders."

—SHIMON APISDORF
Author of *Beyond Survival, Rosh Hashanah Yom Kippur Survival Kit* and *Kosher for the Clueless but Curious*

"As a senior executive who works at the intersection of Judaism and management, I found *The Rabbi and the CEO* an inspiring and indispensible guide and reference. It offers a perfect mix of ancient Jewish philosophy and state-of-the-art leadership tools—a mix that will give leaders an edge in today's complex ethical and global environment. Every nonprofit manager, indeed all leaders who are committed to something bigger than themselves, should read this book."

—SCOTT RICHMAN
Executive Director, Dor Chadash

A confronting (while highly entertaining) read, *The Rabbi and the CEO* summarizes the costs we pay when leadership is insufficient. The authors invite us to explore the possibility of our own leadership and, at the same time, bring contemporary meaning to the Ten Commandments for those who choose to lead.

—MEL TOOMEY
Scholar in Residence, Master of Arts in Organizational Leadership
at The Graduate Institute

The CEO and the Rabbi bring their unique and original insights into the Bible, and its leadership principles, to bear on today's leadership responsibilities. Readers will be inspired to apply the new dimensions of self-knowledge gained from the authors.

—MALCOLM ELVEY
Chairman of the Audit Committee,
The Children's Place Retail Stores Ltd.

"The Rabbi and the CEO: the 10 Commandments for 21st Century Leaders is a transparent title for a book that preaches transparency in everyday and corporate life. Rabbi Raskin and Dr. Zweifel make you look at the Ten Commandments in a new light. The Commandments are the foundation of Judeo-Christian religions and ethics, and religious in nature. The authors manage to approach each Commandment in a new light without denigrating its source and nature. Through a review of each Commandment and its core principles the book is a practical guide to personal growth, finding an ethical base, and developing one's ability to lead others in the private and public sectors regardless of one's personal religious beliefs."

—STEVEN Z. MOSTOFSKY
President, Young Israel

"It's about time someone did what these authors are doing: remind people that the distance from Mt. Sinai to Wall Street can be far or it can be very near. Reminding humans of what their limitations ought to be requires courage. Hoping that people will heed the words on these pages is an act of faith."

—HANK SHEINKOPF
Political strategist and CNN contributor

"Dr. Zweifel and Rabbi Raskin offer the reader a true convergence of worlds. Their work is revelatory in the best sense—a union of the ancient and the modern, the sum of heaven and earth, a compilation of style and substance. Here in brief is a latter-day decalogue of usable wisdom, a Mount Sinai for the 21st century."

—MICHAEL SKAKUN
Author of *On Burning Ground: A Son's Memoir*
and former consultant, Holocaust Memorial Council

"In my work with chief executives around the world I have found that the principles and practices in *The Rabbi and the CEO* have timeless applicability both for those clients and inside my own company. The insights presented by Zweifel and Raskin been very helpful to me in building a viable global business that operates ethically and from clear principles. Regardless of your religious beliefs, the lessons they present are universal and continue to be timely. This is a book executives should read and share with their co-workers."

—JAY GREENSPAN
Founder, JMJ Associates

The Rabbi
and
the CEO

The Rabbi
and
the CEO

*The Ten Commandments
for 21ˢᵗ Century Leaders*

Dr. Thomas D. Zweifel (CEO)
Aaron L. Raskin (Rabbi)

Foreword by Ali Velshi

SelectBooks, Inc.
New York

This edition published by SelectBooks, Inc.
For information address SelectBooks, Inc., New York, N.Y. 10003.

ISBN 978-1-59079-150-9

Library of Congress Cataloging-in-Publication Data

Zweifel, Thomas D., 1962-
   The rabbi and the CEO : the 10 commandments for 21st-century leaders /
Thomas D. Zweifel & Aaron L. Raskin (Rabbi) ; foreword by Ali Velshi. --
1st ed.
      p. cm.
   Includes bibliographical references and index.
   ISBN 978-1-59079-150-9 (hbk. : alk. paper)
   1. Leadership. 2. Leadership--Religious aspects--Judaism. I. Raskin,
Aaron L., 1967- II. Title.

HD57.7.Z94 2008
658.4'092--dc22

                               2007052083

Manufactured in the United States of America

10 9 8 7 6 5 4 3 2 1

The great and wise
Rabbi Simcha Bunam of Przysucha
once said to his students:
"I wanted to write a book, it should be called Adam,
and in it should be the whole human being.
But then I thought of not writing this book."
We were not so wise.

—the Authors

Contents

Foreword

Tradition means giving votes to the most obscure of all classes,
our ancestors.
It is the democracy of the dead.
Tradition refuses to submit to the small and arrogant oligarchy
of those who merely happen to be walking about.
—G.K. Chesterton

During my years at CNN, I've spoken to and worked with countless business leaders. Interviewing them always made me wonder: What makes a truly great leader? Is it something you're born with? Or can leadership be taught? Can someone be coached into leadership, like so many books I see at airport bookshops proclaim? Is leadership a function of the situation (Would Churchill have risen to greatness without facing the menace of Hitler? Remember, Churchill wasn't reelected after winning World War II)? Or is leadership a function of culture, with certain cultures breeding leaders better than others?

The authors of *The Rabbi and the CEO* have arrived at an innovative and powerful answer. Blending time-honored traditions with cutting-edge management methods, this book produces an amalgam that offers leaders (and leaders-in-waiting) a kind of power that's often missing in boardrooms. Steeped in the rich, ancient tradition of Jewish thought, this book makes the timeless wisdom of the ages directly relevant to today's business leaders.

The unique synergy comes from an unusual partnership: the prominent Rabbi Aaron Raskin, eloquent spokesman for Judaism, and author of *Letters of Light*; and Dr. Thomas D. Zweifel, a CEO and leadership professor and consultant in his own right, and the author of four previous books on leadership and people power, including *Communicate or Die* and *Culture Clash*.

Why Judaism? Don't other traditions offer equally profound and rich principles and insightful stories? Yes, all roads lead to Rome, and there are countless ways to reveal essential truth. On the anniversary of a death, for example, Catholics offer a memorial mass; Muslims might read the 36th chapter of the Qur'an; Protestants might gather to sing hymns like the early twentieth-century song "Tell Mother I'll Be There"; Hindus might cook the favorite meal of the deceased, bring it to the temple and serve it to the priest; Buddhists might burn special counterfeit money known as ghost money to repay the dead for their kindness; the Haida Indians of the American Northwest might set out a meal and burn the whole table; and Jews say the *kadish* prayer on the *yahrzeit* of their dead every year. Most everyone, it seems, lights a candle.

But Jews are not universally called the People of the Book by accident. Their book, the Torah—the five books of Moses, also called the Pentateuch from the Greek word for "five"; or, by gentiles, the Old Testament—is a sheer boundless fount of stories about leaders and their moral dilemmas, from Abraham to Noah, from Eve to Sarah, from Moses to David. The Hebrew Bible is chock-full of leaders' trials, tribulations, and triumphs. And if leadership is about freeing yourself from the shackles of the past and achieving a desired future, the Jews undertook one of the boldest collective emancipations of all time when they left Egypt. The Hebrew word for Egypt is *mitzrayim*, which means "the narrows." A core objective of the Torah is to remove us from our own Egypt: to help us transcend our limitations, unleash our indomitable human spirit, and be all we can be. That is what true leadership is all about: enabling people to be themselves, take charge, and fulfill their highest aspirations.

But the Rabbi and the CEO did not stop there. They found that when they married teachings from Torah and Talmud with modern leadership models, the combination yielded powerful insights into today's leadership challenges—trials that would have given even great leaders like Churchill or Kennedy a headache—and useful instruments for tackling any issue that might confront a twenty-first-century manager. How do you keep your moral compass when you face an ethical dilemma? How do you restore the big picture in the clutter of the day-to-day? How do you communicate effectively to mobilize highly mobile knowledge workers for results? How do you manage outsourcing, off-shoring, or virtual teams through remote empowerment across borders? How do you minimize wasteful chatter in meetings, and turn complaints into commitments? How do you keep your eye on the ball, not merely on what's urgent, but on what's important? How do you deal with adversaries who sabotage your efforts? And *the* skill that distinguishes leaders from non-leaders: How do you turn a bitter lemon into sweet lemonade?

To answer these questions, *The Rabbi and the CEO* takes you into the lives of leaders across history, Jewish and non-Jewish, to distill principles and practices based on the Ten Commandments and Jewish teachings. You will go into the wilderness to meet the Jewish leader mentioned most often in both the Bible and the Qur'an: Moses. You will see how Moses became a leader despite his stammer (much like Gandhi in our time), parted the waters of the Red Sea for his people, pioneered a system of delegation (thanks to his father-in-law Jethro, the world's first "management consultant"), and helped his followers keep their vision until they reached the Promised Land.

The result: *The Rabbi and the CEO* arms you with the tools you need to be an ethical and effective leader—now and in the future. And since these tools have stood the test of time, they are built to last, for managers of all stripes. Just as the ad once said, "You don't have to be Jewish to love Levy's rye bread," leaders don't have to be Jewish to appreciate, and apply, Jewish teachings. These principles work: They make for the leadership DNA that has led a tiny group (some 0.2 percent of the world population and 2 percent of Americans) to provide 17 percent of all Nobel laureates in physiology and medicine, 11 percent of physics Nobelists, and 10 percent of U.S. senators.

It's simple: When leaders veer from these teachings, they fail. Great leaders, on the other hand, whether they are Moses or Mandela, transcend themselves. They reach beyond their own narrow interests and embrace the well-being of the many around them. Moses Maimonides, the great twelfth-century scholar in Egypt, wrote that the world is like a scale: one side is 50 percent good, the other 50 percent bad. Any action can tip the scale either to one side or the other. One selfless executive decision can bring salvation, peace, and harmony to the whole world. Churchill put it this way: "You make a living by what you get; but you make a life by what you give." If you truly dare, you can change the world for good. So I hope that people everywhere will enjoy this carefully researched and fun-to-read book as thoroughly as I did, and turn its powerful lessons into practice as they build a better world.

ALI VELSHI
Anchor & Senior Business Correspondent, CNN
New York City, August 2008

Why the Ten Commandments for 21st Century Leaders?

Again and again
Someone in the crowd wakes up.
He has no ground in the crowd
And he emerges according to much broader laws.
He carries strange customs with him
and demands room for bold gestures.
The future speaks ruthlessly through him.
—Rainer Maria Rilke (Über Kunst, 1899)

This book would probably not have come into being were it not for a perfectly clear day in September 2001, an Indian-summer morning when the sky was deep blue. I (the CEO) was sitting on the Brooklyn Promenade—alone except for a few runners and dog walkers—and reading Michel Houellebecq's *Les Particules Élémentaires* when I looked up at 8:46 a.m. and saw something I had never seen before: A plane hit the World Trade Center. Smoke and millions of tiny metallic glitters were in the air; a light wind swept them toward me. The glitters turned out to be countless papers, documents flying across the East River. One of them was a page from a civil law book, blackened on all four sides. Another was a FedEx envelope with a contract that someone had just signed a few minutes earlier.

About a half-hour later another plane flew in from Staten Island, right over the Statue of Liberty. It flew low and accelerated head-on toward those of us now gathered at the Promenade. It banked like a fighter plane, its dark underbelly visible—a terrifying sight that you usually see only in war zones or in movies. Suddenly the plane ducked behind a skyscraper, and a moment later disappeared into the South

Tower. By this time there were about a dozen people watching, speechless and transfixed. I called as many people as I could on my mobile phone, but got through only to my parents' answering machine in Sydney before my phone went dead. Then I saw one tower collapse, then the other. My knees gave in; I staggered to a bench, sat down, and wept. It was hard to breathe.

Like so many others, the only productive thing I could think of doing was to donate blood. It seemed a drop in the bucket. That day of calamity, and the days and years following it, exposed the most pressing issue of our time: Leadership is in a crisis. The Pentagon, FBI, and CIA were all ill-equipped for terrorist attacks or even for reading the writing on the wall. But the crisis affects organizations in all sectors: government agencies, nongovernmental organizations, and international organizations whose leaders struggle with mega-issues like economic volatility, climate change, poverty, or AIDS that transcend national and organizational boundaries. And not least, the crisis is shaking the private sector. When Enron and Andersen, Worldcom and Swissair all collapsed within a year of 9/11, they were just harbingers of things to come. Today, despite an abundance of leadership books (a search on Amazon.com yielded 191,530 hits), the leadership crisis continues unabated. Look at the big challenges facing companies today: Turbulent change such as a U.S. sub-prime mortgage crisis that threatened to plunge the economy into a recession and led Bear Stearns to fall from a record high of $171 a share in January 2007 to near bankruptcy (in 2008, JP Morgan Chase, with heavy lifting by the Federal Reserve, agreed to buy the venerable investment bank for $10 a share); unrelenting pressure for results and corruption born of greed; post-merger pains and a deteriorating labor market ever since the 2000 dot-com crash; culture clashes and threats from India and China; lack of strategy alignment, loss of morale, and brain drain. What do all these issues have in common? Our (the Rabbi's and the CEO's) answer is, they all need leadership. Call us biased, but we see the lack of twenty-first century leadership—leadership that can rise to meet the unprecedented challenges of our time—as the lynchpin issue that underlies all the others. It was of times like these that the economist and philosopher Kenneth Boulding said: "The greatest need for leadership is in the dark.... It is when the system is changing so rapidly...that old prescriptions and old wisdoms can only lead to catastrophe and leadership is necessary to call people to the very strangeness of the new world being born."

Why do we say crisis (and we take the word, much like the Chinese character for crisis, as meaning "danger" combined with "opportunity")? Two reasons: for one, ethical decision-making seems to have taken a long vacation. For too many executives, the game has become about looking good: fudging the numbers in the relentless pursuit of elusive and fickle shareholders. Ken Lay, Jeff Skilling and Andrew Fastow of Enron were only the most visible cases. Witness Maurice Greenberg, the imperial ex-chief of AIG who was subpoenaed and ousted by his own board after a forty-year tenure; Gary Winnick of Global Crossing and Bernie Ebbers of WorldCom; Lloyd Silverstein and other senior managers who lied in a federal inquiry into Computer Associates' accounting; Adelphia and Tyco; Boeing and Putnam; HealthSouth and Prudential; Parmalat and the Bank of Japan; Martha Stewart and Samuel Israel, and—surprise—Greenberg's own son Jeffrey at Marsh McLennan.

Leaders like Steve Case of AOL or Bob Nardelli of Home Depot, once unassailable, have lost much of their luster. And business is not alone; the pandemic of deceit has infected the public and nonprofit sectors. The disgraced former New York Governor Eliot Spitzer was one of the more egregious examples of a state official who failed to walk his talk, gaining national attention as "sheriff of New York" who prosecuted businesses and prostitution rings while being a client of one high-priced sex ring himself. Corruption scandals have tainted more elected officials than we could list here, not to speak of autocratic leaders in the Middle East, or those who were not above poisoning Viktor Yushchenko to derail his campaign for the Ukrainian presidency. A U.S. federal judge presiding over a price-fixing case involving Monsanto conveniently failed to disclose to the parties in the case that in 1997-98 he himself had been a Monsanto lawyer in another case about some of the same issues—a clear conflict of interest.

Senior officials in the Catholic Church and the military have covered up sexual misconduct by priests and soldiers with conspiracies of silence, sometimes for decades. EU and UN bureaucrats have been charged with embezzling millions of euros or dollars. The son of Kofi Annan, the former UN secretary-general who supposedly embodied the moral conscience of the world community, stood accused of colluding with former Iraqi dictator Saddam Hussein to steal billions from the UN's oil-for-food program.[1]

And if you think senior officials are the only ones who cheat, think again. Corruption is wherever the money is. Remember how after Hurricane Katrina tore through the Gulf region, FEMA needed days to mobilize? Another group was on the scene much faster: profiteers. In Mississippi, a couple from Indiana rolled into Jackson and began selling generators out of a horse trailer for as much as $2,600 (they usually cost $700). In Texas, some budget motels charged refugees from Louisiana up to $300 a night—six times the normal rate.[2]

Even the world of sports is riddled with corruption; world records and gold medals have become tainted with suspicions of doping. In the 2000 Sydney Olympics, the U.S. athlete Jerome Young was a gold medalist in the 4x400 meter relays; in 2003 he became the 400-meter world champion; in 2004 he was suspended because of repeated use of illicit substances. And while baseball pitcher Roger Clemens, a seven-time Cy Young Award winner with 354 wins under his belt, issued indignant—and unconvincing—denials during his congressional testimony and in a *60 Minutes* interview in early 2008 ("never happened," he kept snapping at interviewer Mike Wallace), he was widely believed to have been injected with steroids and growth hormones by his former personal trainer, who admitted as much. Far from acting alone, athletes like Young and Clemens conspire with accomplices. "Now we recognize that not only the athlete but veritable teams are involved in the cheating: scientists, doctors, pharma marketers," explained Richard Pound, head of the World Anti-Doping Agency. "One can speak of organized crime…It taught me that people lie. When they're caught, they lie."[3]

Governments have sought to punish and deter ethical lapses. In the United States, after the corporate and accounting scandals of Enron, Tyco International, Adelphia, Peregrine Systems and Worldcom when the collapse of these companies' share prices cost investors billions of dollars and shook public confidence in the securities markets, the U.S.

Congress passed the Sarbanes-Oxley Act (in short SarbOx or SOx, after its sponsors, Sen. Paul Sarbanes, Democrat of Maryland, and Rep. Michael G. Oxley, Republican of Ohio); the 2002 federal law established stricter standards for all U.S. public company boards, management, and public accounting firms and set up an oversight agency. In 2007, China went further when it executed the corrupt head of its State Food and Drug Administration. But the real solution is not legal. Yes, better rules or policing might enhance accountability and transparency, but "There won't be quick fixes," admitted Robert Reynolds, chief operating officer of Fidelity Investments, with $906 billion under management at the world's largest fund manager. (He should know: In late 2003, the state of Massachusetts subpoenaed a salesperson from his own company for improper dealings.) Without morality, without leaders at all levels who can tackle ethical dilemmas, more regulation will not work. Since countless managers have lost their moral compass in the rough seas of globalization and deregulated markets, corporate America and organizations the world over must begin an internal process of renewal.

This book aims to help leaders at all levels find that compass again. *The Rabbi and the CEO* is about a fundamental change that's needed: change from within. It's a type of change that is hardly fashionable; boasting of outward successes is still much more popular. Loud and bossy leaders grab the headlines and thrust themselves into the limelight; think Donald Trump and *The Apprentice*. Quiet leaders are crowded out, lost in the background. The egomaniacs and their scandals are much more fun to watch and read about. Many of these so-called leaders lack the essentials, the fundamentals on which sound leadership is based, and which breed lasting success.

But ethics is only one aspect of the twin crisis of leadership. The other stems from an entirely different quarter: The old leadership model is bankrupt. Why? Because throughout history, leadership was scarce. The vast majority of people never asked themselves what to do. People were subjects; they were told what to do, and their work was dictated either by the nature of their work—for a peasant or a craftsman—or by the lord of the manor. Although Descartes and other later thinkers made a dent with the idea that humans could use their own powers of reason, even the Enlightenment did not fully transform the deeply ingrained culture: people did pretty much what they were told by their parents, superiors, or rulers. The Industrial Revolution that followed in the next century only compounded this mechanistic view; Frederick Taylor's efficiency "improvements" were the culmination of human beings as cogs in a wheel. Even in the 1950s and 1960s, the new knowledge workers (referred to as organization men at the time) looked to their company's personnel department to plan their careers for them. But starting with the late 1960s, the game changed. Young men and women asked, What do I *want* to do?[4] Several waves of democratization gave more and more people the idea that they had rights, they had a voice.

Then, in the 1990s, came the Internet. Google and Wikipedia put knowledge at people's fingertips with the click of a mouse. Now Skype and LinkedIn connect people across the world for free or next to nothing. Blogs have leveled the field of journalism. In the last century, consumers chose among a few TV channels and magazines; by 2007 there were were hundreds of cable channels on TV and 70 million blogs on the World Wide Web. MySpace and YouTube, where 65,000 videos are posted daily, have democratized entertainment and give any-one a shot at being a musician or movie director. Thanks to Macs and Web 2.0, you too can be an industrial designer in the new design democracy.[5] End-users know exactly what they want from the products they buy—more so than manufacturers—and so-called lead users are often on the forefront of innovation and product development, from software to high-performance windsurfing equipment.[6] It is no differ-ent in healthcare, where patients have stopped blindly trusting their doctors and instead demand answers and choice—something unthink-able a generation ago, when doctors were thought to be omniscient demigods whose judgment they never dared question.

Churchill was famous for saying that the higher you rise, the more clearly you see the big picture of vision and strategy. (He also said, somewhat presciently, that the higher the ape climbs, the more you can see of his bottom.) But is that still true today, when the receptionist or the front-line salesperson talks to customers every day and may have as much insight into the market as top managers and board members? Even the military has recognized that soldiers on the ground in Sadr City or Seoul have often more access to local strategic intelligence than the commanders at headquarters and need to take part in strategic decision-making. In complex environments, top-down strategy or leadership is obsolete. The good news is that leadership is no longer confined to the realm of the select few; it has become a public good. More people than ever before in history can now aspire to the mantle of leadership.

That is not to say that they do, or that the leadership craft has become any easier; quite the opposite. In fact people's desire to be in charge has diminished. Take chief executives. Leslie Gaines Ross, chief knowledge officer at Burson-Marsteller, surveyed executives at Fortune 1000 companies and asked how many of them craved being the head honcho. In 2001, 27 percent responded that they had no interest in being CEO; by 2005 that number had jumped to 64 percent in North America and 60 percent in Europe. Ross' explanation: "You take a lot of risk today in choosing the top job."[7] Indeed, in 2005, a record 1,322 chief executives left the corner office, both voluntarily and not; in 2006, departures (or firings, as the case may be) included the bosses of some of America's best-known companies: Ford Motor, Home Depot, Kraft Foods, Nike, Pfizer, RadioShack, UnitedHealth, et al. Sure, many CEOs have their own reasons for leaving. But according to the study, intense global competition, an impatient Wall Street pushing for instant results, and regulators on the war-path all contribute to corner office angst. Many CEOs feel under siege.

Why? Because this new leadership landscape—globalization and democratization, flattening organizational hierarchies and virtual teams, outsourcing and offshoring, the Internet and ubiquitous media—turns leadership into a more complex challenge than perhaps ever before. Even the twentieth century's greatest leaders might have had a hard time leading in the twenty-first. President Franklin D. Roosevelt's debilitating polio would be all over the Internet, had he ever become chief executive. John F. Kennedy's chronic affairs would haunt him while he faced not one but multiple enemies. And Winston Churchill would constantly be shown on YouTube for his battle with the bottle. Not to speak of business leaders like Andrew Carnegie, Thomas Watson, or

Alfred Nobel: They would come under near-constant attack from shareholders bemoaning short-term losses or from the media criticizing their products. More than ever, leadership is in the hot seat, forcing leaders to stay centered in ways that past leaders never had to.

What are the critical competencies leaders must master now? Take a cue from Warren Buffett, the chairman of Berkshire Hathaway and one of the great business leaders and strategists of our time. When Buffett announced to shareholders in 2007 that he planned to hire a younger person (or several) to understudy him in managing Berkshire's investments, he did not mention financial savvy or technical skills or even strategic thinking. Qualified candidates, Buffett noted, must possess "independent thinking, emotional stability, and a keen understanding of both human and institutional behavior."[8]

No question: Leaders of a new kind are called for. But how can such a transformation be brought about? More than two hundred years ago, Michael Faraday took two different fields—physics and chemistry—and married them to create a new phenomenon: electricity. To transcend today's leadership crisis, we (the CEO and the Rabbi) propose to do the same with the two fields of Judaism and leadership. We found that marrying the two makes something new possible: a new type of leadership. Just like the ten vessels (*sefirot*, literally, enumerations) through which God created the world according to the ancient Kabbalah, the study of the mystical meanings of the Torah, each of the ten leadership commandments is interconnected with all others; each is a holographic expression, building on all of the other commandments and leading back to them all. Here is a quick overview:

In Commandment One, Out of Egypt, great leaders start by going beyond their comfort zone; they free themselves and unleash the potential of others. In Commandment Two, No Idols, leaders must build an authentic vision that is not based on idols or external expectations, but is truly their own. Commandment Three, Don't Speak In Vain, shows how to lead through language, how leaders inspire others to act on their vision through a specific type of speaking and listening.

Commandment Four, Keep the Sabbath, is about how transcendent leaders from Moses to Mandela had the courage to prioritize, say no to demands and circumstances, and take time out to reflect and contem-

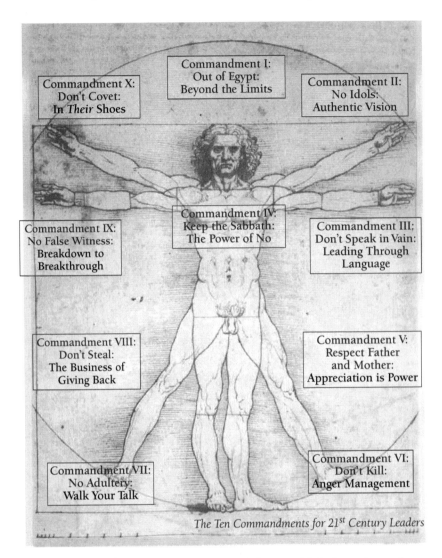

The Ten Commandments for 21st Century Leaders

plate. Commandment Five, Respect Father and Mother, shows how leaders use appreciation as a key management tool; they see the importance of each person and each detail to the overall strategy. In Commandment Six, Don't Kill, powerful leaders regulate their anger and channel their emotions into productive energy.

Commandment Seven, No Adultery, is about *the* source of power for leaders: not their corner office, not their title, not even their authority, but their integrity. They walk their talk and tackle ethical dilemmas.

Commandment Eight, Don't Steal, is about how leaders catalyze—embody, even—the future by the way they invest themselves. In Commandment Nine, No False Witness, the greatest leaders are not afraid to give bad news; instead of being stopped by adversity, they harness breakdowns into breakthroughs. Finally, in Commandment Ten, Don't Covet, global leaders, especially in the twenty-first century, must put themselves in the shoes of their clients, competitors, and even enemies.

These commandments' principles and practices are so fundamental that many managers might overlook them in the rush to show the external, seemingly important characteristics of leaders. But they are the stuff twenty-first century leaders are made of. (In fact we hope readers come to use *The Rabbi and the CEO* as a reference they will keep dipping into for continuous guidance.)

And potent stuff they are indeed. Like fire, leadership can be used to destroy or to build. We assume that you will use the tools in this book for good. Tremendous damage has been done in the world because some have been compelled to put their leadership skills to dishonest or even evil ends. Fueled by greed, intolerance, and revenge, these so-called leaders have perpetrated wars, famine, and commercial or environmental ruin, and have wrought havoc on their companies or whole nations. Under the best leaders, however, people have triumphed over impossible circumstances; fought and won against tyranny and oppression; overcome poverty, hunger, ignorance, and disease; and distinguished within the collective consciousness such notions as equality, freedom, and dignity. In business, they have innovated, made the impossible possible and doable, and mobilized to achieve breakthrough results. (As Herb Kelleher, the former leader of Southwest Airlines, put it recently, "a humanistic approach to business *can* pay dividends—and believe me, I'm *not* off my meds!"[9]) The choice is yours. Use your power wisely.

T.D.Z. AND A.R.
New York City, June 2008

Acknowledgments

Without 9/11 the CEO and the Rabbi might have never met or crafted this book. (From now on, throughout the book, whenever we mention "the CEO" and don't specify further, we mean co-author Thomas D. Zweifel; whenever we say "the Rabbi" without adding a name, we mean co-author Aaron L. Raskin. Maybe our roles will be reversed in another lifetime or two; but that is the way it is for now.)

The day after, both of us went back to mourn the thousands of victims and the loss of the world's innocence (including our own). The CEO sat there with countless others, holding a candle and staring into the smoking, dusty void where the twin towers had stood only the day before, when the Rabbi walked up to him with his full regalia, black hat and beard and *tefillin*[10]—and, because the Jewish New Year was fast approaching, a *shofar* in one hand and a tiny bottle of honey in the other. He asked, "Are you Jewish?" The CEO looked up; he had never met the Rabbi before, and usually would have ignored a stranger or waived him away. But on that somber day, something made him say, "Yes, I am." The Rabbi asked, "Okay, would you like to put on *tefillin*?" The CEO answered, "I've never done this before, but today of all days seems like a perfect day to start." So the two of us, with hundreds of people watching, tied the tefillin on the CEO's left arm and his head, and said the prayer, the Rabbi slowly pronouncing a few holy words at a time, the CEO repeating them haltingly. On that day, a great friendship was forged. Soon the two became collaborators and fellow leaders who coach each other: the Rabbi helps the CEO step back from business and life challenges and make sense of them; the CEO assists the Rabbi in setting strategic direction and tackling leadership challenges.

We thank the readers of our previous books who believed in our ideas. We are grateful to the members of Congregation B'nai Avraham in Brooklyn Heights, led by Stephen Rosen, founder and president, for their generosity and human spirit; Rabbi Simcha Weinstein for his dynamism and ideas; Rabbi Samuel Weintraub and the Kane Street Synagogue in Brooklyn's Cobble Hill and Rabbi Harold Swiss of the Little Synagogue for first opening the door; Rabbi Yitzchak Ginsburgh and Rabbi Dov Ber Pinson for paving the road less traveled; Michael and Sarah Behrman, Jay Greenspan, Elyakeem Kinstlinger, Samuel Mann, Allan Scherr, Motti Seligson, Sam Shnider, Tom Steinberg, and Michael Weinberger for useful insights and inspiring conversations.

We thank Julie Schwartzman and Alexander Reisz for their unvarnished feedback; we thank Lynne Glasner and Nancy Sugihara for their meticulous editing; Kenichi Sugihara for his creative marketing ideas; and Kenzi Sugihara for his unflappable wisdom in the stormy seas of publishing.

We thank the CEO's clients—top managers, entrepreneurs, government and UN officials, and military officers—who have turned the Ten Commandments into results for a quarter-century. We are indebted to the CEO's friends and Swiss Consulting advisers Lawrence Flynn, Florian Goldberg, Peter Spang, and Nick Wolfson for generously sharing concepts and best practices; and to Richard Klass and Lark Bryner for their stories and jokes.

We thank Mina Kim and Yariv Nornberg for research on Perrier; Abril Alcala-Padilla, Jamie Ho, Mihyun Park, Ned Peterson, and Chunyu Yu for research on General Electric; Robin J. Böhringer and Simon Koch for research on Ford; and the CEO's more than five hundred leadership students so far at Columbia University, St. Gallen Business School and Haute Ecole de Gestion Fribourg (both Switzerland), Sydney University, and the Interdisciplinary Center Herzliya (Israel), who researched case studies and helped bring out ideas in this book through challenging dialogue.

We thank our parents and our early teachers and role models Benzion and Bassie Raskin, and Dr. Eva and Dr. Heinz Wicki-Schönberg, who cut the tall grass and showed us what works. We thank Shternie Raskin, a natural leader and manager, for her strategy and intuition from which the Rabbi learned so much, and Yankel, Eliyahu, Mendy, Chaya, and Yehoshua Raskin for encouraging the Rabbi to be a better leader every day. We thank Rabbi Menachem M. Schneerson, the Lubavitcher Rebbe and the Rabbi's mentor, for setting the highest standards of leadership, and Rabbi Jacob J. Hecht, the Rabbi's grandfather, for his inspiration and example. We thank the city of Basel, the CEO's hometown, not only for bringing forth tennis champion Roger Federer, a master of anger management (see Commandment 6 "Don't Kill"), but also for hosting the First Zionist World Congress in 1897 that was attended by the CEO's great-grandfather, Rabbi David Strauss of Zurich. After the Congress, Theodor Herzl, the founder of the Zionist movement, was to write, "To summarize the Basel Congress in one sentence—which I shall be careful not to pronounce publicly—it is this: At Basel I founded the Jewish state."[11]

Last but not least, we are grateful for meeting each other and enriching each other's lives. The terrorists on 9/11 hoped to divide the world and wreak havoc and destruction. Yet as King Solomon said, from darkness comes greater light. Out of the ashes of the Twin Towers our twin souls met; the very calamity brought us together and allowed us to merge our talents with the aim of creating greater good. We present this book with the awe and humility that stem from knowing that we cannot fully grasp the infinite wisdom of the universe. All we can do is open a window and lead the reader to it.

Prologue: Leadership Self-Assessment

Before we proceed, we invite you to assess yourself. Each of the ten chapters in this book explores one of the Ten Commandments and applies it to the twenty-first-century workplace. So before you delve into the book, take a few minutes now to grade your own leadership competencies on the next page. We are aware that readers often skip these types of exercises. Don't. If you take this assignment seriously, the book may give you the power to transform your leadership—for good.

Leadership Self-Assessment
Leading with the 10 Commandments

Rate your leadership competencies below (1=non-existent, 2=weak, 3=fair, 4=competent, 5=masterful). Be honest with yourself: neither negative nor boastful. It is not about looking good.

COMMANDMENT I
Out of Egypt: Beyond the Limits

____ Responsibility for the whole of your organization and mission; willingness to take charge

____ Checking your own assumptions, blind spots, hidden motives, values; staying centered

____ Beginner's mind; remaining a student; openness to coaching Teaching ethical dilemmas

COMMANDMENT II
No Idols: Authentic Vision

____ Creating and articulating a future for people; inspiring others

____ Bringing vision back when people have lost it in the day-to-day details

____ Sustaining an environment of vision, momentum, breakthrough

COMMANDMENT III
Don't Speak In Vain: Leading Through Language

___ Listening for distinctions (e.g., in running meetings);
listening for openings, solutions

___ Making powerful promises, requests (measurable, with deadlines)

___ Cultivating and deepening relationships

___ Giving and receiving feedback effectively

COMMANDMENT IV
Keep the Sabbath: The Power of No

___ Being still; ability to step back; letting go of control

___ Working from priorities; saying no to low-priority demands

COMMANDMENT V
Respect Father and Mother: Appreciation is Power

___ Appreciating what others bring

___ Team skills (e.g., building consensus, alignment)

___ Coaching skills; effective empowerment of people

___ Managing the details, not dropping anything out

COMMANDMENT VI
Don't Kill: Anger Management

___ Regulating your own emotions (e.g., anger, fear)

___ Understanding your own emotions

COMMANDMENT VII
No Adultery: Walking Your Talk

___ Maintaining clarity on your ethical values

___ Matching your words and deeds; integrity

___ Tackling ethical dilemmas

COMMANDMENT VIII
Don't Steal: The Business of Giving Back

___ Contributing to others; always giving more than receiving

___ Adding value to people and/or organizations

COMMANDMENT IX
No False Witness: From Breakdown to Breakthrough

___ Thinking strategically; identification of what is missing, of blockages

___ Being powerful in the face of breakdowns; turning breakdowns into breakthroughs

___ Never ever ever giving up; being fearless; undaunted by No

COMMANDMENT X
Don't Covet: In Their Shoes

___ Enrollment: utilizing and integrating people's existing agenda

___ Managing cultural diversity; standing in the shoes of the other person

___ Decoding another culture (organizational or rational)

The Rabbi
and
the CEO

CHAPTER ONE

Commandment I
Out of Egypt: Beyond the Limits

...in a place where there are no leaders, strive to be a leader.
—Ethics of Our Fathers, Chapter 2:6

No man is fit to command another that cannot command himself.
—William Penn

THE FIRST COMMANDMENT: *"I am Hashem,*[12] *your God who delivered you from the land of Egypt, from the house of slavery."* At its most basic, leadership is about freedom: freeing people up to express their full potential. Leaders dare to go—and take others—beyond their comfort zone. This chapter will show you the most basic leadership competence, and one of the hardest to master: how to leave your own Egypt. How do you unlock people's hidden power? To begin, you need to know their blind spots and understand the nature of power.

Gertrude Boyle marched into her family's clothing factory one winter morning and ordered the foremen to shut down the machines. When the forty workers gathered to find out whether they still had jobs, the silence was louder than the loudest engines. Gert delivered the bad news: Neal, her husband of twenty years and president of the company, had died of a heart attack at age forty-seven; she had buried him just hours before. The second bombshell followed on the heels of the first: Gert had decided to take over and asked that the employees not quit while she learned how to run the business.

"I was a senior at the University of Oregon, studying journalism with a minor in political science," Gert's son Tim recalled. "My intention was to go to law school or buy a newspaper." But when his father died, he rushed home to help his mother manage the firm. "My dad had just taken out a loan, backed by my parents' house, my grandmother's house, all the assets of the family. I made every mistake in the world. It was a tiny business, $1 million in sales in 1970. But by 1971, under our direction, we were at half a million."[13]

No wonder: Tim's mother was a forty-seven-year-old homemaker who did not know how to lead a company. Up to that point, her most significant contribution to the business had been stitching together a fishing vest that Neal had designed at the dinner table one evening. Her bankers, lawyer, and accountants were skeptical of her ability to lead and tried to dissuade her.

Events proved the skeptics right. By 1973, the company had a net worth of minus $300,000, and the bankers pressured Gert and Tim to sell. They agreed reluctantly. A parade of potential buyers ("Buyers?" Gert snorted. "Call them vultures—that's more like it") poured over their books. Only one of them bothered to make a bid. He showed up for the final round of negotiations one rainy spring morning, carrying a long list of conditions. Then came his final offer: $1,400. And in that moment, something snapped in Gert Boyle. She went beyond the narrow confines of the meek housewife who did not speak up at meetings and transformed herself into the indomitable leader of Columbia Sportswear. She ordered the potential buyer out of her office, shouting after him: "Why should I let you have all the fun? For $1,400, I'll gladly run the business into the ground myself."

The rest is history. Needless to say, Gert Boyle did not run Columbia Sportswear into the ground; quite the reverse. Under her leadership (and Tim's, now the president and CEO), the firm has become a leading maker of outerwear and skiwear and one of the fastest-growing manufacturers in the footwear and sportswear markets. Some 10,000 retailers and catalogue companies in Europe, Asia, and the United States carry its jackets, jeans, boots, and hats. Even the sexy lingerie retailer Victoria's Secret has featured Columbia's Bugaboo Boots on its catalog cover. In 1997, Columbia posted $535.5 million in sales and $44.3 million in operating income—a growth of 30 percent and 35 percent respectively from a year earlier. In 1998, Gert and Tim took the business public and realized a paper fortune of $350 million, while keeping 75 percent of Columbia's stock and paying a dividend of $95 million to themselves and key managers.[14] By 2006, the company's market capitalization was just shy of $2 billion.

Some 3,300 years before Gert, another human being stood up—in Egypt. One day, Moses walked outside the palace and witnessed injustice: he "saw an Egyptian beating a Hebrew, one of his kinsmen. He turned this way and that and, seeing no man, he struck down the Egyptian." The Hebrew word *ish* can mean "man" as well as "leader." Moses saw no other leader defending this man, so in a split second, without thinking, he took charge. Moses had lived comfortably among Egypt's elite;[15] but now came a reckoning that forced him to show his true colors, and in one instant he changed his life and gave up everything he was and had, his money, his position, and his connections in the top echelons of society. What for? Essentially, it was his chance to leave his limitations and become truly himself. There was no one else who would lead; he knew another human being depended on him, and he chose to step into the gap.

Where did Gert Boyle find the strength to make the shift from homemaker to business leader, and a wildly successful one at that? What made Moses, raised among the privileged princes of Egypt, throw in his lot with slaves and become a transcendent leader who would free his entire people from the yoke of Egypt and guide them to the Promised Land? What gave Moses and Boyle the power to stand up? Both experienced that defining moment when, as the poet Rainer Maria Rilke put it, "someone in the crowd wakes up, he has no ground in the crowd, and he emerges according to much broader laws"[16] It's the ultimate leadership question: What makes a leader?

The Rabbi and the CEO say it's the First Commandment: *I am your God who delivered you from the land of Egypt, the house of slavery.* The Hebrew name for Egypt, *Mitzrayim*, from the root *metzar*, means also narrow, limited, constrained. So "I delivered you from Egypt" really means "I freed you from your limitations." The job of a leader is to lead people—starting with themselves—out of narrowness into openness, and to create freedom wherever people are locked up.

The exodus from Egypt is a defining moment in Jewish history. Each year during Passover, Jews all around the world—even those who barely remember their roots—relive their liberation and have done so for many centuries, even in times of intense oppression, such as in fourteenth-century Spain, seventeenth-century Poland, 1938 in Germany, or 1960 in Russia. The exodus is not merely a historic event that happened thousands of years ago; in every genera-tion, it is incumbent on leaders to leave the places where they have been confined, where they have been less than themselves, where they have not been fully expressed, and free themselves and others. The exodus is hard-wired into the Jewish psyche. It created a new human being: a person who yearns for liberty and will never succumb to subjugation.

But that liberty is a far cry from reality. Who of us working in organi-zations—no matter whether on the front lines, as a middle manager, or as CEO—has not seen examples of the Egypt of corporate life? Man-agers cover their backsides; direct reports pass the buck; colleagues are afraid to speak up and say what they really think; people reduce them-selves to going through the motions in their nine-to-five routine, or they let someone else boss them around. When the CEO (co-author Thomas D. Zweifel) asked an executive coaching client, a managing director at a New York financial services firm, for his objectives, he said, "My CEO expects me to double total revenue." Was this *his* vision or the boss's vision *for* him? "The CEO's," he admitted. It dawned on him that his basic modus operandi was to play exclusively within the rules other people had set for him, rather than participating in *making* the rules that would maximize productivity. This blind spot greatly ham-pered his leadership.

Hasidic tradition (from the word *hesed*, an Orthodox Jewish move-ment founded by the eighteenth-century Rabbi Israel ben Eliezer, also known as the Baal Shem Tov, literally "Master of the Good Name") and the Kabbalah (literally "receiving," a mystical Jewish tradition resulting in the *Zohar*, widely considered the Kabbalah's most important work, say that the inability to fully express yourself means you're in exile: you're not free, you're still a slave. If a pharaoh doesn't own you, then your circumstances, or your outdated beliefs, are running your life. Leaving your own Egypt and achieving full self-determination are the essence of redemption and liberation.[17] (This is also expressed in the word "education"; *educare* is Latin for to teach, but literally means to lead out.) But leaving your own Egypt can be frightening, messy, and far from glamorous. In the beginning Moses had grave doubts about whether he could fulfill his mission. He was marked by imperfections. He stammered. When God called on him, he made excuses and conditions: "I am slow of tongue and slow of speech." He asked, "Who am I?" and begged God to choose someone else to lead:

> Who am I that I should go to Pharaoh and that I should take the Children of Israel out of Egypt?...they will not believe me and they will not heed my voice, for they will say, 'God did not appear to you.'...Please, my master, I am not a man of words, not since yesterday, nor since the day before yesterday, nor since You first spoke to Your servant, for I am heavy of mouth and heavy of tongue....Please, my master, send whom-ever you will send![18]

In that moment, Moses regretted his choice to become a leader and would have given anything to avoid the burden of leadership. But God would have none of it. He told Moses:

> Therefore, say to the children of Israel, "I am God, and I shall take you out from under the burdens of Egypt; I shall rescue you from their service; I shall redeem you with an outstretched arm and with great judgments. I shall take you to Me for a people and I shall be a God to you; and you shall know that I am Hashem your God, Who takes you out from under the burdens of Egypt."[19]

Moses was right to be scared. Once you leave your own Egypt, where do you go? There is an old Jewish saying that some attribute to Rabbi Menachem Mendel Morgensztern of Kotsk, the Kotsker Rebbe:[20] It is one thing to take the Jews out of exile, but it is quite another to take the exile out of the Jews. Where do you find your power as a leader when you venture into the unknown?

The answer lies in one of the first portions of the Torah (the five books of Moses, also called the Old Testament), *Lech Lecha*: Go to Yourself. What does that mean? Didn't we just go beyond ourselves? Why do we have to come back to ourselves? It means you are on a life-long journey to unfold who you *really* are. The eighteenth-century Rabbi Zusya said about himself, "In the world to come, I shall not be asked, 'Why were you not Moses?' I shall be asked, 'Why were you not Zusya?'"[21] And the wise Rabbi Simcha Bunam said in old age, when he had already gone blind: "I should not like to change places with our father Abraham! What good would it do God if Abraham became like blind Bunam, and blind Bunam became like Abraham? Rather than have this happen, I think I shall try to become a little more myself."[22] Or, as another leader of an entirely different kind was to put it centuries later, "Where I was born was very far from where I'm supposed to be, so I'm on the way home." Who said this? It was Bob Dylan, one of the key innovators in the field of music. "I had ambitions to set out to find—like an odyssey going home somewhere—I set out to find this home that I had left a while back, and I couldn't remember exactly where it was but I was on my way there..."[23]

His ambition to be on a life-long search for home—or his true self—gave Dylan (whose real name was Robert Zvi Zimmerman[24]) the courage and creativity to lead music into an entirely new realm. He committed what some fans considered heresy by playing electric guitar at the 1965 Newport Folk Festival. His push to break through the boundaries of music was not exactly earning him roses; a full one-third of the audience that night booed him for destroying the folk music they knew and cherished. While he walked back and forth on stage tuning his electric guitar, a heckler yelled, "Hey, traitor, why don't you hear yourself?" Others cried, "Bobby, go home!" When he recalled the incident four decades later, Dylan still struggled for words: "The booing didn't really—it didn't really—you know—I have a perspective on the booing because you gotta realize you can kill somebody with kindness too."[25] At the time, he was undeterred. He smiled sheepishly like a naughty schoolboy, shrugging his shoulders as if he didn't quite know what was happening, as if things were out of his hands. Unperturbed, like an indifferent teenager who simply didn't care what people thought, he abruptly started singing in his rough, snarling voice, turning his back to the audience, hunched over, cradling the guitar as if to protect his new "baby" from the audience and its outrage.

Looking back on the incident decades later, Dylan explained: "I didn't want to give something away that was … [he fell into a long silence, weighing whether to say the word] *dear* to me, or something," He kept doing his unique thing, escaping his own immense popularity that had become an obstacle, inventing a style that would transform for all time what was possible in music. "I wrote a lot of songs in a quick amount of time," Dylan said. "I felt like I discovered something no one else had ever discovered, and I was in a certain arena that no one else had ever been in before, ever—although," he quickly inserted a disclaimer, "I may have been wrong about that." Wittingly or not, Dylan became a leader of his generation because he gave voice to what that generation wanted to hear. At the source of his leadership was leaving his own Egypt—an intense desire to find his own power, a power not based on a job title or wealth or popularity.

No two humans are alike. Dylan's task, just like Rabbi Zusya's and Rabbi Bunam's, was not to emulate the heroes or sages of the past, no matter how great they were. Rather his job was, and is, to know himself, find his unique purpose in life, and stay true to that purpose. This concept, unfolding the unique you and doing something that has never been done before, is central to the Jewish concept of leadership. The *Zohar* (one of the greatest kabbalistic works) says that the *neshama*, the human soul, is so great that it precedes even creation itself.[26]

Dylan ended up reaping rich rewards for his courage to be himself. He became a star, and he rewrote music history. In business too, leaving your own Egypt and venturing into the unknown pays dividends: You can build an entire company on people transcending their limits. Sergey Brin and Larry Page did. Even the name of their company showed their playfulness on the journey to freedom and innovation: They took a typo, a misspelling of "googol," the number represented by a 1 followed by 100 zeroes, and made it into the name of their project: Google. They got venture capital and quickly built one of the world's most visible brands. But they kept their own unique strategy and management style to stay on the cutting edge. Hiring the best minds they could find, they prized originality, to a fault. Google engineers—among them such brains as Rob Pike, one of the creators of the Unix operating system; Adam Bosworth, a pioneer of the XML programming language; and Louis Monier, an inventor of the Altavista search engine popular in the 1990s, and later director of eBay's advanced technology research—are encouraged to work the equivalent of one day each week not on Google but on their own pet projects. It's a zany culture built on the tenets of leaving your own Egypt and of the uniqueness of each person as a leader.

And you don't need to be a rock musician or a math genius. In an industry not exactly known for prizing originality, Herb Kelleher did it with Southwest Airlines, where new hires are asked to bring "a warrior spirit and a fun-loving attitude." To be sure that job candidates got a grip of Southwest's culture, Kelleher did not leave the hiring process to the human resources department, but asked model employees to interview new people and top managers to train them in leadership. "We ask, how did you use humor to extricate yourself from a situation? You hear some of the damndest stories. ...We hire you because you are you, not because you're a robot."[27] Southwest's focus on people freeing themselves from the shackles of corporate existence paid off. From 1972 to 2002, the airline produced the best return to investors in Standard & Poor's, netting an average 76 percent growth compounded annually. An investment of $1,000 in 1972 was worth $1 million in 2002. Today, Southwest Airlines is still a top performer, producing profits in a struggling industry by enabling its people to leave their limits behind.

* * *

The joke goes that a Buddhist monk entered a pizza shop and asked, "Make me one with everything." He got his slice and handed a $20 bill to the proprietor, who pocketed the entire bill. After a befuddled pause the monk protested, "Where's my change?" The pizza man shot back: "Change? Change comes from within."

Jokes aside, on a deeper level the pizza man was right. Unless you monitor your blind spots, the inner motives, conscious or not, that drive your actions, and above all your ego, you're enslaved; you risk running around like a headless chicken, victimized by others' demands or by circumstances beyond your control.

How do you do it, though? How do you go about leaving your own Egypt? We propose three fundamental tools: first, taking full responsibility; second, checking your own beliefs, assumptions, and blind spots; and third, being aware of how you exert power.

Responsibility = Ability to Respond

In the extreme, when people are utterly enslaved, they become robots that can be used by whoever gains control over their minds. To see the consequences of such complete lack of self-determination, one need only recall how the German masses followed the *Führer* (German for leader) before and during World War II. It was above all their individual and collective refusal to think for themselves that turned them into accomplices to a monster on his twisted march to utter destruction. Such lack of independent thought is unthinkable in Judaism, which has always asserted that each human is directly responsible to God. Jews have a direct link to the divine. There is no pope, no vicar of the divine on earth; no human has the ultimate authority to tell you what to think; two Jews, three opinions, for better or worse. (When Richard Nixon told Golda Meir that "I am the president of 200 million Americans" she reportedly quipped "And I am the prime minister of four million prime minsters.") Their responsibility (unlike guilt, which they have often confused it with) is, quite literally, the ability to respond; the words are derived from the same roots.

In Jewish teachings, a human being first becomes a leader of the self, then of the family, the community, the nation, and ultimately of the world. To free others, you must be in charge of yourself; you have to know yourself and take full responsibility for your actions, responsibility not as in guilt, but as in a basic willingness to be the cause, never the victim, of what happens in your life. "People are always blaming their circumstances for what they are," George Bernard Shaw once observed. "I don't believe in circumstances. The people who get on in this world are the people who get up and look for the circumstances they want, and, if they can't find them, make them."[28]

In the *Amidah*, the most self-confident of the daily prayers, Jews take three steps forward to address God directly and without intermediary. They stand up to God and face their own responsibility. (*Amidah* means standing up; when you face God, you go beyond your limitations, stand up for yourself, and hold your head high.) Yes, they're humble: "To those who curse me, let my soul be silent; and let my soul be like dust to everyone."[29] But they're in charge.

Some Jews took responsibility to an extreme that may strike some as borderline heretical. Adam himself was not above bargaining with God. The story goes that God and Adam were playing around in Eden and had a lot of fun—at least for while. Eventually God got a bit bored and decided to make Adam an offer. "I will give you a creature unlike any you have ever seen: her name will be Eve. She will be gorgeous and smart, she will be your life partner, she will give you beautiful children, and she will make you laugh for the rest of your days." "That sounds awfully good," Adam said. "What do you want in return?" God answered, "Your right arm and right leg." Adam thought it over, then came back. "That sounds fantastic," he replied, "but giving up an arm and a leg is a bit much, don't you think? What do I get for a rib?"

While this is of course a joke, that Adam was willing to haggle with God set the stage. Many generations later, Abraham, the father and first leader of the Jews, again took it upon himself to negotiate with God over the fate of the evil cities Sodom and Gomorrah. Reportedly God said to Abraham, "Without me you would not exist." Abraham responded swiftly, making clear he saw eye to eye with his creator: "Yes, God, that I know. But you would not be known were it not for me."[30] It was straight talk on the verge of impertinence. He argued that even if only fifty good men lived there, the cities as a whole should be saved. Then he started bargaining like a rug dealer in the souk of Tunis.

> Here I have begun to speak to my Master and I am but dust and ashes. But suppose they lack five of the fifty righteous? Will you destroy the whole city because of five? [God] said: "I will not destroy if I find forty-five." [Abraham] continued to speak to him and said:

"Suppose there are forty found there?" [God] said: "I will not do it for the sake of the forty." [Abraham] said: "Let not my Master show anger and I will continue to speak. Suppose thirty are found there?")[31]

Abraham did not stop wheeling and dealing until he had won a huge concession from God: Sodom and Gomorrah would not be destroyed if a mere ten good men could be found among the whole evil population. (Of course not even ten could be found, so God annihilated the cities; only Lot and his family were saved.)[32]

> **Tip:** Remember, you always have a choice. You're in charge; nobody can tell you how to live your life. As the sages say, "You are not obligated to complete the work, nor are you free to desist from it."[33] It's a fundamental paradox of being human: you're free, and yet that freedom comes with a price: you are to meet yourself and your purpose. The choice is yours.

But responsibility goes deeper. It is the willingness to be 100 percent accountable for your actions and choices. Consider the story of Rabbi Shneur Zalman of Liadi, known as the Alter Rebbe.[34] Early in the nineteenth century, the government of White Russia (today Belarus) put the Alter Rebbe in jail in St. Petersburg after the *mitnagdim* (adversaries of Hasidism, from the root *neged* meaning against) of Vilna had denounced him for his practices and principles. The rebbe was awaiting trial when the chief of the gendarmes entered his cell. The majestic and quiet face of the *tzaddik*,[35] who was so deep in meditation that he did not at first notice his visitor, suggested to the chief, a thoughtful man, what caliber of man he had before him. He had read the scriptures and began talking with his prisoner, bringing up several clever questions. The chief saved his best weapon for last: "How are we to understand that God, who is all-knowing, said to Adam: 'Where art thou?'"

It was a trick question, one of those riddles with no way out. If God is really infinite and omniscient, why would He have to ask where

Adam is hiding? And if He does not know everything and has to ask, then He is not God, right?

True to Jewish form, the Alter Rebbe responded with a question of his own: "Do you believe that the scriptures are eternal and that every era, every generation and every man is included in them?" "I believe this," said the chief.

"Well then," the Alter Rebbe said with a smile, "in every generation, God calls out to every man, 'Where are you? So many years and days allotted to you have passed; how far have you gotten in your world?' God says something like this: 'You have lived forty-six years. How far along are you?'"

When the chief of the gendarmes heard his own age mentioned, he gave a start, put his hand on the rebbe's shoulder, and exclaimed, "Bravo!" But his heart trembled.[36] Just like Adam, the first human being, he had come face to face with his own responsibility for his life.

Questioning Your Assumptions and Blind Spots

Visitors to the ancient oracle at Delphi were greeted with the words "Know Thyself" chiseled in stone on top of the massive entry gate. Self-knowledge is the foundation of ethical and effective leadership; without that groundwork, talking about such grand leadership topics as charisma or vision or empowerment is frivolous. Devoid of self-awareness, leadership is a castle built on sand. The question is, can you achieve, and cultivate, self-knowledge? Say you're in a difficult meeting with one of your managers, and he really rubs you the wrong way; can you check your own blind spots?

First of all, whenever we make observations, we have to know where we stand. Scientists do so (or should do so) routinely to calculate mechanics: they have to take themselves and their relative vantage point into account. For example, if a physicist wants to determine the speed of the Earth, he or she needs to be aware of making that calculation within a framework called the solar system, which is itself spinning through space. This is even more salient when humans are involved. Brain scientists know that it is extraordinarily difficult to observe the human brain at work without damaging it. Anthropologists and sociologists use a similar intellectual discipline: They have to be aware that the very act of observing a particular system may influence—and change—the system they're observing. In a series of well-known experiments at the Hawthorne Works of the Western Electric Company in Illinois between 1924 and 1932, three organizational psychologists from Harvard studied the effects of lighting on workers' productivity. They brightened the lights in a factory; the workers' output promptly went up. They turned the lights *down*, and productivity went up further. In a phenomenon that came to be called the Hawthorne Effect, it finally dawned upon the scientists that it was not the lighting or other changes that influenced performance; it was the fact that the workers knew they were being observed.[37]

Just like these researchers, it behooves us to check where we stand when we see what we see. Knowing your own perspective and value-system, knowing where you stand, is crucial if you want to lead. One question is surely, why do you want to lead at all? Are you perhaps a control-freak who doesn't give others the freedom to make mistakes? Do you resist the role of follower when a colleague takes the lead? Is your motive to avoid domination by others, or even to hold others down so you can shine and advance? People come up with pretty twisted strategies to avoid being dominated. (For more on this, read Eric Berne's *Games People Play*.) The CEO once had a boss whose chair at the conference room table was just slightly higher than the chairs of the rest of the senior management team. So another question to ask is, are you blind to certain character traits in yourself? What is "unthought in the thinker's thought," as the German philosopher Martin Heidegger put it? What is automatic in your thought?

> **Tip:** When you observe something, get in the habit of catching yourself. What are you assuming about this "reality"? What if the opposite assumption were true? If a colleague rubbed you the wrong way recently, how do you know your perception is reality? How do you know your blind spots are not playing a trick on you and somehow distorting what you see?

Your world view influences the reality you see; what you call reality is not fixed, but fluid. (This perspective is based on the suggestion of constructivist theory that reality is constructed by intersubjective understandings, meaning by group or societal consensus. During the Cold War, so many people in the West agreed on the Soviet Union being an "evil empire" that everything the USSR did only provided more evidence for this "fact." In a more recent and more pleasant example, researchers at the California Institute of Technology confirmed that a $90 bottle of wine really does taste better than a $10 bottle—even when it actually is a $10 bottle. When wine drinkers sipped a $5 bottle of wine, they rated it much higher when it was disguised with a $45 price tag. The study found that the higher price tag primes the brain to expect pleasure, fooling people into what they actually experience. "Subjects believe that more expensive wines are likely to taste better," neuroscientist and economics professor Antonio Rangel explained. "These expectations end up influencing their actual experience."[38] In other words, what you think shapes your reality.

It helps to ask yourself what fundamental beliefs you have that may be causing you to see what you see, to think what you think, to feel what you feel, and to do what you do every day automatically, without thinking. This way you can see the unexamined assumptions that drive your thinking and your actions—the invisible strings that make the puppet dance. One of the CEO's clients, a managing director in a global energy company, was a poor listener. His direct reports loved to hear him speak, they found his talks brilliant, but they soon tuned out; they saw no reason to lead around him and finally left it all up to him. While consulting with this top executive, the CEO helped him reveal his blind spot: his internal background conversation that drove all his actions was something like, "I'm the most brilliant guy in the room anyway. Why should I listen to other people? It's a waste of time." The CEO called him "the preacher." Once he had identified his background conversation, he could transform it into a new one ("My listening is a source of power for other people") and discipline himself to ask questions instead of giving all the answers.

Tip: A good way to access your own blind spot, or defense mechanism, is to recall a recent moment when you were suffering, not physically suffering, but, for example, a situation in which you felt slighted, humiliated, or anxious. Say an outstanding idea of yours was flatly rejected by the management team, and your automatic reaction was, "I've had it with these people, I'm taking my marbles home." Ask yourself, why am I hurting here? What button is being pushed? How old is this defense mechanism; when did it all begin? And what fundamental decision did I make at that time? Most defense mechanisms are pretty old and deeply entrenched; they have served us all our lives to get results; but they may no longer be optimal strategies for leading today.

There are those who believe that strong leaders never question themselves, that flip-flopping betrays a weakness of character. But questioning one's own beliefs is essential for innovative leadership. The British economist John Maynard Keynes put it this way: "When the facts change, I change my mind. What do you do, sir?"[39] The physicist and Nobel laureate Richard Feynman once observed that "if we did not have doubt ... we would not have any new ideas." Feynman wanted to "teach that doubt is not to be feared, but that it is to be welcomed as the possibility of a new potential for human beings. If you know that you are not sure, you have a chance to improve the situation. I want to demand this freedom for future generations."[40] Or as the French philosopher Voltaire wrote centuries ago, "Doubt is not a pleasant condition, but certainty is an absurd one."[41]

Tool 1.1
The Five Fallacies of Fuzzy Thinking

Unless we're trained to do so, most of us do not naturally appreciate how automatic our thinking is; and even if we do, we live with the unrealistic but confident sense that we know already—that we've figured out the way things really are and have done so objectively. Here are the five most common fallacies of fuzzy thinking:[42]

"It's True Because I Believe It."

(Innate Egocentrism) I assume that what I believe is true, even though I have never questioned the basis of many of my beliefs.

"It's True Because We Believe It."

(Innate Sociocentrism) I assume that the dominant beliefs within the groups to which I belong are true, even though I have never questioned the basis for many of those beliefs.

"It's True Because I Want To Believe It."

(Innate Wish Fulfillment) I believe in, for example, accounts of behavior that put me (or the groups to which I belong) in a positive rather than a negative light, even though I have not seriously considered the evidence for the more negative account. I believe what "feels good," what supports my other beliefs, what does not require me to change my thinking significantly, what does not require me to admit that I have been wrong.

"It's True Because I Have Always Believed It."

(Innate Self-validation) I have a strong desire to maintain beliefs that I have long held, even though I have not seriously considered the extent to which those beliefs are justified, given the evidence.

"It's True Because It's In My Selfish Interest To Believe It."

(Innate Selfishness) I hold fast to beliefs that justify my getting more power, money, or personal advantage, even though those beliefs are not grounded in sound reasoning or evidence.

Most of us, most of the time, are not willing or able to go beyond these self-serving beliefs. We are truly the self-deceived animal. To be a leader, by contrast, means to be self-determined and requires a high level of competence in questioning your perspective. So the next time you face a particular issue, ask yourself, How am I looking at this? What are my assumptions? Am I basing my judgment on information I failed to verify? Might I be biased or blind to beliefs I never questioned before?

If you are a leader who intends to empower leaders around you—literally, to be a source of their power—part of your job description is to be cognizant of the clever, yet palpable and often destructive games people play, either to dominate others or to avoid domination by others. This can happen with the best of intentions. One top manager at a global bank was unaware of the huge impact his words had on his direct reports and all those below them. By virtue of his authority, people anxiously hung on every word he uttered, and an offhand remark of his might have huge ripple effects down the line. The idea is to make power conscious, which is essential if you want to exert it wisely. There are five distinct types of power; let's look at each in more detail.

Tool 1.2
The Five Types of Power

Reward Power
Reward power is the authority leaders have to grant financial, status, and promotional rewards to their organization's human resources. A boss has reward power; he or she can give, or withhold, compensation, perks, or favors. A country's government might have reward power over another country's government if it can apply economic or diplomatic sanctions. It's important to understand where you exert reward power since your followers might fawn all over you and say how brilliant you are, when in fact it is just your reward power over them that has them say those nice things. (Especially if you're

a professor ...) Worse, they might tell you only what they think you like to hear instead of what you need to hear; the consequences can be disastrous.

Expert/Information Power

Information power and expert power both come from knowledge, expertise, and access to information sources that others do not have. Professors have expert power vis-à-vis their students. Financial analysts enjoy expert or information power over their clients (who can only pray that they won't abuse it). Knowledge workers have expert/information power to the extent that they know more than their bosses, which they do more often than not. Knowledge workers take their expert power home with them every night when they leave the office.

Legitimate Power

Legitimate power is conferred by the organization itself, not by the person who occupies a particular position. An elected official has legitimate power as long as the election's legitimacy is not contested. But you need not be in a democracy to have legitimate power. The Pope is elected only by the Cardinals, rather than by all Catholics; yet you could say his power is legitimate. A CEO is not elected but appointed, but his or her power is legitimate as long as the appointment happened according to clear rules and not by shooting their way into office.

Coercive Power

If someone comes to power not through clear rules but through a violent coup, they have coercive power. Jerry Rawlings, the former president of Ghana, did precisely that in the 1980s (but later subjected himself to free and fair elections and thus gained legitimate power). Coercive power is the ability of a leader to force others to do things they would not otherwise do. The most colorful example of coercive power is the mafia, but it's not alone: the government enjoys coercive power over its citizens—it can extract taxes from us, and it can send some of us into battle or to prison (in some states it can even have us killed). And managers have the power to force tasks on employees or fire them if they don't perform certain functions.

Referent Power

Referent power is derived from the esteem in which a leader is regarded by others. A star (Bono) or a supermodel (Kate Moss) might enjoy referent power; they get people to do things they would not otherwise do, such as putting on strange or expensive outfits. Mahatma Gandhi also had referent power: he never held office, and his influence came from his charisma and the power people gave or referred to him. In business, the boss's executive assistant might have very little nominal power, but her (or his) referent power can be enormous: she (or he) knows who's who in the firm and controls access to the boss and the boss's agenda.

You have probably gathered that these types of power are not entirely separate but can overlap. Bill Gates, for example, can have expert power and reward power. States have legitimate and coercive powers. Arnold Schwarzenegger enjoyed referent power as a body-builder and movie star, but also, more recently, legitimate power as governator (sorry, governor) of California.

The Sun Will Set Without Thy Assistance

We feel a big disclaimer is needed here. Stand up for yourself and go beyond your limits, yes; but don't get carried away with your power or you'll get into trouble, like Leona Helmsley (née Leona Mindy Rosenthal), a former model who had posed in Chesterfield ads as a cigarette girl and who as part of a husband-and-wife team built up a real estate empire of $50 billion at its peak, and owned or controlled such New York City landmarks as the Empire State Building, the Flatiron Building, 1 Penn Plaza, and six of New York's top hotels. The Helmsleys traveled in a 100-seat private jet and lived opulently among several homes; in addition to their 10-room duplex with indoor pool atop the Park Lane Hotel, she added a mansion in Connecticut and a condo in Palm Beach, and kept a minimum of twelve pictures of herself in every room. A liveried butler bearing a silver platter of freshly-cooked shrimp was required to stand at attention while she did her early-morning laps in the pool; at the end of each lap he would hand her a shrimp. She overdid it, and her fortunes collapsed amid charges of greed and personal tyranny. When her only son died in 1982, she sued for his estate, leaving her four grandchildren with just $432 apiece (her husband sued even for the money it had cost to fly the body to New York). The high life ended in 1989 when the couple was charged on 235 counts of evading more than $4 million in taxes. Among other misdeeds, they were accused of buying personal items ranging from a $210,000 mahogany table down to an $8 girdle and charging them as business expenses.[43] Reportedly, she declared, "We don't pay taxes. Only little people pay taxes." Helmsley paid $7.1 million in fines, served eighteen months in prison, and came to be reviled by the public as "the queen of mean."

Or take Maurice ("Hank") Greenberg, the former chief of the insurance giant AIG who regularly dressed down analysts. "You don't mess around with Hank," one of them said on condition of anonymity for fear of Greenberg's wrath. "He could squash me like a bug."[44] Once a month, the imperial chairman would assemble his division presidents around a rectangular table in a large plain room on the sixteenth floor of AIG's headquarters. To start the chairman's meeting, as it was called, he would swing his eyes around the room and, like a stern law professor putting students on the spot, would finally let his gaze rest on one executive, who had a minute or so to rattle off current sales, expenses, profits, and any unusual developments. It was a crisp, charged atmosphere. Greenberg cowed even AIG board members with his dismissive treatment. "That's a ridiculous question," he reportedly snapped at a director who dared ask about AIG's books in a board meeting, "You don't understand the insurance business." Greenberg thought he had both the board and the regulators in his pocket. "That technique," said David Schiff, editor of *Schiff's Insurance Observer*, "stonewalling and pushing people around, worked for him for forty years."[45] As late as 2000, Greenberg's approach was hailed by the *New York Times* as superior to that of even Warren Buffett, a model of corporate integrity and philanthropy, who spent his career of many decades seeking to integrate personal values like honesty, trust, and openness with the business and political worlds around him. But Greenberg's arrogance came back to haunt him when his own board fired him in 2005 from the very company he had built, and he himself came under scrutiny when federal regulators renewed their investigation into whether AIG had cooked its books. Within weeks, Greenberg's reputation was shattered and the company's value had fallen by as much as $1.77 billion.

Not only that, Greenberg's son Jeffrey, who was his heir apparent before resigning from AIG in 1995 and becoming CEO of Marsh & McLennan, was forced to resign from that insurance giant amid three government investigations and accusations of bid-rigging, misleading customers, and raising the cost of insurance artificially to increase Marsh's profits. What had once been perhaps the most influential family in the global insurance industry lay in ruins, the *New York Times* wrote in a 180-degree reversal of its earlier adulation.[46]

To be fair, Greenberg and Helmsley were not the only ones to have outsized egos; notorious leaders tend to have them. And in fact, the idea of an individual with an ego (defined by *Webster's* dictionary as "the 'I' or self of any person...distinguishing itself from the selves of others and from objects of its thought"[47]) was a product of eighteenth-century enlightenment, after Descartes had came up with his dictum "*Cogito, ergo sum*" ("I think, therefore I am") that paved the way for all people to no longer be mere subjects of their kings or lords, but be individuals capable of conscious and independent thought. This powerful innovation once helped topple hereditary elites. But today, the ego has got out of hand. Authentic leaders need to know how to keep their ego in check. The access to greatness, the possibility to stand up and see eye to eye with the greatest rulers, and even with God, is a double-edged sword. It brings with it great power, but also great obligation; as the French say, *noblesse oblige*.

Already in the time of Exodus, God said: "And you shall be to me a nation of priests, and a holy people."[48] This direct link of every human to divine holiness, and ultimately to God, has a price. A leader has an obligation to make the maximum difference with his or her life and do what is possible for human beings. Great leaders focus not on themselves but on others and on the difference to be made. Leaving your own Egypt must be tempered with humility because you're never quite done becoming yourself. You don't pretend being someone you are not. You are like the people an old British philosopher addressed before his departure from the United States: "In 1776," he told them, "you Americans conquered your father. In 1861, you conquered your brother. In 1918 and again in 1945, you conquered your neighbors. Now all that remains for you to conquer is yourselves."[49] Mastering yourself is the pinnacle of all conquests, and ultimately it is the only conquest available. No mortal ought to lord over another. That is why Jewish thought does not approve of lordship; there is only one Lord who heads up the universe. The Hebrew word *lehishtamesh* expresses this beautifully: a reflexive word, both active and passive, it means to use, but also to be used. We use life and life uses us.

The Hebrew language provides an even more profound reminder of humility. The word for I (*ani*) has the same letters, slightly rearranged, as the word for nothing (*ayin*). I have to remember that "I" am "nothing." Humility, Hasidic philosophy explains, means remembering that you are nothing by yourself. No matter what you have achieved, no matter how great a person you have become, none of your talents and qualities is of your own making. Whether you have a lot of creativity for innovation or a knack for languages, these gifts are God-given (that is why they are called gifts). And you have to assume that if someone else had been given these same gifts, they would have accomplished much more than you. Ultimately, being humble means to be aware of the divine as the source of all your life and successes. We are but specks in the all-encompassing universe. The greatest leaders knew this; Winston Churchill said, "We are all worms; but I am a glow-worm." Golda Meir put it even more wryly: "Don't be humble; you're not that great."

Humility for the 21st Century

Even Rashi, the great eleventh-century commentator whose words appear on every page of the Torah, was not above saying a humble and well-timed "I don't know"; admitting his limitations only strengthened Rashi's credibility. Humility is a timeless virtue prized in Hasidic philosophy,[30] but it also happens to be a better fit for today's world. We are at the end of the era of larger-than-life leaders—be they Churchill or Roosevelt, the Baal Shem Tov or the Lubavitcher Rebbe, Greenberg or Welch—who towered mightily over their followers. In this new era, leadership will be in the hands of many, and a healthy dose of humility is crucial in a global market where you have to produce results across borders and respect the values of other cultures; a world of democratization and flattening hierarchies where frontline people or soldiers may know more than you do about reality on the ground, where shareholders or patients demand more voice, where knowledge workers may walk out if they find a better job, and where you cannot simply tell people what to do.

So if you're self-confident enough to check your ego at the door, it could be your best investment in the leadership of those around you, not to speak of your own peace of mind. Moses Maimonides, a rabbi, physician, philosopher, and pioneer of global citizenship far ahead of his time, lived in Spain, Morocco, Israel, and Egypt from 1135 to 1204, during the Golden Age of Jewish and Muslim partnership. His Hebrew name was Rabbi Moshe ben Maimon (RaMBaM or Rambam for short), and his Arabic name was Abu Imran Mussa bin Maimun ibn Abdallah al-Qurtubi al-Israili; he is most commonly known by his Greek name Maimonides, which also means son of Maimon. Maimonides was by far the most influential figure in medieval Jewish philosophy. A popular saying that also was his epitaph states: "From Moshe (of the Torah) to Moshe (Maimonides) there was none like Moshe." Despite (or because) of his great leadership, Maimonides warned that pride, arrogance, and an inflated ego are the main obstacles to happiness. He quoted Proverbs: "Do not glorify yourself before the king."[51] Don't focus on your own glory. You will bring no honor to yourself. On the other hand, making your own ego small allows for divine inspiration and wisdom. Great joy is born from the spiritual womb of nothingness. When you surrender your ego to serving others, making them happy, the result will be joy.

> **Tip:** Humility might be the willingness to let go of your infantile will to power—the belief that "I want, therefore I should have." If unchecked, your limitless desire can be the source of much anxiety and psychic suffering. The Hasidic kabbalist Rabbi Yitzhak Ginsburgh said a few years ago: "Depression is ego. If I lower my ego, if I deserve nothing, then the worry vanishes."[52]

The problem is, you're never quite done letting go of your petty ego. What's beautiful about the commandment of leaving Egypt is that it's about the process, the journey of freeing yourself. "Somewhere, you always have to realize that you're constantly in a state of becoming," as Dylan put it once. "And as long as you can stay in that realm, you're sort of gonna be all right."[53] But the ego is a formidable adversary, tough as nails and deeply ingrained, and it started with the first man, Adam, who let his ego go to his head. He thought that since he was God's creation, nothing could destroy him. His hubris is precisely what led to his downfall and exile from Eden. He forgot that his very name, the Hebrew word for human being (*adam*), has the same root as the word *adamah* (earth). Humans are made from dirt, and we would do well to remember at all times that in the words of King Solomon, we "all go to one place, all are of the dust, and all return to dust."[54]

Humility is not something you get once and for all; it's not an item you can cross off on your checklist; you have to check your arrogance over and over again. And the ego is so cunning that it may pose even as modesty! Once two Hasidic rabbis came into a town and were greeted enthusiastically by thousands of people who streamed to the town square to meet the VIPs. One of the rabbis was so disgusted with the adulation that he proceeded to throw up. The other said to him, "Why do you get so excited? If you are *ain*, you are nothing. It's not about you." The other rabbi knew that refusing admiration can still be a manifestation of ego.

Humility is not false modesty, nor does it imply that you should be a doormat and let people run all over you. Being a victim has nothing to do with humility. By contrast, when you're humble, you're still crystal-clear about who you are, your unique qualities. You don't let anyone trample on you or kick you around. You're still a force to be reckoned with, and you're standing in your full power—just not in your egoic arrogance. This is the essence of leaving your own Egypt.

Unlike Adam, Moses was a living example of this combination of selflessness and confidence, the Torah says: "And the man Moses was exceedingly humble, more than any man on the face of the earth."[55] When God said that Moses would die as soon as he had seen the Promised Land and would in fact never himself enter the land, Moses acquiesced and was willing to let go of his leadership role: "Let the Lord, source of the breath of all flesh, appoint someone [else] over the community."[56]

Luckily, we need not go as far back as Moses to find humility; we can find it in modern leaders, in science, art, education, politics, and business. Take Albert Einstein, one of the most influential thought-leaders of our time. The story goes that one afternoon he was playing the violin with some friends in a chamber group. Unfortunately it was not going well. Finally, after several false starts, the conductor turned to him, scowled in frustration, and asked, "Einstein! Can't you count?"[57] Even the most revered scientist of the twentieth century, a man richly deserving of portrayal as genius, was a human being with weaknesses just like the rest of us.

Physicists call the year 1905 Einstein's miracle year because in those twelve months alone, he achieved the unimaginable: publishing four papers, each of which resulted in deep changes in how we understand the universe. One, about quantum mechanics, challenged not only previous laws of physics, as the other three (two about relativity and one proving conclusively the existence of atoms) had done, but called into question the entire century-old framework of physics itself, in particular its ability to make definite predictions. After Einstein, it became forever clear that the most physics can do is predict the *probability* that things will turn out one way—or another way, or still another. And true to form, far from resting on the laurels of his place in the pantheon of humanity's greatest thinkers, Einstein was gnawed by doubts about his own discovery. As long as he lived, he was never comfortable with it.[58] He was intellectually too humble for that.

In the arts, humility is rare; so many stars are so full of themselves. But not every star is a diva. When Sonny Rollins, arguably one of the most innovative and original jazz musicians of our age, was asked how his big concert at the 2005 Montreal Jazz Festival had gone, he answered in his froggy voice: "Well, I don't know. I look at all that from the inside, so you'd probably have to ask someone else." He constantly laced his comments with humility. "I don't want this to sound self-aggrandizing," he said. "In my later years I've become very self-effacing. I have decided that I know what greatness is, and I don't want to put myself in that category." Asked if there were any of his recorded performances that didn't pain him with thoughts of how it could have gone better, he hesitated. "It's hard to say," he finally answered, "because I haven't listened to any of my stuff in a long time. Unless it's on the radio, and I can't leave the room." But then he gave a hint of the irrepressible human spirit that is the theme of this chapter: "This is what jazz is: jazz is freedom."[59]

If you're an expert or teacher, it's tempting to think that you already know everything, that you have the answers, and that you're miles ahead of your students. Meet the opposite of that attitude: doctor and teacher Henryk Goldszmit, who wrote under the pen name Janusz Korczak and whom some called the Dr. Seuss of Poland, is virtually forgotten today. His bestsellers, such as the 1919 *How to Love a Child*, and his radio show in the 1930s (until it was canceled due to complaints by Polish anti-semites) changed how parents treated children in a society that still clung to stern Victorian ideas of education. In the 1930s, he founded an orphanage in the Warsaw ghetto and was a light in the heart of darkness. Because of his fame, Korczak's non-Jewish friends offered him more than one chance to get out. They had bribed Nazi guards and gotten him forged identity papers. But he refused to abandon the children. "When a child is sick, you don't leave him alone in the middle of the night," he told them. Korczak was a rare hero of his time. But he didn't like the idea of heroes.

Oversized characters, he taught, dwarf our imagination and make us forget that ordinary people can do extraordinary things, too.

During the time of the Warsaw ghetto, a local newspaper published an article that lauded Korczak for his efforts to keep the orphanage going. In the next issue, a dissenting letter to the editor said, "The Orphans Home has never been, and will never be, Korczak's orphanage. That man is too small, too weak, too poor, and too dimwitted to gather almost 200 children, house, clothe and feed them. This great task has been accomplished by the joint efforts of hundreds of good-willed people."

The letter was signed by Janusz Korczak.[60]

Yes, there are even political leaders who are humble. After Abraham Lincoln won the presidency, he made an unprecedented decision. Possessing enough self-knowledge to know that he did not bring all the qualities needed for effective governing, he had the humility, and the guts, to appoint the most brilliant political minds of his generation, some of whom had been bitter rivals for the nomination and openly disdained the backwoods lawyer who had come out of nowhere, to key posts in his cabinet. His competitors came to revere Lincoln as the greatest leader they had ever known.

Five generations after Lincoln, the CEO met another newly elected president in 1994 and was immediately struck by the South African leader's humility. Nelson Mandela was clearly reluctant to talk about himself. When asked what he considered his greatest accomplishments, he snapped, "Such a question is very important and should be put in writing first." In any case, "they are not my accomplishments," he said. "Everything I have done is to do with the ANC [African National Congress]. I do not make the decisions alone. When I decide to act, it is something that we discuss. I think it is a mistake to think in terms of the Mandela years. It is the era of the liberation forces." This is not just pseudo-modest talk. When Mandela was elected, he gave up the presidential mansion to his co-president (and former archrival) Frederik de Klerk. And after being in office barely a year, he invited the widows of former presidents, his sworn enemies who had locked him away in prison for twenty-seven years, to tea; guests included Betsy Verwoerd, whose husband Hendrik F. Verwoerd had been a principal architect of apartheid. The 94-year-old former first lady was too frail to come, so Mandela traveled to the whites-only enclave where she lived to meet her.[61]

Last but not least, humility yields rich results even in business. Paul Flessner, senior VP of server applications, grew Microsoft's database business from $50 million a year (when he took it on) on to over $1 billion a year. Today Flessner leads about 2,500 people, but he seems to keep his ego in check; he hates publicity and usually insists that photographs of him also include his team members. "Good managers in general are a rare thing," Barry Goffe, a group manager who used to work for Flessner, said; "and good managers capable of overseeing a vast collection of rocket-scientists who have egos and opinions are even rarer."[62]

At the Finnish telecommunications giant Nokia, humility has become a cultural norm. Task forces at all levels of the organization take on major tasks. Almost every assignment of any importance at Nokia is given to a team, even running the whole firm. A five-person team—the CEO, the president, the head of mobile phones, the head of the network equipment business, and the CFO—has been at Nokia's helm for so long that they seem inseparable. "First of all it comes from how the management team works, how they communicate," former CEO Jorma Olilla said in an interview. "Is it a political setup, one with lots of hidden agendas? I think we have had through the years, particularly through the '90s, a particularly strong culture of none of that nonsense."[63] Egos or superstars have no place at Nokia; the company has systematically bred a culture of teamwork. The spirit reaches even outside Nokia: Executives are committed to open standards and interoperability in wireless devices with an almost religious zeal, and periodically sign deals with competitors to develop shared operating systems and standards.

The Finnish telecom is far from alone. Judaism has long known the importance of teams as a check and balance of leadership. God told Moses to gather 70 elders , and a Jewish court consists of 23 rabbis (the minimum is three) since God is the only leader who can lead alone. Team-based organization designs at senior levels have replaced more traditional executive structures in many firms. A study of 277 Fortune Service 500 and Industrial 500 firms showed that in the 1960s, top-level teams existed in only 8 percent of companies (modern teamwork had been spear-headed by the Swiss pharma industry). By the 1980s, 25 percent of firms had established top-level teams, a threefold increase.[64] Today, the team model is a strong alternative to the two-person CEO/COO structure; it has emerged to tackle increasingly complex internal and external demands on organizations, as well as to the age-old issue of executive succession. In many firms, team-based organization designs improved coordination among the departments and functions of a complex enterprise. The result was a synergy in which the added value of a team was greater than the overhead costs of coordinating their collective work. With this synergy came productivity: by the late 1990s, research of over 2,000 firms in Great Britain showed that teamwork clearly improved their financial performance on average (although it also showed that autonomous teams didn't do any better than closely supervised teams); and an analysis of 131 studies of teamwork and productivity found that of all organizational development interventions, team-building has the highest impact on financial results.[65]

The Bottom Line

- To earn the right to lead, you begin by leading yourself out of your own Egypt (the Hebrew name for Egypt also means the narrows). Leadership is in large part a commitment to self-determination, to ending the slavery, and to taking charge of yourself.

- Before you can envision the future, you examine yourself—your motives for leading, your assumptions, your principles and values, your blind spots. Leaders who failed to practice self-knowledge, from Nero to Hitler to Ken Lay and Jeff Skilling, wreaked havoc around them.

- How do you practice leaving your own Egypt? You take 100 percent responsibility (Jews are directly accountable to God). You constantly check what principles and values your actions are based on. You decode your own background conversations and blind spots.

- As you lead, be aware of what type(s) of power you exert over other people, and what type(s) of power they exert over you, or you might be in for a rude awakening later.

- Going beyond your limits must be coupled with humility. The costs of hubris can be huge, while checking your ego yields rich results.

CHAPTER TWO

Commandment II
No Idols: Authentic Vision

The idols of the nations are silver and gold, human handiwork.
—Psalms 135:15

I don't want to achieve immortality through my work.
I want to achieve immortality through not dying.
—Woody Allen

THE SECOND COMMANDMENT: *"You shall not recognize the gods of others before my presence. You shall not make yourself a carved image nor any likeness of that which is in the heavens above, or of that which is on the earth below, or of that which is in the water beneath the earth. You shall not prostrate yourself to them nor shall you worship them."* Are you worshiping idols? Are you acting out someone else's dream or expectation, or truly pursuing your own? Money, power, and fame are not goals but false gods; they are only a means to an end. A leader's true vision is larger than life, includes many others, and often outlives the leader. What difference will you make? What legacy will you leave behind? This chapter will show you how to unfold your own authentic future, and how to make it real. First you must put the past back where it belongs: in the past.

One day Moses returned to camp and was in for a shock: The people had made a golden calf; they had turned the unspeakable and infinite Being, the divine essence, into a thing and were praying to gold.[66] In keeping with his character, Moses acted decisively: The moment he saw the gilded sculpture, he smashed the tablets and had three thousand of the idolatrous revelers killed. Gone was the stuttering shepherd; he had transformed himself into a mighty leader marked by divinity. The last sentence in the Torah reads: "Never again did there arise in Israel a prophet like Moses—whom God singled out face to face ... and for all the great might and awesome power that Moses displayed before all Israel."[67]

Why did Moses intervene with such holy fury? Because an idol is a mirage that leads people away from their real mission. The Commandment "You shall have no idols" is about keeping your eye on the future without being distracted by short-term gratification or glory. And yet we live at a time when many seem to have their eye on the wrong ball: on themselves and their material stuff. A 2007 study by San Diego State University showed a 30-percent increase over the last twenty-five years in the number of young Americans with symptoms of what the researchers called "elevated narcissism." More people than ever agreed with statements like "I like to be the center of attention" and "I am special."[68] Contrast that with a generation earlier. In 1967, a survey of college students found that their highest priority was to find "a meaningful philosophy of life."[69] Scroll forward to 2006 when more than 80 percent of students listed "wealth" as their top priority in life, with "fame" as a close second. The television show *American Idol* epitomizes this trend. Why would people want to turn themselves into idols?

There is nothing wrong with wealth or fame, to be sure. But they are, at best, side-effects, not the real thing, and at worst false idols. In fact, fabulously rich and famous people like Bill Gates or Warren Buffett, Oprah Winfrey or Michael Bloomberg did not get rich or famous by having money or stardom as their life purpose. None of them set out to be a star or a billionaire; they each committed to a vision larger than themselves, a vision that was about adding value and creating a new quality of life. Indeed, when leadership theorists Warren Bennis and Burt Nanus studied ninety successful business leaders—from Ray Kroc, the founder of McDonald's, to Lee Iacocca, who revived Chrysler in the 1980s—in search of their single most-common trait, they found that these leaders all built, and acted upon, a vision shared by their followers. Bennis' definition of leadership is "the capacity to create a compelling vision and translate it into action and sustain it." Successful leaders have a vision others believe in and treat as their own.[70] For that, a leader's vision has to be larger than life, larger than the leader's self-interest.

A Nation of Visionaries

Judaism is inextricably linked to the vision of a brilliant future; the drive to reach the Promised Land—or the coming of the Messiah—is its very essence. So it comes as no surprise that the Bible is filled with a plethora of visionaries. The second volume of the *Tanach*[71] is the Book of Prophets, from Joshua to Samuel and Isaiah, who could castigate leaders ("O my people, your leaders mislead you, and they have corrupted the direction of your ways"[72]), but could just as easily conjure up a stirring vision of peace ("They shall beat their swords into plowshares and their spears into pruning hooks; nation will not lift sword against nation, and they will no longer study warfare"[73]). The training and development of prophets was even institutionalized; by the time of the First Temple, there were many schools of prophecy. The investment paid off: While only forty-eight male and seven female prophets (yes, women broke through the glass ceiling then) are mentioned by name, there were in fact over *1.2 million* prophets in Jewish history.[74] In fact, some thought there were too many. When Joshua found out that people were prophesying in the camp, he went straight to his leader. "My master Moses," he implored, "imprison them!" But Moses rebuffed him: "Are you jealous for my sake?" He had no desire to keep others down; on the contrary, he wanted all people to be visionaries and rise to his level, if not higher. His fervent wish was, "If only all the people of God were prophets!"[75]

Visionaries vs. Realists vs. Dreamers

Unlike Moses, some leaders have no patience for visionaries. Former German chancellor Helmut Schmidt quipped that if people want vision, they should go see an eye doctor. (Schmidt's view is understandable. Germans were badly burnt; they have been skeptical of grand, big-picture ideas ever since Hitler brought them his ill-conceived dream of an Aryan master race dominating the world.) There is nothing wrong with realists like Schmidt; they are concerned with controlling uncertainty and making reliable predictions. There is a place for past-based projections. Reducing uncertainty is a key task of management, and it is only human to want to reduce the often unbearable tension between the now and the future you want.

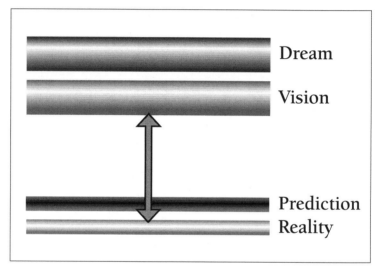

Figure 2.1: Vision vs. Prediction vs. Dream

If the bottom bar in Figure 2.1 is the current reality, leaders cannot stop at the second level—the merely predictable. The only future-oriented statements so-called realists are willing to make are forecasts, for example, "I predict that given our flat performance last year, we should again have 1 percent growth this year." Such a statement puts you to sleep. For the realist the future is pretty much an extension of the past—the opposite of leadership, which is about bold vision, even if that brings more uncertainty. Leaders are not merely about changing what is, because what exists now is a result of yesterday; they are about creating what isn't, which means venturing into uncharted territory, working toward a vision. This is not the same as a dream, the top bar.

Isaiah's dream of total peace, or Martin Luther King, Jr.'s dream that we will all be brothers one day, is worth aspiring to but ultimately out of reach.

A vision, to deserve the name, is unpredictable and yet possible to achieve. It is desirable; it offers a new quality of life; it is a magnet for action that gets you out of bed in the morning. A vision serves as a strategic filter to weed out irrelevant actions; and it should not be merely self-serving ("I want to make $250,000 a year" is not a vision) but inclusive, owned by all key stakeholders and implementers. Bill Gates's vision—to solve everybody's computer problems everywhere—is all-encompassing: Many, many people can get behind it.

But since stretching for the future in the day-to-day is inherently uncomfortable, many people want to reduce the tension between their current reality and their goal by doing one of three things: they curb their enthusiasm and cut their vision down to a mere prediction; they live only in dreamland and forget about reality altogether, for example by taking drugs; or they swallow the tension and get ill or depressed. Leaders, by contrast, live in the tension between reality and vision— every day. When Colin Marshall became chief executive of British Airways and promised it would become "the world's favorite airline," realists derided his bold declaration as a frivolous pipedream. At the time, BA was so second-rate that people quipped it was short for "Bloody Awful." Undeterred, Marshall acted consistent with his vision. He constantly searched for new areas and levels of customer service that would yield stronger customer loyalty at lower price realization than they cost to create. Marshall's motto was "Putting people first" (customers *and* colleagues); he greatly spruced up service, improved the in-flight food so people would no longer joke that hell in Europe was a place with a British cook, refurbished all major airport lounges, and put all employees through a two-day seminar designed to put them in the customer's shoes, and mandated that passengers be greeted by their names, as in "Have a good flight, Mr. Jones." As then-BA general manager Chris Swain put it, "It's customer, customer, customer."[76]

Marshall improved quality by paying attention to BA engineers, revamping key subcontracting and union agreements, and streamlining maintenance. And he made money by freeing engineers to service other airlines. Perhaps being the world's favorite airline is never quite fully achieved, but British Airways came awfully close: In 1992 it was rated best transatlantic airline by *Business Traveler*. Fifteen years later, Marshall (who had meanwhile become Lord Colin Marshall, Baron of Knightsbridge) wasn't resting on his laurels: by then he was pushing his latest vision—the ambitious Terminal 5 project to double the size and operations of London's Heathrow airport.

Resignation Wins All the Votes

Before delving further into the future, the French adage, *Il faut reculer pour mieux sauter* (You have to recoil to leap better), reminds us that we first have to take a step backward. All of us tend to burden ourselves with at least some resignation, resentments, or regrets that come from past experiences and cloud our outlook. It comes with the territory of being human. But already Moses knew that it was easier to take the people out of Egypt than to take Egypt out of the people. The past had a way of pulling people back to it. And he knew that as the going got tough, people would idealize the way things used to be.[77] People tend to be addicted to the past. When you set out to design and commit yourself to a new future, be cognizant of several obstacles: resignation; the hold of the past; and addiction to old and obsolete tools.

Proverbs warns unequivocally that "Where there is no vision, people perish."[77] But our concerns tend to be short-term: Will the stock price go up or down this quarter? How do we get through this week's e-mail backlog? How do we survive the endless meetings, the office politics, the gossip at the water cooler? Managers spend an inordinate percentage of their time running the present, not creating the future. And how can you get to the future if you work on it only when you have time left over? Most managers spend most of their time managing the status quo—on what is, not on what could be.

What is the status quo based on? The past. And what happens when the past has such a grip on the future that vision is virtually absent? We get the opposite of vision: resignation to the status quo. When the CEO lived in India in 1987, defeatism was everywhere. At that time, it took seven years to get a new phone line—if you were willing to bribe officials. Nearly every morning, when the CEO got up and looked outside his bedroom window, he saw a dead person being carried off on a cart under a white shroud. All he wanted to do was crawl back into bed and forget about his job. The resignation was pervasive and nearly too much to bear. (This has changed; at least in the urban areas, where India's professional class has caught the globalization train, a sense of optimism and good fortune prevails.)

But you don't need to go to India to find resignation. A lawyer in New York City making $200,000 a year might be completely down about his career chances if he hasn't made partner by his mid-thirties. And resignation can creep into any meeting; a colleague might say, "Come on. We tried that already; that's not going to work," or people might mumble among themselves, "Here they go again; yet another change effort that's going to fail. Good luck on that one." Others might be overly risk-averse or concerned about losing their job if they try something new. Resignation may even pose as business-as-usual. As *New York Times* columnist David Brooks put it in one of his riffs:

> Your DVD collection is organized, and so is your walk-in closet. Your car is clean and vacuumed, your frequently dialed numbers are programmed into your cordless phone, your telephone plan is suited to your needs, and your various gizmos interact without conflict. Your spouse is athletic, your kids are bright, your job is rewarding, your promotions are inevitable, everywhere you need to be comes with its own accessible parking. You look great in casual slacks.[79]

Most of us (at least those who live in industrialized countries) sail in quiet and lukewarm waters toward retirement, and then toward the end of our lives. Even if we have to put out the occasional fire, we react to circumstances; we tend to live our lives from the past—unless we are struck by a shocking change of destiny, like the death of a loved one, a sudden bout of cancer, or a calamity like 9/11. One man who had a brutal awakening from going through the motions was Alfred Nobel, a reclusive Swede who had amassed a fortune by producing ammunition for war; among other things, Nobel was the inventor of dynamite. When his brother died unexpectedly, Nobel's life changed.

One newspaper confused the two brothers and believed Alfred was the dead brother. So one morning, the war manufacturer got an opportunity never afforded to anybody: to read his own obituary while he was still alive. He was shocked; it was not a pretty picture. The article described Nobel as a man who had made it possible to kill more people, more quickly, than anyone else who had ever lived.

In a flash, Nobel realized two things: that the world would remember him for this death-laden legacy, and that he was loath to leave such a legacy. He established the Nobel Prize, which soon became the ultimate honor in the fields of economics, literature, physics, medicine, the sciences—and peace. Today, some one hundred years after his death, Nobel's lasting legacy is not chiefly his contribution to war and death, but to peace and life.

Putting the Past Back in the Past

To be sure, you can learn valuable lessons from the past (indeed this book would not exist without past experience). Your mind is like a machine that constantly likens everything that happens—yes, *everything*, without exception—to other past experiences. And 99 percent of the time, this Bayesian updating (as it is called in statistics and econometrics) is sensible. Since the sun has risen each day your entire life, it will probably rise again tomorrow. Likewise, it's not sensible to sit on a hot stove when you know from experience that the results are painful. Most of the time, being burned, learning from past mistakes, is useful and indeed can be crucial for survival. It can also be important for improving your skills. For example, a tennis pro knows, from past practice, exactly where the ball will fall if he or she hits it with a backhand slice. But there is a pitfall in equating everything that happens in the present to the past. If every time something happens we say, "Aha, here we go again," then we cannot have truly new experiences. We are stuck in our own past—not a good thing if we want to lead others into the future.

Yet it happens all the time. Especially when managers face a crisis, they tend to get bogged down in their own past and revert to what worked last time. A classic example can be seen in U.S. foreign policy: In the twentieth century, successive U.S. governments tended to fight their previous wars. It was like an evil spell: When the United States went to war in Korea, Harry Truman used military strategies he had learned in World War II, thereby failing to foresee the massive attack by North Korean forces that nearly drove the outnumbered U.S. and R.O.K. defenders into the sea. Lyndon Johnson and Richard Nixon used the Korea strategy in Vietnam, but U.S. forces were ill-prepared for the highly mobile Vietcong cells that had infiltrated every village in the South. George Bush (both the elder and the younger) used state-of-the-art technology like stealth aircraft and infrared sensors that detected heat from tanks and made them into easy targets, as well as overwhelming air strikes the United States had learned in Vietnam. In fact, George W. Bush framed Iraq in terms of Vietnam; when defending his administration's Iraq policy, he said that "one unmistakable legacy of Vietnam is that the price of America's withdrawal was paid by millions of innocent citizens."[80] But both Bushes suffered from the Vietnam Syndrome in Iraq.

Whether in politics or business, when you graft the past onto a new situation, you may pre-program failure. In the 1970s, Swiss watch companies held on to obsolete rules of the game, doggedly producing the same old expensive watches with high-quality and expensive manual labor. They were quickly outmaneuvered by nimble Japanese copycats who dumped low-cost, high-quality watches on world markets. Swiss watchmakers had dominated the global watch industry for sixty years; by 1968 they commanded over 65 percent of the world watch market and over 80 percent of industry profits. Ironically, it was Swiss researchers who developed the first electronic quartz watch. But when they introduced the cutting-edge idea at a 1967 conference of Swiss manufacturers, it was roundly rejected. Yes, the quartz watch performed like a watch, but it lacked "real watch" components like gears and mainsprings. It did not fit the Swiss watch paradigm. Japanese watchmakers like Seiko had no such past baggage; they embraced quartz watches immediately. The result: The Swiss watch industry took a nose dive, and 50,000 of 62,000 Swiss watchmakers lost their jobs.

The Hebrew word for "sin" or "wrongdoing," *averah*, comes from the same root as the word for "past," *avar*. According to the Talmud, all you have done in your past, even your proudest accomplishments, is insufficient for the future: it will not lead to success if you have lulled yourself into complacency. Rabbi Saadia Gaon, a great Torah scholar and community leader in Babylonia more than a thousand years ago, wrote that we should "repent" for yesterday, no matter how good it was, for yesterday compared to today and tomorrow is limited.[81] You can never be satisfied with what you did yesterday, since today you have already added knowledge and understanding, and tomorrow you will add even more. The daily lighting of the candles during the Hanukkah holiday symbolizes this principle. Each day Jews kindle one more candle than the day before: one on day one, two on day two, and so forth, through the eighth day. Every day you have to bring more light to the world than the day before. Senegal's former president Abdou Diouf knew that. After he received the Africa Prize for Leadership in 1987, he kept his award, an elegant gold sculpture by the Japanese artist Igarashi, on his desk as a reminder "that no matter what I did yesterday, I must earn the prize again today."[82] Every day he had to do his utmost as a leader again and earn his award anew. He was never done.

Dropping Your Tools

Sometimes the very tools that have led to all your successes and brought you to today can become a hindrance. On July 6, 1994, disaster struck at South Canyon, Colorado. According to the inquiry board, the fire

> moved onto steep slopes and into dense, highly flammable Gambel oak. Within seconds a wall of flame raced up the hill toward the firefighters on the west flank fireline. Failing to outrun the flames, twelve firefighters perished. Two Helitack crew members on the top of the ridge also died when they tried to outrun the fire to the northwest.[83]

Worst of all, the fourteen firefighters and crew members died needlessly. They could have outrun the fire had they dropped their heavy tools. So why didn't they? One of the survivors, Clinton Rhoades, testified, "at some point, about 300 yards up the hill... I then realized I still had my saw over my shoulder! I irrationally started looking for a place to put it down where it wouldn't get burned. ...I remember thinking I can't believe I'm putting down my saw."[84] For years, the firefighters had been drilled that their tools were crucial and they had to save them at all costs. It had become part of their conditioning. Faced with the decision to save either themselves or their tools, the fourteen who instinctively did the latter suffered the consequences, and died.

Leaders often face a similar dilemma. We fail to jettison the tools—the methods, beliefs, or rules—we have used so successfully throughout our lives, even when those tools prevent further progress, or keep us from moving on and being who we can be. We have gotten so used to them, they are so ingrained and automatic that it's hard to let them go. The failure to drop our tools seldom costs us our lives, as it did the firefighters at South Canyon, but it does rob us of our ability to build something new. Leadership entails facing new situations in which old solutions no longer work. As a quote attributed to Albert Einstein says, the significant problems we face today cannot be solved at the same level of thinking we were at when we created them.[85] If we cannot let go of outdated tools and rules, we cannot survive as leaders. We could take our cue from the Torah: When God speaks to Moses for the first time, He instructs him to "remove your shoes from your feet" so that Moses has nothing between him and his sacred mission; when Moses sees the buring bush, he shifts from his old point of view, "Let me turn aside and see this great spectacle,"[86] and when David prepares to meet Goliath, King Saul offers him armor for the fight;[87] but David knows it would only hold him back. So before he fights, he drops the armor.

That's exactly what Intel had to do when Japanese companies were conquering the memory market and Intel's found itself on a slippery slope down. Andy Grove, then the company's president, sat in his office with Gordon Moore, the co-founder and then chairman and CEO; he turned to Moore and asked, "If we got kicked out and the board brought in a new CEO, what do you think he would do?"

Moore answered, "He would get us out of memories." (No pun intended.)

After a moment of reflection, Grove said, "Why shouldn't you and I walk out the door, come back and do it ourselves?"

It was easier said than done. Intel was synonymous with memories; Grove found it was unimaginable without them.

> As I started to discuss the possibility of getting out of the memory chip business with some of my associates, I had a hard time getting the words out of my mouth without equivocation. It was just too difficult a thing to say. Intel equaled memories in all of our minds. How could we give up our identity?[88]

To cut a long story short, Grove and Moore did jettison Intel's memory business. It was not easy for Grove or for anyone else in the company. But it turned out to be their best move ever. Intel had developed the microprocessor as an alternative computer chip. The 8086 and its next of kin, the 8088, helped launch the personal-computer revolution by providing the brains for IBM's pathbreaking PC. Grove and Moore had the guts to shed all past activities that were not a match for their goal. They gave up what Intel had been for what it could be.

In order to build a new future, managers have to unshackle the present from the past. One way to do this is by finishing unfinished business, in particular unwanted and repetitive patterns of behavior that draw their energy from something unresolved.

Tool 2.1
Unfinished Business

This tool helps you put the past where it belongs: in the past. List all unfinished business that drags you into the past. (The acid test is this: Is the item taking up bandwidth in your head? Do you catch yourself repeatedly thinking about the item and do you spend more time justifying why you don't get it handled than it would take to simply handle it? List your unfinished business by category, as follows:

Finances
(e.g., someone owes you money; you owe someone money; your taxes are overdue, etc.)

Physical environment
(e.g., you have too many old shoes in your closet; your jacket needs to be fixed; your desk drawers are a mess; a book from the library is a year overdue; your filing cabinet is bursting with obsolete files, etc.)

Communications
(e.g., you have unanswered and long overdue mail or e-mail; you have withheld uncomfortable information from a colleague, friend, or family member, etc.)

Relationships
(e.g., you have lost touch with someone years ago and keep thinking it would be nice to reconnect, but don't quite ever get around to it; you have never quite forgiven someone for a past transgression; you had an upset with a colleague, family member, or friend and never cleared the air, etc.)

Health
(e.g., you keep postponing that dentist appointment, you wanted to get that medical checkup a year ago, you have neglected flossing your teeth, despite a fervent New Year's resolution you just don't use that gym membership, etc.)

For each item, set a deadline for handling it. (As the jazz musician Duke Ellington supposedly admitted, "Without a deadline, baby, I wouldn't do nothin'.") You may want to ask a trusted colleague or friend to hold you accountable, especially for tough items that you might be resisting. This week, close at least three open cycles.

> **Tip:** Instead of waiting for unfinished business to accumulate and bog you down, dedicate half a day each week to completing unfinished items.

At times your unfinished business is more internal than external; that's when it can play the most devious tricks of all. A generation ago, the CEO participated in a leadership workshop in Zurich. The facilitator had a shock of premature white hair and a slightly obnoxious smile, and opened the session in a loud and confrontational style. The CEO's reaction was immediate and overwhelming: the urge to get out of there. He said to himself, "I can't stand this guy and his fascist voice."

Then, in a flash, he discovered that he had instinctively compared the facilitator to his paternal grandmother, with whom he sometimes stayed during vacations as a child. Each morning, she would storm into his guest bedroom at seven o'clock, and shout cheerfully, "Good morning, Thomas! It's a new day!" She would rip open the window with zest and force the sleepy eight-year-old to do morning gymnastics. For breakfast, he had to eat strange foods like sunflower seeds that looked and tasted like bird-droppings. As an adult, the CEO realized that his grandmother had meant well and that indeed her health practices had been ahead of her time; but back then, it was a nightmare.

So decades later, as he heard the workshop facilitator, all these memories flooded his brain. In a flash, he was the eight-year-old again; reflexively, his mind screamed at him to escape—at all costs—from that white-haired maniac with the penetrating voice. In that very moment, the workshop leader yelled, "You cannot even hear what I'm saying right now. I'm sounding just like your father, or your teacher, or some other person in your life."

The CEO's ears perked up; his game had been called. It occurred to him that he might learn something from this facilitator, so he chose to stay in the workshop. (Later the facilitator and the CEO became good friends and colleagues.) Equating a leadership trainer with your grandmother may sound like an odd example; but how often do we shoot ourselves in the foot, losing precious opportunities, because we get bogged down by our past patterns, which prevent us from seeing a new situation from a new perspective? Had the CEO yielded to the imprints from his past, he would have missed a priceless chance to develop his leadership.

Building a Shared Vision

Once you have cleaned up the past and put it to rest in the past, you can finally move back to the future. Most leadership theorists agree that a key characteristic shared by great leaders is having a compelling vision. But using the word "vision" over and over does not a vision make. A vision arises in a conversation between people; it is shared. No matter how great your vision is, if you don't share it with others, it will die. The Hebrew word for prophet, *navi*, means literally "words from lips." Moses Maimonides writes in the twelfth century that if a prophet keeps a vision to him- or herself, he or she is liable to the death penalty at the hands of God.[89] That's a bit harsh, but it gets the point across.

Abraham Lincoln might have had a vision of a country without slavery, but until a critical mass of his contemporaries shared that vision, it couldn't become an historical imperative. John F. Kennedy might have dreamed of space travel, but his vision of an American landing on the moon and returning safely became a reality only once enough other people shared it. Jürgen Schrempp's vision of a global DaimlerChrysler company, by contrast, never materialized, despite being hailed initially as a "merger in heaven." Schrempp failed to ensure that Daimler's and Chrysler's visions were aligned; Daimler's vision ("Nur das Beste," Only the Best) and Chrysler's (whatever the customer wants) didn't match. The question is, how do you co-create vision? How do you have others buy into, and own, your vision?

Tool 2.2
Co-creating Vision

What can you do to build a compelling future, one that inspires others to go beyond themselves (and their past)? Here are some ground rules.

Ask people what they want.

Don't tell—ask. So many managers simply state their vision instead of asking questions. Vision is, quite simply, the answer to the question, what do you want? If you ask, people might at first answer with trivial things, e.g., a new copy machine, but will soon get to the bigger picture. You could ask, "where do you see yourself and/or this organization three years from today? Where do you want to be? What can you not even imagine in the current environment? If you could wave a magic wand, what would you have (or do, or be) that you don't today?"

Don't censor any ideas.

In a brainstorming session, all ideas are equally valid. Once the vision has traction, you can always check its feasibility or prioritize ideas. But cross that bridge later. For now, make it safe to speculate, entertain bold ideas, and propose seemingly impractical solutions.

Manage the conversation.

If you don't, the discussion about the future can easily deteriorate into mere opinions or conversations based in the past, with complaints, excuses, or blame.

Write it down.

Like exhaling on a cold winter day, a vision of the future can just as easily vaporize into the atmosphere of today's current battles and circumstances. A great way to keep your vision of the future alive is to write a newspaper article for your favorite publication (for example *The Economist*, *The Wall Street Journal* or *The New York Times*) about your organization and/or yourself as a leader. Date the article five years into the future and use the third person to describe yourself. What did you accomplish? What difference did you make? What was unique or different about you and/or your organization's approach? What do customers, colleagues, suppliers, end-users, or VIPs say about you/your organization? How do you spend a typical day? Be bold and creative, and have fun with this.

Make it a common future.
Avoid the DaimlerChrysler fiasco. Be sure your colleagues
share your vision and own it as theirs. Again, a simple way to
do that is to ask, What do you want? What do you see? Is anyone in the room not aligned with this vision? Any objections?

Institutionalize the conversation.
Part of managing the conversation is to create occasions for
developing the future. For example, you may want to hold
weekly or monthly meetings or teleconferences in which you
allow yourself and your colleagues to speculate wildly, without
any accountability or obligation to deliver on the possibilities
created. Each Friday, the CEO and his colleagues like to ask,
What if …?

When top managers are willing to let go of control and allow for co-
creation, people will take ownership of the vision and see is as theirs,
and they will be more likely to beat the odds. In October 1990—on
Mahatma Gandhi's birthday—The Hunger Project, an international
organization dedicated to ending world hunger and on the rosters of
the UN Economic and Social Council (ECOSOC) and the UN Millenium Project Hunger Task Force, worked with the planning commission of India to call together all stakeholders, from government people
to the grassroots in the villages, from media people to experts, to
develop a vision and strategy for ending hunger, at a time when some
11,000 people died of hunger-related causes in India *every day*. The
stakeholders in the planning process were not inspired by the organization's mission to "end hunger in India." After much deliberation, they
came up with their own vision, consistent with that of The Hunger
Project: "Cross a threshold where every man, woman and child has the
capacity to lead a healthy and productive life in harmony with nature."
Indian culture is known for flowery language, so the planning commission's vision was a bit more verbose than, say, Canon's pithy strategic
intent to "Beat Xerox," but the important thing was that the stakehold-

ers in India owned it as *theirs*. All implementers were inspired, and the vision pulled them into action. For example, their strategic intent required catalytic action in order to end the marginalization and oppression of women (who produce some 80 percent of the food, bear the brunt of providing nutrition, safe water, child-rearing, and education, and often work from 4:00 o'clock in the morning until they drop late at night in developing countries) and to foster women leaders. Since only men could inherit land from their parents, the planning commission and The Hunger Project pushed through new banking laws so women could get bank loans for their business ventures without land as collateral; to transform the age-old monopoly of men in the *panchayats* (village councils), they pushed through a new national policy: one-third of all *panchayat* leaders had to be women. This led to a landslide: in the 1994 election, in what is perhaps the largest leadership experiment of our time, 330,000 women were elected to leadership positions. The number soon rose to over *1 million women* in government.[90]

Co-creating a broad-based vision works in business too. Nokia did it routinely in what came to be called the "Annual Nokia Way." Each year, Nokia offices around the world submit their local vision and strategy recommendations to Helsinki headquarters, which synthesizes them into the overall company vision and strategy. Because Nokia employees have a stake in Nokia's strategic intent ("to create personalized communication technology that enables people to shape their own mobile world") and because they feel part of the strategy team, they rally for seemingly impossible objectives. One short-term goal Nokia executives set for themselves at the end of 1994 was to sell 400,000 phones. The company was so revved up, and the market conditions so favorable, that when the project was over, Nokia sales reps had sold not 400,000 but *twenty million* phones.

Be the Future Today

The Native American Iroquois Confederacy considered the consequences of their actions for seven generations, and the Japanese company Matsushita reportedly operates from a 250-year plan.[91] But we are talking about more than foreseeing the future; leadership, in Gandhi's words, is the capacity to "be the change change you wish to see in the world."[92] Can you live today as if the future were already here?

In Jewish thought, the rooster embodies the capacity to stand in the future; it is the only animal that wakes up while it's still night. In that sense, the rooster is a symbol for leadership: It can see the light while others still see only darkness. It is not a victim of circumstances. (The Hebrew word for "rooster" is *gever*, the same word as for "man.")

> **Tip:** Are you willing to be a rooster? To be the future now while delaying gratification? When you make a fundamental change in the company, or bring an untested new product to market, are you willing to live with no results for a while?

The Talmud asks, "Who is wise?" and gives its own answer: "He who sees what is to be born."[93] Wisdom includes seeing the future possibility in everything that exists. In the words of the Spanish-born philosopher George Santayana, "To love things spiritually, that is to say, intelligently and disinterestedly, means to love the love in them, to worship the good which they pursue, and to see them all prophetically in their possible beauty. To love things as they are would be a mockery of things: a true lover must love them as they would wish to be."[94]

To stand in the future while that future is not yet here calls for yet another leadership capacity: delaying gratification. The rooster cries as if dawn has already arrived, but he doesn't get his reward until after daylight. When Moses led his people out of Egypt, many of them thought the Promised Land was just around the corner. But Moses was far from naïve; he knew the long-term journey would demand countless short-term sacrifices before his people would reach their destination. At times he had to ask them to take action consistent with their vision while the jury was still out. When the Jews were sandwiched between the endless waters of the Red Sea and the rapidly approaching Egyptian army, Moses realized the only action that would save them was to walk into the water. He gave the command; they were aghast;

nobody followed suit. What—into the *sea*? It was the most ridiculous thing they had ever heard. When Moses had told them to leave Egypt for the uncertain vision of the Promised Land, they had heeded his call and trusted him. Enough was enough; now their leader surely had lost his mind? Everybody hesitated, frightened to death. Then one of them, Nachshon ben Aminadav, prince of Judah, stepped up and waded into the waves; his legs disappeared, then his chest, then his shoulders. The Jews crowding the beach gave a collective gasp. He was in the water up to his nostrils—and then, the sea parted. "God drove back the sea with a powerful east wind all that night, and He transformed the sea into dry land."[95] Nachshon had to stand in the future, in the vision, without any evidence that it would work. He was like a proverbial tightrope walker who has to keep his gaze firmly fixed on the horizon. If he loses sight of his goal and looks down at the gaping void below him for even a moment, he will be lost in fear and plunge to his death.

As a prisoner held by the South African apartheid regime for twenty-seven years, Nelson Mandela did not know whether he would disappear into oblivion; in addition to the courage of his convictions, he had to muster extraordinary discipline—including an unusual capacity to delay the gratification of success—until finally, impossibly he made his triumphant entry on the world stage. Winston Churchill found himself alone in the wilderness, cast out from Britain's government from 1932 to 1940 while appeasers in the cabinet fell prey to Hitler's treachery. In 1940, when the war seemed lost and the Germans readied to storm the British beaches, Churchill finally became prime minister at an age when most of us retire.

Martin Luther King, Jr., was less fortunate; just like Moses, he would not be allowed to see the Promised Land. In the last speech of his life he said:

> Well, I don't know what will happen now. We've got some difficult days ahead. But it really doesn't matter to me now, because I've been to the mountaintop, and I don't mind. Like anybody, I would like to live a long life. Longevity has its place. But I'm not concerned about that now. I just want to do God's Will, and He has allowed me to go up to the mountain, and I have looked over, and I have seen 'The

Promised Land.' I may not get there with you, but I want you to know tonight that we as a people will get to 'The Promised Land'! So I'm happy tonight, I'm not worried about anything! I'm not fearing any man! 'Mine eyes have seen the Glory of the Coming of The Lord!'[96]

The next day King was dead.

The willingness to incur short-term costs and, in the extreme, make a personal sacrifice for an uncertain future is a hallmark of great leaders. It seems to work for the rest of us too. In a series of classic experiments in the 1960s, psychologist Walter Mischel showed how important delaying gratification is to a child's future development and achievement. In the preschool on Stanford University campus, Mischel left four-year-old children in a room with a marshmallow and a bell, and told them that if they rang the bell, he would come back and they could eat the marshmallow immediately. But if they did not ring the ball and waited for him to return, they would get two marshmallows. The "grabbers," the children who lacked the discipline to wait for their treat, Mischel found, later struggled in school, and as he followed them over the next fourteen years, they were far more likely to succumb to teen pregnancy, drugs, gambling, truancy, and crime. On the other hand, the "waiters," those who could delay their marshmallow for the promise of future rewards, had higher SAT scores, were accepted at the more competitive and prestigious colleges, and had more satisfying adult lives.[97]

> **Tip:** The CEO's clients often create a "sculpture" of their future by carving out their seven fundamental life commitments. (Why seven? Don't ask...It just seems to work for managers, and seven is a large enough number to include all aspects of life.) What are the commitments that, unless you fulfill them in your lifetime, will make your life less than truly fulfilled?

One client, the president of a multinational energy company, came up with fundamental life commitments like these: "Create an environment where people fully express themselves. Continually expand my knowledge and spiritual satisfaction. Have my family be fulfilled.

Honor my word—no frivolous talk. Have the whole repertoire of language at my disposal." Another of his commitments was particularly startling. He told the CEO, "I want to make people laugh." The CEO was nonplussed. Was this the same top manager who intimidated most of his workforce; the same guy who used to dress down subordinates in his office which most of them hadn't ever seen from the inside, the same guy whose conference calls were exercises in corporate routine, with zero creativity or leadership? Yes, the president said. He had long held the dream to be an entertainer and let the sparks fly. He wanted to open a bar with a friend of his where he would perform on stage and tell war stories and jokes about corporate life. So the CEO gave his client the benefit of the doubt and asked him, "Why are you waiting until retirement to make people laugh? How about living that commitment *now*?" Three months later, the CEO was invited to the company's holiday party and saw the president on stage, giving a hillarous performance that had everone in stitches. At dinner, several managers came up to came up to the CEO's table and whispered, "What did you do with do with the boss? He is a new man. He constantly cracks us up. He's actually fun to work for—we look forward to meetings with him!"

Keeping the Big Picture Alive

Last but not least is perhaps the most important skill of leaders: How do you keep your vision alive in the endless details of day-to-day management? What do you do when you or a colleague have run out of steam and given up on his vision? What did Moses do when he realized that the Promised Land would take a long, long time—forty years, something he hadn't known when he had ventured out of Egypt—and his people lost morale and wanted to give up? If you can bring the big picture back whenever it goes out the window, it will be hard to stop your leadership. Restoring people's vision is a five-step process.

Tool 2.3
Restoring Vision in Five Steps

Step 1

Let the person speak and listen with compassion. Once you have seen how pervasively the past reigns supreme, open the lines of communication and simply allow the person to communicate fully and explain where they are. (It may help to get intelligence about the person and their situation from their peers or people who know them well.) Don't try to persuade the person or change his or her mind.

Step 2

Ask the person when he or she gave up. Find out exactly when the vision became "impossible" and what the exact blockage was that got in the way. It could be that someone missed an interim milestone, or that an important gatekeeper dismissed the entire project, or some problem outside of work got in the way. No matter what the interruption was, identify the precise moment, not only to fix problems that may have arisen at that point, but also to hear how the person interpreted what occurred.

Step 3

Separate what *actually* happened from the *interpretation* of what happened. What did the person decide? What conclusion did he or she draw? Be sure that the person makes a distinction between the facts and the *perception* of the facts. In 1987, when the CEO coached teams in twenty-seven countries in their strategies to meet their annual financial goals, he called the managing director in Finland and asked how he was doing. There was a long silence on the phone (not untypical for the Finns); the CEO thought the line had gone dead. He asked, "Are you there?" Finally the answer came in a thick and dark voice, "I think I shall kill myself." In a flash, the CEO realized that his colleague took his goal so seriously that he would

rather die than live with the shame of missing it. The CEO had
to help him see that the facts (he was behind in meeting his
financial goals) were not connected to his interpretation (he
was a loser who did not deserve to live) at all.

Step 4

Revisit the person's original vision; why did he or she commit
to that goal in the first place? If the person stopped, what
would be missing in his or her life, in the organization, or in
the world? The person may have to step back from the current
project or goal, wipe the slate clean, and create the vision again
from scratch.

Step 5

Invite the person to recommit to their vision. You may have to
act as a "wall" for people's commitments so they close the
back door, as it were, and kill the alternative of giving up. In
many ways, the job of a leader is encouraging team members to
recall their commitment to the future when they forget.

As you build your organization's future, the key is to choose your
own, and not sink money into pipedreams (however tempting they
may be) that are not really yours to achieve. For Michael Dell, inventing
the Next Big Thing was never his mission; it was building the Current
Big Thing better than anyone else. Dell started selling PCs from his college dorm room; his vision to serve the end-user directly and cut out
the middlemen made his fledgling company into a $60 billion giant.
The clarity of this single-mindedness has saved Dell a lot of money:
its R&D budget, for example, is much lower than that of its rivals.
But Dell's startling success comes not only from its focus. Perhaps
even more important is another key success factor that is the topic of
Chapter 3: its founder built a corporate culture of wide-open communication. This did not come naturally, to say the least.

The Bottom Line

- As Proverbs says, "Where there is no vision, people perish."[98] Without a future you and the people around you die, if not physically, then at least as leaders.

- A key quality leaders need is the capacity to see the future before others do. But most managers have little time or resources left over for the future; they are consumed by running the present—managing the clutter and current circumstances, which are all based on the past.

- A vision is not a dream; neither is it a prediction. It is the statement of a future that is desirable, possible, achievable, measurable, and inclusive.

- The opposite of vision is resignation to the status quo, a rampant condition in our lives, organizations, and societies. To clean up the canvas on which you can paint a future, you need to put the past where it belongs: back in the past. You can achieve this by finishing unfinished business (in your finances, physical environment, communications, relationships, and health).

- You can build a vision for yourself and others by conducting an uncensored conversation for the future, by carving out seven fundamental commitments, or by writing a news article now about yourself five years hence.

- A key leadership skill is to enable people to get their vision back when it has gotten lost in the day-to-day detritus. You can restore someone's vision by revisiting the moment he or she gave up. What happened that led the person to conclude that the vision was not achievable and/or worth pursuing anymore? Separate what happened from the person's interpretation of what happened. Then revisit the original vision, and see whether the person is willing to recommit.

- Build visionary practices into your day-to-day business, for example, by encouraging weekly speculation days and what-if conversations.

- The best leaders live the future now. They embody the change they wish to see in their world.

CHAPTER THREE

Commandment III
Not in Vain:
Leading Through Language

For God is in heaven and you on earth, therefore let your words be few.
—Ecclesiastes 5:1

It's so simple to be wise.
Just think of something stupid to say and then don't say it.
—Sam Levenson

THE THIRD COMMANDMENT: *"You shall not take the name of your God in a vain oath."* We tend to use words carelessly, whether in kvetching or slander, excuses or blame. But words are oaths: commitments that become reality. They are either bricks that build up or weapons that destroy, especially for leaders. Communication is the water in which leaders swim; top managers are not paid primarily for their technical skills, their financial acumen, or even their strategic thinking. They are paid for communicating effectively, which makes the difference between a vision achieved and a fiasco. This chapter will show you how to make words count—both in your speaking and listening—to build the future you want. The bigger your repertoire of listening, the more in charge of the conversation you are.

The ability to be a great communicator lies at the heart of leadership in the framework of Judaism. In Hebrew, communication and leadership are intimately intertwined: the word for leader, *daber*, literally means "spokesman." From Abraham to Moses, being a great communicator and speaking for others lay at the heart of effective leadership. The fourth book of the Torah is known in Hebrew as *Bamidbar* (in the desert). But the root of the word desert (*midbar*) is *daber*, and *medaber* means "speak." While the Jews wandered in the desert, they were riddled by constant communication issues—disputes, open rebellion, blame, complaints, slander, and rumors.[99] How did Moses, and his siblings Aaron and Miriam, persuade their followers to keep tackling endless trials and tribulations?

For Moses, it was hard enough to give up a life of wealth and power, stand up to an intransigent Pharaoh, and lead the Israelites out of Egypt; but the real hardships were yet to come. The Jews, "six hundred thousand men on foot," were in the desert for forty years; they faced wilderness and uncertainty, almost died of thirst, lost faith, and mutinied. "They said to Moses, 'Were there no graves in Egypt that you took us to die in the Wilderness? What is this that you have done to us to take us out of Egypt?" They bickered about the whole idea of venturing into the unknown: "Is this not the statement that we made to you in Egypt, saying, 'Let us be and we will serve Egypt'? For it is better that we should serve Egypt than that we should die in the wilderness!"[100]

Unlike Moses, Michael Dell did not face open rebellion. But in an internal 2001 survey, subordinates thought Dell was not a great leader; he was too impersonal and emotionally detached. What happened next says much about why Dell is one of the best-led companies in the technology space. Within a week, the chairman faced his twenty top managers and surprised them with a frank self-critique. He acknowledged that he was hugely shy and granted that it sometimes made him seem aloof and unapproachable. Days later, every manager in the company saw a videotape of his talk. Dell didn't stop there; the firm institutionalized an annual 360-degree review in which workers are urged to speak their minds, question everything, and challenge their bosses, including Dell himself, who insisted that every manager submit to periodic feedback by his or her subordinates.

Dell knew that full communication was the key to his company's ongoing learning, innovation, and agility (he cited Digital Equipment

Corporation's Ken Olsen as someone who failed to build a learning organization, stuck with his rigid strategy, and let the market pass him by). He knew that communication is not an item you can tick off on a checklist; it needs to be practiced every day. As a reminder that he might fall back into his old noncommunication patterns, he kept a prop on his desk: a little plastic bulldozer cautioned him not to ram through his ideas without including others.

The bad news (well, good news for Dell if you believe that communication makes the difference between a good and a great company) is that most leaders in most companies are nowhere near Dell's communication capacity. Many leaders constantly violate the Third Commandment: "Don't use my name in vain." Both the CEO and the Rabbi have sat through countless meetings in which people wasted hours with indecisive talk that went nowhere.

Humans are not very inventive with language, especially in organizations. A 2006 survey of office workers found that the management jargon used by bosses lowers employee morale. Workers said they were particularly depressed by terms like like "get your ducks in a row" and "thinking outside the box"; and "helicopter view" or "heads up" fared only marginally better.[101] When you think about it, many phrases business people use when they mean to be powerful come from the military (for example "strategy," "campaign," "plant the flag," "taking territory") or from sports (for example, "hit the ball," "the whole nine yards," "a walk in the park," "move the ball down the field," "this side of the net"). With automatic jargon like that, as George Orwell wrote, we end up with language that is "designed to make lies sound truthful and murder respectable, and to give an appearance of solidity to pure wind."[102]

> **Tip:** Instead of using clichés like "thinking outside the box," come up with genuine language that says what you want to convey in your own terms.

Too often we carelessly use words that originated five hundred years ago. In the sixteenth century, in times of war and pestilence, it was appropriate to use language like "I'm dying, I'm starving, I'm struggling here," since people literally did face death on a daily basis. But today, for most of us in the so-called developed world at least, saying "This heat is killing me" when the air conditioner happens to be down is hyperbole and is speaking in vain (except of course in extreme situations such as in France, where over 14,000, mostly elderly people, did in fact die in the 2003 summer heat wave because they lacked A/C; but you get the drift). There is nothing wrong with military or sports analogies or with old language, but if language is the wellspring of reality, you have to be conscious of what you say. The language you use has to be real and cannot be automatic jargon. Don't ever go on autopilot. See if you can say what you want to say in your own words.

Even otherwise effective leaders may have communication blind spots that can hamper them. A good example is Bill Gates of Microsoft, whose combative communication style spurred people into innovative action inside Microsoft but made for poor negotiations outside (in *Communicate or Die*, the CEO used Gates to illustrate the "deadly sins of speaking"[103]). To be sure, Gates is one of the undisputed greats among business leaders and strategists; few people have done more than he has to spur the PC revolution in the twentieth century; and (thanks to his wife Melinda) he may well be one of the greatest philanthropists of the twenty-first. But during Microsoft's legal battles against the U.S. Justice Department in the late 1990s, Gates did it again: he spoke in vain and committed communication gaffes that set his company back unnecessarily.

Gates's slip-ups make for an often entertaining textbook case for how not to do it.[104] In 1997, arch-rivals Microsoft and Apple struck a deal that shocked the industry: Apple agreed to replace the Netscape Navigator, the Mac's default browser, with Microsoft's Internet Explorer. Justice prosecutors had reason to believe that the headline-grabbing agreement had been a result of Microsoft's threat to cancel Office for the Macintosh unless Apple complied.

In August 1998, Gates and David Boies sat down in a windowless conference room in Microsoft's Building 8 in Redmond. Boies, arguably the most brilliant litigator of his generation, had "expected the Bill Gates I'd be facing would be the same Bill Gates I'd been in a room with that spring," he said later.[105] "The Bill Gates I'd met was smart, tough, and articulate, a very passionate and effective spokesman for his point of view." Boies grinned. "Needless to say, that was not the Bill Gates who showed up for the deposition." The Gates who showed up was cantankerous, petulant, and obscurantist. He professed not to recall countless e-mails he had written, and not to know about key company strategies—strategies he had evidently masterminded himself. He took five minutes to concede that when one of his Microsoft executives had talked about "pissing on" Java, it was not, as Boies put it, a "code word that means saying nice things." When asked who had attended a Microsoft executive-staff meeting, he replied, "Probably members of the executive staff."

This went on for three days. On the third day came one of the priceless exchanges. Boies handed Gates an e-mail he'd written and offhandedly said that at the top of the message Gates had typed "Importance High." "No," Gates said curtly.

"No?"
"No, I didn't type that."
Then who did?
"A computer."
"A computer. Why did the computer type in 'High'?"
"It's an attribute of the email."
"And who sets the attribute of the email?"
"Usually the sender sets that attribute."
"Who is the sender here, Mr. Gates?"
"In this case, it appears I'm the sender."
"Yes. And so you're the one who set the high designation of importance, right, sir?"
"It appears I did that."[106]

The results of Gates's communication blunders speak for themselves. Microsoft not only lost the trial, but also took a serious hit to its reputation, corporate morale, and stock price. Key talent like Paul Maritz and dozens of Microsoft's best and brightest left the company within a few months after the verdict. And a decade later, the battle was far from over. In 2004, the EU hit Microsoft with a fine of 497 million euros ($725 million); and in 2008, the EU Commission ruled that Microsoft was still acting monopolistically and not sharing data with competitors, and fined it 1.4 billion euros ($2.082 billion), the highest EU fine ever. A commission spokesman said, "In the 50 years of European antitrust policy, it's the first time we've been confronted with a company that has failed to comply with an antitrust decision."[107] The EU threatened Microsoft with a $4 million fine *per day* of the company's delinquency—not good for Microsoft's reputation, or its shareholders.

Corporations are not the only places hampered by bad communication. In the medical profession communication can either heal people or make them sicker. By 1984, researchers showed that on average, doctors interrupted eighteen seconds after patients began explaining their problems. We have all been there: you walk into a doctor's office, and he asks, "What brings you here today?" You start to answer. Eighteen seconds later, the doctor interrupts you mid-sentence. The study found that fewer than 2 percent of patients got to finish their explanations. When Dr. Wendy Levinson, vice chairwoman of the University of Toronto's department of medicine, studied malpractice suits, she found that bad communication is a common theme. What often prompts people to sue their doctors, she said, "is the feeling that they were not listened to, that they didn't have the doctor's full attention."[108] Problem physicians come in many guises, patients say: the arrogant or dismissive doctor, the impatient doctor with his hand on the doorknob, and the doctor who is callous and judgmental.

Ideally, doctors would have "a combination of the most technically sophisticated skills and knowledge and the best communication skills," Dr. Levinson said, "because that will get us the best outcomes from our patients."[109] Research has shown that good doctor-patient communication resulted in lower blood sugar levels in diabetic patients, and lower blood pressure in hypertensive patients. Other studies have found connections between positive patient-physician encounters and the reduction of pain in cancer patients, improved physical health in people with various illnesses, reduced stress and anxiety, and better adherence to prescribed treatments.

Patients don't even need face time with doctors to experience positive results. Researchers discovered that phone calls from nurses or other clinic staff members to provide emotional support go a long way to help people quit smoking, stay on medication, or shake low moods. In a large-scale, 18-month study, doctors in Seattle found they could significantly improve recovery rates for patients taking antidepressants by providing a few 30- to 40-minute counseling sessions over the phone. Have these findings changed practice? In 1999, a follow-up to the 1984 study found that doctors no longer interrupted their patients at 18 seconds—now it was after 23 seconds, a 5-second improvement in fifteen years.[110]

To be fair, the grievances are mutual. While patients say that doctors don't answer their emergency calls, keep them waiting endlessly during office visits, and don't take time to explain things properly, doctors counter that patients don't comply with their treatment regimes, ignore professional advice in favor of sketchy information on the Internet, and don't come clean about their complete health histories. It's all part of a changing relationship between patients and doctors. The ability to easily gather information through Google, Wikipedia or WebMD makes patients much more aware of their rights and gives them a sense of empowerment. Joanne Wong, a software engineer in Sunnyvale, California, suffered from abdominal pains and nausea. Her doctor told her to have a blood test, then ushered her out of his office, ignoring her when she asked what the test was for. "The test came back, and he said I have a virus," Wong said. "He said, 'Take this medicine for two weeks.' I asked, 'What kind of virus do I have? How did I get it?' But he just said, 'Take the medicine and come back in two weeks.'" Two weeks later, she still felt ill. "He said, 'You're fine, you're fine.' I said, 'At least tell me the name of the virus.' He just patted me on the shoulder and sent me out," she related, and told her to come back in three months for yet another blood test. She never returned to that doctor. When she got her medical records, she learned that she had hepatitis A, a viral liver infection.[111]

All too often, patients don't dare speak up, said Dr. Richard Frankel, a professor of medicine and geriatrics at Indiana University who teaches medical faculty how to communicate with patients. "You hear their sad story, and then you ask, 'Well, did you say anything to the person who was offensive to you or treated you poorly?' In 99.9 percent of the cases, the answer is no." But unless you make your views known, nothing will change. You need to say something like, "I had a bad experience today, and I'd like to tell you why." Most doctors, Dr. Frankel said, have no idea they are difficult, and "if you don't give feedback—this is unacceptable, this is inappropriate, this hurts my feelings—you reinforce the behavior."[112]

There are solutions. By 2011, all new residents at Harvard Medical School will have to show empathy by examining an actor posing as a patient. And Dr. Howard Beckman, the medical director of the Rochester Independent Practice Association, said there is a simple method that works. "You use continuers. As you're working with people, you say 'uh huh' three times." For example, he advised a colleague: "The patient says, 'I've been having chest pains.'" Instead of jumping in and suggesting tests, the doctor says, "Uh huh." The patient says, "I've also been having headaches." The doctor says, "Uh huh." So the patient says, "It all started when my brother died of an aneurism in the brain. And I wonder if it's related." The doctor, Dr. Beckman said, "looked at me like I'm a little nuts," but agreed to try the procedure. Later he returned—elated. Dr. Beckman recalled him saying: "I can't believe how different it is. I hear things I don't usually hear."[113]

Language Is the House of Being

The Hebrew word for "word," *davar*, also means "thing." So the word *ledaber*, "to speak," also means "to create a thing." (It is a bit like the English word "matter" that can also function as either a noun or a verb.) From the beginning of the world, every word counted. In the Book of Genesis, God spoke ten times, and each time gave birth to another aspect of creation—with words that became things. "God said, 'Let there be light,' and there was light." On the sixth day, "God said, 'Let us make Man in Our image, after Our likeness. They shall rule over the fish of the sea, the birds of the sky, and over the animal, the whole earth, and every creeping thing that creeps upon the earth.'"[114] (Hasidic kabbalists say that today these words still hang in the firmament and continue to give vitality to the world.) Every morning service,

Jews reaffirm "Blessed is the One Who spoke and the world came into being."[115] And since humans are created in the image of God, they too have the capacity to speak life into being.

Jews are often called the People of the Book; the root of the Hebrew word for "book," s-f-r, can mean three things: *sefer* (book), *sefar* (number), and *sipur* (story). Books, stories and even numbers are language, and the power of language to create life is fundamental to Judaism; ultimately, without language, there is no life.[116] And if (as both the Bible and constructivist theory say) reality is indeed made from language, you have the power to change it through language, no matter your job title or how much money you have. Even a penniless woman barely surviving in a slum on the outskirts of Mumbai or Port-au-Prince has the power to speak and listen, hence the power to build reality, and ultimately to lead, through language.

The playground adage most children learn, at least in the United States, "Sticks and stones may break my bones, but words will never harm me," is wrong: words have tremendous power to inflict pain. The story goes that in the middle of the eighteenth century, two citizens of Medzhybizh (a small town which had once been in Lithuania, then Turkey, Poland, and Russia, and today is in Ukraine) had a quarrel in the synagogue of Rabbi Israel ben Eliezer, the Baal Shem Tov (literally master of the Good Name)) who founded Hasidism and made the study of Torah, previously the exclusive domain of rabbis and scholars, available to laypeople. The two angry men circled each other like boxers. In the heat of the action one of the disputants threatened the other, "I will tear you apart like a fish!" The Baal Shem Tov immediately asked all his students to stand around him, to hold one another's shoulder and to close their eyes. He then placed his hands on the shoulders of the two disciples standing next to him. The students gasped in terror: behind their closed eyelids they had seen one of the quarreling fellows actually dismember his adversary![117] Chastened, the two disputants stopped their fight. They had been struck by the power of their own words; the Baal Shem Tov had shown them that their words had congealed into reality.

Every word you utter has the potential to affect reality, both your own and that of others.[118] (In fact, as the Rabbi shows in his book,

Letters of Light, every single letter in each word has a specific shape, energy, and set of attributes that influence each moment of creation.) In Hasidic thought, speech comes from a higher source, a place even more elevated than intellect or emotion. The Hebrew word for "emotion" is *ruach*, the same word as "wind," a fickle thing that comes and goes with the weather. Words are more stable than feelings—as long as they are meant for real and not spoken in vain.

Giving and Getting Feedback

Despite the power of words to shape reality, many managers are inept at using them skillfully; and even though leaders may succeed or fail as a result of the quality of their speaking and listening, most have never bothered to tone their communication muscles. As George Bernard Shaw said, "The single biggest problem in communication is the illusion that it has taken place."[119] When communication breaks down, "There's often a big disconnect between how managers think they are doing and how employees think they're doing," said Robert Morgan of Hudson Talent Management. In a 2006 survey, 92 percent of managers told Rasmussen Reports they were doing an "excellent" or "good" job, while only 67 percent of their subordinates thought so. "Most managers don't think they're doing a bad job," said Morgan. "But if you're not getting feedback from your employees on how well you're doing, where else do you get it from?"[120]

Some bosses never even get feedback, simply because they don't ask for it. Leslie A. Perlow, a Harvard leadership professor, has seen a "vicious spiral of silence" do its dirty work at countless companies.[121] Take the big office equipment company whose software engineers spent hours each week preparing for weekly meetings with their boss, though they all thought these meetings were a complete waste of time. Despite the wasted hours and frustration caused by the meetings, none of the engineers would take it upon themselves to say something to the boss. Worse, even the boss thought the meetings were useless, but he didn't want to cancel them; he feared that doing so would discourage the engineers from bringing new ideas to him. The inability of both sides to voice their true feelings cost the company thousands of man-hours in lost time, loss of productivity, and lots of overtime for engineers. "We all know how hard it is to talk back to superiors," Perlow said, "but often we forget how hard it is for bosses to speak up to us."[122]

Tool 3.1
Effective Feedback in Six Steps

What if a team member really riles you, is constantly late, goofs off instead of doing his or her fair share, or dominates the group? A key leadership skill is giving effective feedback and knowing when and how to do so. Two centuries ago, Rabbi Schneur Zalman said that if your neighbor wrongs you, you're right to rebuke him; straight talk is both appropriate and necessary. But, the Alter Rebbe went on to remind his students, always be close to someone you criticize;[123] rebuke them privately, never in public; and pare your nails beforehand,[124] lest you tear into the person with claws too sharp. Following are the six steps of a feedback process designed to promote solutions rather than escalate the problem in business or organizational environments.

1. Don't barge in.
Don't withhold your feedback—but time it wisely. Unless your counterpart is open to your feedback, you're wasting your time. Ask: "Do you have a moment? I'd like to tell you something" or "Would you mind if we talked on Thursday?" Make sure your asking is so neutral in tone and content that you don't already jump the gun or make the person uncomfortable. Saying "I have an issue with you" is not a good opener.

You might frame your feedback in appreciation: "You know I think the world of you and am totally on your side. There is one area that would make a big impact on the business if we could improve it. ..." But be aware that praise that comes just before feedback might be seen as manipulative or even dishonest; make sure that you stay genuine and don't give the impression that you are sugar-coating the real issue or buttering up the person.

2. Don't blame the person – state the facts.

Talk straight, but do everyone a favor: avoid complaining or hurling accusations like "Why do I always end up doing all the work?" Blaming or complaining are no-nos; it's communication that points to the past and only reinforces the very reality you want to change. Say what happened, avoid judgments, and avoid characterizing the person or personalizing the issue. Statements like "You're a liar" are not going to resolve anything. Don't say "You're indiscreet" but rather "You brought up our confidential conversation in the all-staff meeting." Be specific and stay away from broad statements like "that presentation was a disaster" (in fact even "that presentation was wonderful" is much too generic to be useful).

3. State the consequences.

Say what outcome the behavior led to. For example: "When you put a thousand pages of legal briefs on my desk Friday afternoon, it took me most of the weekend to read them, and I had zero time for my family. Now my spouse thinks I should leave the firm." Limit the feedback to one incident or behavior. Avoid words like "always" or "never."

4. State your feelings.

Rabbeinu Tam said your words must come from your heart; words that emanate from your heart enter into the other person's heart.[125] Once you have clarified the facts and consequences, you can express your feelings. Don't talk about what *your colleague* did wrong but about *your* experience. For example: "When I had to read the legal briefs over the weekend, I felt tired and frankly had little desire to come back to the office today." Don't say "You make me angry," but instead say "I feel angry."

5. Co-create a solution.

Ask if the other person is open to working with you to find a mutually acceptable solution. Make your expectations clear. Leaving things ambiguous may lead to unintended outcomes. If you tell an employee that you're disappointed with his or her performance and would have expected more, you've got to specify clearly what you expect or you are not likely to get the results you want.

6. Thank the person.

> **Tip:** Avoid giving feedback via e-mail; it's a terrible vehicle for resolving issues, and conflicts can easily spin out of control if you cannot speak in real time.

Dishing out feedback is one thing; being open to receiving it is quite another. Rabbi Sholom DovBer (1860–1920), the fifth Lubavitcher Rebbe, wrote to his students: "Cherish criticism, for it will place you on the true heights."[126] That's easier said than done, especially for a large organization in the fishbowl of public scrutiny. Imagine your company is coasting along nicely, but one day it gets branded as one of the country's most reviled companies because visitors to Consumerist.com, a heavily visited consumer Web site, have voted it the second "worst company in America," and the human rights group Privacy International has just given it the 2005 "Lifetime Menace Award."

This is what happened to ChoicePoint. In addition, in January 2006, the Federal Trade Commission hit the company with a $10 million fine—the largest civil penalty in the agency's history—for security breaches and record-handling procedures that violated consumers' rights. But instead of getting defensive, ChoicePoint decided to reach out. It sought feedback from its adversaries, its most vocal critics, and asked them, "What are we doing wrong?" Even its most ardent detractors were forced to admit that the company's open listening was a key factor in turning around its negative image and restoring its credibility in the market. "I have to give them a lot of credit," said Daniel J. Solove, an associate professor at George Washington University Law School who had long been counted as one of ChoicePoint's most persistent critics. "ChoicePoint had the attitude: 'We want to make our privacy practices exemplary.' They wanted to find out what kinds of things they could do better and get feedback about some of the ideas they were thinking about." And in fact the company found that the very same people it had once cast as shrill and ill-informed were the ones who now proved crucial to its plans to shore up its security and tend to its tattered image.[127] What had King David said again? "From my enemies I became wise."[128]

But you need not wait until your reputation is in tatters to ask for feedback; it's immeasurably better to be proactive about it. A few years ago, on a rainy day in London, ten people gathered around a conference table at Vodafone to give unvarnished straight talk to the world's largest mobile phone company outside of China. They included a telecom analyst, a local government planning officer, someone from a think tank, a sustainable development campaigner, the editor of an environmental journal, and a reporter. In a polite but lively debate facilitated by an external consultant, they took turns telling the Vodafone representative exactly what they thought about the company, and they talked about several controversial issues, from the siting of mobile phone masts to the protection of children from adult Internet content. The Vodafone rep sat quietly and took lots of notes.

Seeking out the views of stakeholders has become accepted practice, especially among large companies. Vodafone holds many such meetings around the world each year. "You've really got to take the whole thing seriously and be prepared to listen to people and take on board their views," said Charlotte Grezo, Vodafone's corporate social responsibility officer.[129] Another British company, the high-end retailer Marks and Spencer, talks (or rather, listens) to some 160 different groups. Among other factors, this helped the company; from 2005 to 2006, it climbed from 493rd to 458th among the Fortune 500 and increased its profits by 33.8 percent.

Arrest Slander

When we have an issue with someone and are uncomfortable letting them know our feelings directly, it often seems easier to talk to others who might commiserate. Idle talk about someone who is not present—in a word, gossip—is understandable; after all, getting your colleagues to agree with you is much easier than confronting the culprit.

Gossip has its uses. According to the evolutionary psychologist Nigel Nicholson, it was a skill needed by our Stone Age ancestors to survive the socially unpredictable conditions of the Savannah Plain. Over time, gossiping became part of our mental programming. Nicholson argues that executives trying to eradicate gossip at work might as well try to change their employees' musical tastes.[130] Similarly, Don Cohen and Laurence Prusak write that "Telling and listening to stories, chatting, sharing a little gossip, are the main ways that people in organizations come to trust and understand one another."[131] Maybe so; but when people are fearful of being straightforward and honest with colleagues, when they have to resort to the rumor mill, the organization is in trouble. Continuous slander is like a cancer that can destroy teams and organizations.

In Judaism, *lashon hara* (Hebrew for evil tongue) is one of the deadliest sins. Referring to a person who repeats a slander they heard elsewhere, the Talmud warns that "the third tongue kills three persons"[132] *in addition to* the person being bad-mouthed in absentia: first, the originator of the defamation; second, the person who relates it; and third, the witness who listens to it. People who habitually commit *lashon hara* are not tolerated in God's presence.[133] When Moses led the Israelites through the desert, the spies who slandered against the promised land of Israel met with a gruesome punishment: their tongues grew long into their own bellies, and worms grew from their tongues even before they died.[134] The Talmud lists bad-mouthing as a cause of *tzaraat* (leprosy)[135] and people who slandered, maligned, and debased others were afflicted by a special illness that only a *kohen* (priest) could quarantine.

In *Communicate or Die*, the CEO called slander one of five capital sins of speaking that can paralyze whole organizations. (The others are excuses, blame, judgments, and threats.) A few careless, or worse, maliciously and carefully placed words can destroy something that took years to build. At an Australian high-tech company people had never been trained to express their thoughts directly to one another. In public they said only what they thought their superiors wanted to hear; but behind people's backs they bad-mouthed their bosses. The chairman and the managing director took it to the extreme: Each of them called the CEO overseas to complain about one another, even though their own offices were about a three-minute walk apart. The company's culture of gossip and slander was only one factor, but it certainly didn't help. The firm soon went out of business.

The term *lashon hara* in this context includes complaining about an issue to people who lack the power to do something about it. Most of us have that nasty habit. We complain to anyone and everyone except the person who can make something happen to resolve our complaint. If you're an account executive, complaining to other account executives about the vice president of sales will only aggravate your issue; all you are doing is gathering evidence for your existing viewpoint instead of speaking to the vice president directly. Complaining only to co-workers who cannot act fuels the perception that "nothing matters," "we have no power to change things," "they never listen," or "life here sucks." When enough people in the organization add enough of this fuel, it becomes a self-fulfilling prophecy—reality begins to mirror their complaints. (Of course, the people doing the slandering have no idea that they had everything to do with shaping the environment they so vigorously oppose. They don't see that they literally speak that environment into being.)

Replacing *lashon hara* with more productive communication is essential for the health and productivity of your enterprise. How can you do that? Based on our own experience with organizations of all stripes, the CEO and the Rabbi recommend three ground rules. First, ask people to stop *lashon hara*, and refuse to participate whenever you hear it. Second, complain only to the person who can do something about fixing the problem. Most often, that person is either the manager in charge of the area or the very person at the root of the issue. For instance, if you have a complaint about how people are promoted at your company, the person to talk to might be the company president, the department chief, or the head of HR. If that person cannot handle the issue satisfactorily, then you can both determine who is better positioned to resolve it. Third, if you are going to a superior, be sure to offer not only the problem but one or several options for resolving it. Aleksandr Kuzmin, the mayor of Megion in western Siberia, said he was tired of subordinates telling him that problems were impossible to solve, rather than offering practical solutions. So in 2007 the mayor issued a list of twenty-seven forbidden phrases, including "I don't know," "What am I supposed to do?" "We're having lunch," "The working day is over," "Somebody else has the documents" or "I think I was off sick at the time."[136] You don't need to go as far as Mr. Kuzmin, but don't allow people to delegate problems to you; hold them accountable for finding the solution themselves.

Tool 3.2
From Kvetching to Commitment

Yiddish is the language par excellence of complaint, which we consider speaking in vain. As Michael Wex, the author of *Born to Kvetch*, puts it neatly: "Judaism is defined by exile, and exile without complaint is tourism." An innocent question like "How are you?" amounts to a provocation in Yiddish, which recoils from happy talk as if it were the plague. A fairly neutral answer to the question is usually another question, with an undertone of vexation: "How *should* I be?" Yiddish can be beautiful, soulful, poetic—or a lethal weapon. While Americans generally stick to short, efficient four-letter words when doling out abuse (drop dead, for example), you could say in Yiddish, *a viste pgire af dir* (a dismal animal death to you), which suggests that "you should spend the rest of your tiny life in a Colorado feedlot, then be herded off to some nonunion slaughterhouse to be turned, *painfully*, into fast-food burgers for one of the less prominent chains." Wex asserts that kvetching has its roots in the Torah, with the "nonstop grumbling of the Israelites, who find fault with everything under the sun."[137] When the Israelites found themselves trapped before the Sea of Reeds, Moses cried out to God to save them from the fast-approaching Egyptians. But kvetching was not an option. God told Moses, "Why cry to me? Speak to the children of Israel that they go forward."[138]

Thousands of years later, we humans still haven't learned the lesson. We tend to whine a lot—about the weather, our ailments, our relationships, our politicians, not enough sleep, or the stock market. How do you turn this all-pervasive kvetching into commitment and move the action forward? The answer is, ironically, by treating the kvetching itself as a commitment. If you consider everything a person says an oath, the next time someone complains and says, for example, "my boss is such an idiot," you can ask the person, "Are you committed to that?" As annoying as it may be, this simple device teaches people to wake up to the effects of their language.

The other tool for turning complaints into commitments is to use promises and requests. The philosopher Friedrich Nietzsche wrote that the chief difference between humans and animals is that the human being is "an animal that may promise, meaning he or she treats the future as something that depends on him or her and for which he or she stands."[139] The CEO's consulting work often encounters management teams that have no idea how to weed out their ineffective interactions, which are all too often couched in cheap talk, excuses, blame, judgments, gossip, rumors, opinions, or brick-wall statements like "I told them this would never work—now they can just fend for themselves" or "Why am I always the one that everybody dumps on?" The CEO's experience has shown that when teams cut out such wasteful talk and instead use action-oriented conversations like promises, requests, offers, and invitations, their productivity grows significantly (one team in the energy field increased shop sales in one year by 11 percent while industry sales dropped by 1 percent). The added bonus: making and keeping promises builds trust.

To have any chance to be fulfilled, a promise needs three things: a clear deadline, a clear deliverable, and a clear receiver. "I will be more open to feedback" is not a promise; "Count on it, I will get feedback from at least three direct reports this month" meets the criteria. The same is true for requests. Bear in mind that people need the freedom to accept, decline, or counteroffer; if they don't have that choice, the request is, in truth, a command, or even a threat. When the former CEO of the Zurich Kantonalbank (ZKB) said, after a 56-year-old manager of the bank shot both of his bosses and then himself in the Swiss canton of Ticino, "As long as people deliver, they have nothing to fear,"[140] that was not a request but a thinly-veiled threat.

According to the Torah, "He must carry out all that has crossed his lips."[141] Once you say something, you are obligated to do it.

> **Tip:** Treat all statements as if they were a commitment, an oath. When someone kvetches in your presence, ask, "Do you have a request or promise?"

R U Listening?

This chapter would be incomplete without highlighting the flipside of speaking in vain: listening in vain. One captain of industry, reminded of the importance of two-way communication, snapped, "*Of course* I use two-way communication! I communicate to my people both verbally and in writing." He had no inkling of a crucial key to finding solutions and increasing productivity: listening. Powerful listening can lead to vast accomplishments. According to tradition, God dictated the entire Torah to Moses, who listened extremely well. His undivided attention allowed him to transcribe the dictation word for word. But today the power of active, attentive listening is lost on many leaders; no wonder, since our leadership role models on TV seem to never be listening, but talking nonstop.

The legendary rock musician Jimi Hendrix used to say that "Knowledge speaks, but wisdom listens." Yet many managers don't know how to listen as if words really count. If they don't ignore what they hear altogether, they pretend to listen while answering an e-mail or fiddling with their BlackBerry; they project their prejudices onto the speaker; or they control—with their body language, their facial expression, or by glancing demonstratively at their watch—what the other person can can get out of their mouth.[142] But listening is not just a luxury for the human resource people—though its absence may lead to disenchanted and bickering employees or lawsuits—it is a strategic skillset. If you don't listen, you miss out on useful intelligence. Imagine a seven-level hierarchy in which managers at each level communicate 50 percent of what they know to the next higher level (quite an optimistic assumption). Guess what percentage of the available information is shared with the boss at the top? Quantitative types know the answer: 1.6 percent. The boss can only pray that based on this tiny fraction of the company's knowledge, he or she calls the right shots, that the 1.6 percent he or she knows are the right 1.6 percent, and that the relevant knowledge is not buried in the other 98.4 percent of information the boss never receives. The front-line people, and even the receptionist who talks to the public (including the customers) every day, often know more about the business and the market than the lone man or woman at the top. The only way to get strategic intelligence to the CEO and the board is to institutionalize listening throughout the corporate pyramid.

Tool 3.3
Texts and Subtexts

How do you listen effectively and get access to hidden intelligence in what you hear, whether in a negotiation or a conversation at the copy machine? The key is to train yourself to listen to the subtext of the words you hear. As the Jewish adage goes, don't answer the question, answer the person. The German communication theorist Friedemann Schulz von Thun suggested that everything we say, every "text," is only the tip of the iceberg: the invisible ice hidden under the water is huge.[143] Three subtexts underlie any given text, as shown in the chart.

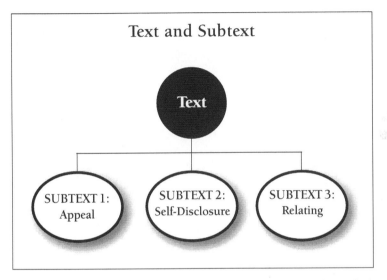

Figure 3.1: Text and Subtexts (based on Friedemann Schulz von Thun)

When a wife asks her husband, "Aren't you cold?" there are three sub-texts. Wittingly or unwittingly, she is making a hidden **appeal**; it might be, "Turn the heat on already" or "Give me your sweater." In **self-disclosure**, she, deliberately or not, is saying something about herself, perhaps "I feel cold myself" or "I feel helpless." **Relating** contains a secret message about the relationship or a desire to relate; it might be, "I care about you," "You're my husband, my protector," or "You could pay more attention to me." Even in a book, the author might be pleading with the reader to agree with him or to recognize how brilliant he is. He might be self-disclosing something about his own life. (And he might wish to get closer to reader. So reader, beware!)

By listening actively and training your listening muscle to listen not only to the obvious content but to listen *for* the subtexts of any communication, you'll be a much more effective communicator, equipped to deal effectively with any communication that comes your way, especially with brick-wall statements like "When will you finally get this report right?" This deeper understanding will help you decode hidden meanings, put undiscussables on the table, and diffuse difficult issues. Ultimately, it will put you in charge of any conversation.

You *can* communicate too much, as we shall see in the next chapter.

Tip: Instead of listening for the mud (what's wrong, and whether to agree or disagree) listen for the gold (what's valuable, what's brilliant) in what people say to you. What if the quality of your listening had the power to triple productivity—both your own and that of your direct reports?

The Bottom Line

• So much of what people say to each other on a daily basis is spoken in vain. But words matter. God created the world in ten utterances; and even the words of ordinary humans have the power to create or destroy. The Hebrew word *daber* means both speaker and leader. Leaders lead through language; their language crafts reality; their (and their people's) productivity is a direct result of how effectively they communicate.

- You build trust—one of the most crucial ingredients of successful business dealings under complexity and globalization—by a simple two-step process: making commitments, and keeping them.

- The six steps of effective feedback are: 1. Ask for permission, 2. State the facts, 3. Say the consequences, 4. Share your feelings, 5. Ask whether the other person is willing to work out a solution, 6. Thank them.

- Every communication has three subtexts: 1. Appeal, 2. Self-disclosure, 3. Relating. Listening for subtexts in whatever you hear puts you in charge of the conversation. Effective listening gets your hands on the levers and dials of enhanced productivity.

- A great way to cut through the pea-soup of kvetching and talking in vain is to ask "What is your request or promise?"

CHAPTER FOUR

Commandment IV
Keep the Sabbath: The Power of No

The feeling of being hurried is not usually the result
of living a full life and having no time.
It is, to the contrary, born of the vague fear
that we are wasting our life.
When we do not do the thing that we ought to do,
we have no time for anything else.
—Eric Hoffer

I once wanted to become an atheist, but I gave up—
they have no holidays.
—Henny Youngman

THE FOURTH COMMANDMENT: *"Remember the Sabbath day
to sanctify it. Six days you are to work and accomplish all your
tasks. But the seventh day is the Sabbath to your God; you may
not do any work—you, your son, your daughter, your manservant, your maidservant, your animal, and the convert within
your gates—for in six days God made the heavens, the earth, the
sea and all that is in them, and He rested on the seventh day."*
True to its name, business is busy-ness. Every day brings a bar-
rage of e-mails, meetings, decisions, deals. Lest we lose our
center or go under, we have to stop periodically and be still.
Stillness has been the hallmark of the most distinguished leaders; those who incorporated periods of stillness in their lives
were able to develop a resolve of steel and make choices that
would stand the test of time. In this chapter you will learn how

to reduce stress, step back, recharge your batteries, and right your compass, including how to set clear priorities. In a 24/7 world, the Sabbath is an ingenious institution for saying no to mindless activity, however pressing. If you cannot say no, you are not a leader but a pinball of circumstances or other people's agendas.

In the evening of April 17, 2007, the unthinkable happened—the BlackBerry network went down for an interminable twelve hours. To many BlackBerry customers, even twelve minutes would have been too long. What if they missed *the* e-mail message that would make or break their happiness, or their bank account? The hiatus in service revealed the accuracy of what experts call the obsessive compulsive behavior, addiction, and acquired attention deficit disorder of BlackBerry users (and users of other personal digital assistants). Dr. John Ratey, a clinical associate professor of psychiatry at Harvard, coined the latter term several years ago to describe the condition of people accustomed to a constant stream of digital stimulation, and bored to tears in its absence. Whether the stimulation is from the Internet, TV, or cell phone, the brain is hijacked. "I liken it to a drug," Dr. Ratey said. "Drug addicts don't think; they just start moving. Like moving for your BlackBerry." Many users themselves half-joke that they've become junkies. "I push that button like a nervous habit, all day, all night," said Los Angeles music executive David Hyman. "When you don't get your e-mail, you're like a drug user cut off from your source."[144]

By 2006, the number of BlackBerry users worldwide had surpassed seven million. One of them is Brad Garlinghouse, a seemingly normal technology executive who lives in California. Mrs. Garlinghouse, he says, has forbidden laptops in their bedroom; but the BlackBerry is granted admission to the inner sanctum. The sleek device rests on his night table, handily close, in case he wakes up in the middle of the night with an idea that must be committed at once to e-mail.

People like Mr. Garlinghouse would rather tap away obsessively and risk the "CrackBerry" or "BlackBerry Thumb," a type of carpal-tunnel syndrome or joint pains from excessive e-mail indulgence using PDAs, or even broken marriages, than to ban their beloved mobile toys from their bedrooms or homes. And the problem reaches far beyond PDAs; portable e-mail has allowed work to penetrate into homes and flow into nonwork time, blurring the distinction between work and leisure. Skype, Facebook or LinkedIn are wonderful tools for building virtual communities, but many managers complain about being too connected. You *can* communicate too much. Stanford University professor Steve Barley estimates that Silicon Valley executives have added nearly one hour to their average work day by staying connected outside the office.[145] That's one work week per year. Are these hours really adding productivity? "People on cell phones are now reachable in their cars on their commute, and time that used to be downtime or transition time is time used by employers," said Gerry Sussman, a professor in the School of Urban Studies and Planning at Portland State University. "Electronic communications makes possible a much deeper penetration for the commercial use of anything," he added, citing as examples unwanted e-mail, phone solicitation made from computer-generated lists, and television advertisements.[146]

The result: virtually no quiet time. In an end-of-2006 survey conducted by the Harris Poll, only 3 percent of respondents said they have no stress in their lives; 56 percent said they're stressed out from having "too many things to do," and 33 percent from having "too much information." According to another poll by Pew Internet & American Life Projects, 77 percent of people are annoyed by spam, and 53 percent have trouble sleeping.[147] Peace of mind, and with it the space to reflect and contemplate our lives, has become the scarcest of commodities.

A Commercial for Stillness

An unusual slant on leadership is a component that is usually overlooked, but that both the CEO and the Rabbi have found to be the most powerful, and the hardest to sustain: stillness. Stillness is about allowing (even institutionalizing) periods of silence in your life. In a world of multitasking, where ads blur the promise of 24/7 service, where we surf more than five hundred cable channels or the countless

Internet sites with our wireless devices, where 411 numbers edit out our superfluous fillers like "Uh" from "Uh, Domino's" so they won't waste the operator's time, where hurried parents read One-Minute Bedtime Stories to their children, and where a restaurant in Tokyo charges customers by the minute rather than by the amount consumed,[148] the idea of taking time out for quiet reflection may seem rather outdated. It is a quality and behavior virtually overlooked in the media's depiction of leaders; rarely do we see leaders being still. TV and movies portray them as being always in action: debating, moving, performing, and acting (in both senses of the word). Yet, as Hemingway said it perfectly, "Never mistake motion for action."[149] Without stillness, leadership is but a hollow shell of blind activity; it lacks insight and wisdom, precisely the qualities that are at a premium now that our lives are perhaps more complex, the stakes higher, and the choices harder than ever. Stepping back from day-to-day activities compels us to go deeper, takes us from doing things right to doing the right things, and brings us to the fundamental values that allow us to make the right choices, choices that stand the test of time. Robert E. Rubin announced on May 12, 1999, that he would step down as U.S. treasury secretary; two days later, he received a letter from then-Enron chairman Ken Lay, offering Rubin a seat on Enron's board. At the time, Enron was being hailed as a model company by the most reputable business magazines, including *Fortune*. Few if any people had any idea that the star company and its financial wizards would go down in flames within three years. But Rubin had the foresight to decline Lay's juicy offer, and after leaving the government became a co-chairman of Citigroup instead. We do not know why Rubin chose to turn down Lay's offer; but the fact is, he did. Where did he get the clarity to say no to Enron and to avoid a possible conflict of interest given that Citigroup was a major Enron creditor? By stepping back from the action long enough to see beneath the glitter. (Once he was a Citigroup executive, Rubin did lobby his old agency on behalf of Enron in the Fall of 2001, which exposed him to charges of a conflict of interest; but Senate investigators later cleared him of violating any federal law or regulation.)

Through stillness, you can filter out what is merely urgent from what is truly important, reduce stress and burnout, and perhaps find that which is permanent and timeless. Stillness has little to do with passivity, and much to do with balanced and centered action. Life without respite from situations of high stress, such as wars or other crises, compounds the likelihood of bias and bad decisions. In a study of a dozen international crises, political scientists Glenn Snyder and Paul Diesing found that misperception, miscalculation, and other cognitive malfunctions were common in crisis management.[150] Stress comes from the perception that the time horizon for decision-making is extremely short, that we have no time to think, and that we must act right away. Other studies found that under severe time pressure, people's verbal self-monitoring system broke down, and otherwise normal people made errors similar to those committed by schizophrenics.[151]

The ability to step back and gain perspective, and ultimately to come up with the right judgments, has been a hallmark of the most distinguished leaders in history. Great leaders, both Western and non-Western, regularly withdrew from the world to be still, reflect, or meditate, so that the right choice could reveal itself to them. Winston Churchill was born in a much slower century, when declarations of war still took months to arrive in diplomatic pouches. He used to sit outside his house most days after lunch, at the edge of the pond he had made with his own hands, thinking, brooding, and watching the ducks. He would not permit himself to be disturbed. He would sit there, sometimes for hours, and then return to Parliament in a decisive spirit. Churchill's success in defeating Hitler in World War II stemmed at least in part from his courage to step back from the heat of the action.

Churchill's contemporary (and adversary) Mahatma Gandhi sat, fasted, and prayed at his spinning wheel in order to see what was next in his mission to free India; "Freedom," he wrote, "is often to be found inside a prison's walls."[152] And in the second half of the last century, Nelson Mandela spent twenty-seven years of enforced isolation in prison. During that time of isolation, he developed a resolve of steel. Upon his release from Robben Island, Mandela emerged with utmost clarity on what was needed to end apartheid and build a modern democracy in South Africa.

These leaders acted and took time to be still on behalf of countless people who depended on their wisdom and insight. Each had to find inner clarity in the midst of turbulence; each knew that his decisions would affect countless lives. Stillness allowed these leaders to rise above the fray, to get their priorities clear, and to say no to things that were urgent but not really important, even to pressing or popular demands for which there was loud clamor. Just as they did, those of us who aspire to be leaders, whether in politics, industry, or daily life, have to find the silence within that is conducive to purposeful action. It is in stillness that you can find your way, your ethical compass as a leader. No person or book can ever give enough advice to cover even a fraction of all the challenges a leader might encounter. Unless you can be silent and access the quiet power that stillness makes available, you miss out on one of the most valuable leadership tools.

The effects of mind relaxation on happiness for body and soul are palpable. Researchers at MIT and the University of Wisconsin, Madison, conducted laboratory tests in which the French-born Buddhist and molecular biologist Mathieu Ricard and other Tibetan monks agreed to have their brain activity observed during meditation.[133] The tests showed, among other things, increased activity in the prefrontal cortex, the part of the brain associated with feelings of happiness, alertness, and well-being. Similar tests were run on stressed-out workers from a biotech firm, half of whom had participated in an eight-week meditation course by Jon Kabat-Zinn, author of the meditation book *Wherever You Go, There You Are*. Among the major findings: not only did the meditation novices show much greater activity in the left prefrontal cortex than the control group, they also were found to have significantly enhanced immunity when researchers injected both groups with an influenza vaccine; and those with the greatest left-prefrontal-cortex activity showed the highest levels of immunity. Other studies have shown that meditation not only reduces stress but lengthens lives, and helps prevent, slow, or at least control illnesses such as cancer, heart disease, and even AIDS. So while we've just begun exploring the links between meditation and healing, there are clear signs of a positive correlation.[154]

Stillness works in sports too. Swiss Consulting Group advisor Peter Spang, a former tennis pro who played against Ivan Lendl and Boris

Becker in the 1980s, found stillness in the midst of the tennis court: "I understood that in my most beautiful and blissful moments on the tennis court I must have been playing in a state of meditation—with no thoughts, no emotions, just crystal-clear awareness."[155] Phil Jackson, one of the great basketball coaches of our generation, uses meditative practices to find his and his players' power in the midst of battle. He says, "The best stress reliever that I've found is meditation. That's what I do to start every day. It's a discipline and a setting of priorities." When Jackson still played for the New York Knicks, many years before he became known as the "Zen master coach" who taught his players meditation techniques, "I created a space in Madison Square Garden where I could become quiet, serene and focused." To do this, he used a breathing technique: "Of course the mind will race in to fill the gaps, but every breath brings me back to an inner silence and inner stillness," he explained. "A good metaphor for this is the action of the Samurai. The Samurai use meditation to be calm in the midst of violent fighting."[156]

Jackson and Spang are not alone: An estimated ten million Americans, among them business leaders like Thomas S. Monaghan, the founder of Domino's Pizza, the world's largest pizza-delivery chain, now use meditation to center themselves and make better decisions. They say that stillness and prayer are good for business.

(Have you heard the one about Moishe who comes into the synagogue? He has agreed with Shawn that they would meet there to discuss the sale of a diamond. Shawn has not arrived yet, so after waiting a bit, Moishe decides to start *mincha*, the silent afternoon prayer. Shawn comes in, sees Moishe standing silently praying, goes up to him and offers $10,000. But Moishe cannot stop his own prayer; even motioning with his hand would be prohibited. So he keeps praying. Shawn thinks Moishe's silence means his proposal is not high enough, so he offers $20,000...)

On a more serious note, business leaders today, even those not known as yogis, take time out for reflection. Andy Grove, the ex-leader of Intel famous for his restlessness (his memoir is titled *Only the Paranoid Survive*), steps back from the action regularly to reflect and try to foresee long-term trends in the industry. Bill Gates takes "think weeks" offline, without access to computers or other gadgets, from which he returns with fresh ideas distilled from reading and exploration, alone and with others. "The idea is to synthesize and focus on priorities— go up to the 15,000-foot level and really think about directions," said a Microsoft spokeswoman.[157]

Finally, non-doing may even be good for the environment. *The Idler* magazine has pointed out that it is our culture of busy-ness that makes us gobble up fossil fuels and spew out greenhouse gases at disastrous rates. If we just stopped our ant-like running, even for one day a week, by not using the stove or the lights, or the car, or the plane to jet off on a holiday, and instead spent some time walking in the park or talking to friends, we would reduce our fuel consumption significantly. Do nothing and save the planet?[158] How about that for a stillness commercial!

Torah and Stillness

Thousands of years before Churchill, Gandhi, and Mandela, the Torah gives us early role-models who withdrew from the action, as well as the costs of blind activity. Jacob, Moses, and David were all shepherds at one point in their lives. They developed their leadership in the quiet meditation of the desert. The all-encompassing silence and great emptiness allowed these leaders to become invincible. Many of the prophets also took to the desert to receive prophesies and visions.

The eighteenth-century Rabbi Israel ben Eliezer, the Baal Shem Tov, liked to meditate for hours in the forest. Hasidism, the movement of pious Jews and kabbalists he founded, teaches that the three great sins of humanity—the sin of Adam and Eve who ate from the tree of knowledge; the sin of the Jews who danced around the idolatrous golden calf; and the sin of David who took the beautiful Bat Sheva as his wife even while she was married to Uri, whom he sent into battle and certain death to remove him from the scene[159]—all involved impatience, the urge for instant gratification, and the inability to await the proper time for action.[160] On the other hand, when Noah built an ark for all species to survive the great flood, he had to build for 120 years, and then wait another year until it was all over (an almost inconceivable amount of time for those under pressure to perform for the next quarter's earnings).

Modern-day Noahs may need even more patience. The joke goes that in the twenty-first century the Lord came again unto Noah, who now lived in the United States, and said, "The earth has again become wicked and over-populated, and I see the end of all flesh before me. Build another ark and save two of every living thing along with a few good humans. You have six months to build the ark before I will start the unending rain for forty days and forty nights." Six months later God looked down and saw Noah weeping in his yard, but no ark. "Noah!" He roared, "I'm about to start the rain! Where is the ark?" "Forgive me, Lord," begged Noah, "but things have changed. I needed a building permit. My neighbors claim that I've violated the neighborhood zoning laws by building the ark in my yard. Then the Department of Transportation demanded that we post a bond for the future costs of moving power lines and other overhead obstructions, to clear the passage for the ark's move to the sea. I told them that the sea would be coming to us, but they would have none of it. When I started gathering the animals, an animal rights group sued me. They argued it was cruel and inhumane to put so many animals in a confined space. Immigration and Naturalization is checking the green-card status of most of the people who want to work. To make matters worse, the IRS seized all my assets, claiming I'm trying to leave the country illegally with endangered species. So, forgive me, Lord, but it would take at least ten years for me to finish this ark."

Suddenly the skies cleared, the sun began to shine, and a rainbow stretched across the sky. Noah looked up in wonder and asked, "You mean you're not going to destroy the world?"

"No" said the Lord. "The government beat me to it."

Noah and his problems aside, the Hebrew word for waiting (mechakeh) is composed of the same letters as the word for wisdom (chachmah). Only the period of seeming inaction allowed Noah to leave behind the old world that had existed before the flood and build a new one.

An Island in the Sea of Time

The Sabbath is an ingenious institution. It is the one day each week
when we're still, not pushing our lives forward, not engaging in the
usual hyperactivity. On what Jews consider the highest holiday—
higher even than the High Holidays of Rosh Hashana and Yom Kippur
—we are free to simply be. This is why the twentieth-century Jewish
philosopher and civil-rights activist Abraham Joshua Heschel, who
famously marched with Martin Luther King, Jr. in Selma, in his tribute
The Sabbath, called it an "island in the sea of time":[161]

> In the tempestuous ocean of time and toil there are islands of still-
> ness where we may enter a harbor and reclaim our dignity. The island
> is the seventh day, the Sabbath. ... Six days a week we live under the
> tyranny of space; on the Sabbath we try to become attuned to holi-
> ness in time. It is a day when we are called upon to share in what is
> eternal ..., to turn from the results of creation to the mystery of cre-
> ation; from the world of creation to the creation of the world.

The Mishnah (the first written recording, around 100 C.E., of the oral
Torah) spells out thirty-nine labors used to build the holy temple and
hence prohibited on the Sabbath (since even building something holy
was off-limits on the Sabbath). You shall not thresh the land, nor water
the plants, carry loads, plow, make a fire, cook, bake, sow, slaughter, nor
build. By extension, no financial transactions, no driving, no phone calls,
no CD, no DVD or TV, no PC. You are neither to write nor to erase writing, since moving a pen across paper, or typing a document on the computer, would alter the structure of the paper or the harddrive, which
would create something and is therefore inconsistent with the "island in
the sea of time." You are to live: spend time with friends and loved ones,
pray and study the Torah, sing and dance, eat, drink, and yes, make love
with your spouse). Every week, from sundown on Friday through night-
fall on Saturday, Jews who observe the Sabbath withdraw from the action. It is a sort of defragmenting of the brain, becoming whole at least
once a week. The feeling starts right at the lighting of the Sabbath candle before sunset on Friday. By kindling the candle, a line is drawn in the
sand: from now on, it is family time, quality time—holy time. The Sab-

bath has begun. No more rushing, no more pushing for results, no more management, no more transactions, no more business or busy-ness. The struggle has fallen away, a sense of peace is all-enveloping, things are okay the way they are, nothing has to change. The freedom to simply be is a feeling of quiet delight.

> **Tip:** At the beginning of the Sabbath meal, after the blessing of the wine, Jews wash their hands, and then don't talk until they say the blessing for the bread. These minutes of silence are a blessing in and of themselves. You don't have to chit-chat, impress someone with your wit, or somehow move the action forward. What if you created other pockets of time when you don't have to push the ball down the field, when you allow yourself to simply *be*? This state of being may be the source of all your clarity of purpose. From your being comes the power of your doing. As Hamlet said, "To be or not to be, that is the question."

Practicing Stillness

Sabbath observance gave rise to the idea of sabbaticals: every seventh year is a sabbatical year in the land of Israel. Farmers let the land lie fallow, creditors annul and forgive debts owed to them, and observant Jews rededicate themselves to studying and praying.[162] If this works for keeping the land fresh and fruitful, it certainly works for refreshing the human spirit. And if, as Abraham Lincoln is supposed to have asserted, "I had eight hours to chop down a tree, I would spend six sharpening my axe," then the Sabbath is precisely that: sharpening the axe so that you're unstoppable when the next week starts.

But how do you practice stillness during the day-to-day activities? A good place to start is to acknowledge that you don't know how to stand still for a single minute. Sometimes, we are tempted to rush on and want to be farther along than we really are. But it's a truism that peace comes only from being fully wherever you happen to be; in fact that's the only place where you will ever be: here, now. You've never been anywhere else. That's why Buddhists say that all suffering comes from desire. It's the ceaseless wanting of something more, or something different, or simply plain wanting, that causes pain. If you can be fully present in this moment, you might be surprised to find that nothing is lacking. You are fulfilled.

That sounds great; but how can you live totally in the now when thoughts rush to your head a mile a minute, broadcasting regrets and resentments from the past, "I should have …" "I can't believe she didn't …," or fears and worries for the future? How does the Dalai Lama, perhaps *the* icon of peace and tranquility in our time, relax? "I like to let my thoughts come to me each morning before I get up," he said. "I meditate for a few hours and that is like recharging." A few *hours*? What if we don't have a few hours to meditate? "I garden … gardening is one of my hobbies. Also, reading encyclopedias with pictures." He laughed. "I am a man of peace, but I am fond of looking at picture books of the Second World War."[163]

If the world's leading exponent of nonviolent political change finds tranquility by looking at war photography, you are free to explore whatever works for you in achieving stillness. A run? A walk? A bath? Your call. One of the CEO's coaching clients, the managing director of a multinational energy company, used to take his state-of-the-art BMW on the German autobahn and drive at 225 km/h; when the car was at full throttle, he was in the zone. So there are no rules for what constitutes a practice of stillness (as long as you don't find peace by killing people or hurting yourself); you have to decide for yourself. And don't say you're too busy: Rabbi Shlomo ben Aderet (widely known by his acronym Rashba), a world-renowned thirteenth-century Torah scholar with a packed schedule, still found time to take an hour-long walk every day.

Many Jews follow Rashba's example and study Torah; according to the Kabbalah, "Torah preceded the creation of the universe" by two thousand years.[164] When you delve into the Torah, God studies with you; you become one with the infinite. In fact, almost anything you do wholeheartedly, with total focus, can give you access to stillness. Whether it is doing the dishes and paying complete attention to the warm water swirling around your hands, the sensation and smell of the soap, the clinking of the cutlery against the cups, the brilliance of a dripping glass; or walking deliberately and being aware of each step, the feeling in the heel and ball of your foot, the position of your toes in your shoes, and the feeling of your skin brushing against the fabric; or whether it is making love (no comment on the details here, just find out yourself), the key is to be there fully, forget about the opportunity costs of what you might be missing out on (since you're here and not there, you're not missing a thing), and to let yourself live right now to the fullest. You have a choice every moment of every day: are you trying to get through it, get it done, survive it as it were, or are you allowing yourself to get lost in it, which turns that moment into the perfect place to be and opens a window to eternity?

Leadership Means Saying No

Since leaders, by definition, take on more than they can handle, their lives can get so full that windows of stillness are not enough. One of the factors that create much stress for managers is what one of the CEO's clients, a high-tech developer, aptly calls "focus anxiety": the inability to focus on doing any one thing at a time without thinking about all the other things you could or should be doing instead. Hence, this chapter would be incomplete without a key discipline that brings the peace of Sabbath into your daily life and work. In one word, it is: *No*. The Danish philosopher Søren Kierkegaard wrote: "Purity of heart is to will one thing."[165] What gives you real peace of mind is to focus on one thing: to prioritize and have the courage to say a well-reasoned no to lower-level priorities, even to demands that seem urgent or for which there is loud clamor. Take your cue from Jack Welch, who introduced just five major initiatives in his eighteen years as GE's chief executive; he simply refused to focus on other opportunities. Or from nineteenth-century entrepreneur Andrew Carnegie, the father of the American steel industry, who changed a famous adage to suit his purposes: "Put all your eggs in one basket and then watch that basket." Carnegie wrote in his autobiography:

> I believe the true road to success in any line is to make yourself master in that line. I have no faith in the policy of scattering one's

resources, and in my experience I have rarely if ever met a man who
achieved preeminence in money-making—certainly never one in
manufacturing—who was interested in many concerns. The men
who have succeeded are men who have chosen one line and stuck to
it…My advice to young men would be not only to concentrate their
whole time and attention on the one business in life in which they
engage, but to put every dollar of their capital into it.[166]

Tool 4.1
Managing from Priorities

Imagine a big empty glass jar on the table in front of you. Now
put rocks in it until they reach the rim. Once the jar is full, fill
it with small pebbles. You realize there's more room than you
thought. Now put sand in it; there's still more room. Finally
pour water in. Is it full now? Yes. What's the lesson? That no
matter how full your life is, you can always squeeze in more?
No, that's not the lesson. The real lesson is: prioritize. Put the
big things in first. That's the meaning of the word "priority":
actions that come *prior* to other actions.

Most managers think they know what priorities are. But if
you asked ten people for their priorities, most would give you a
to-do list. Tasks are not priorities, which are the single most
important practice for living effectively, and for staying sane in
a world that offers a dizzying surplus of opportunities. Clearly
articulating and managing from priorities reduce focus anxiety
(constantly thinking of what you're *not* doing). No matter what
a great leader you may be otherwise, working without priorities
is like driving a car without a map or GPS and only a vague idea
of where you want to go—you may drive as fast as you can and
still not get there. Even Martin Luther King, Jr.'s soaring ora-
tory suffered from being overly abstract and convoluted whenever he was not single-mindedly focused on the clear and
present pressure of a bus boycott or the threat of jail time;[167]

and Winston Churchill became a rather lackluster leader once he had completed the almost superhuman task of vanquishing Hitler and returned to being a peacetime prime minister (in fact he lost the first peacetime election in 1945).

To put priorities to work for you, they need to be declarations of what comes first. But how do you know what comes first? Your priorities should emanate from your long-term goals, as discussed in Chapter 2. If an insurance agent's objective is to earn $200,000 this year, her priority actions might be to write 30 percent more policies than last year, increase her prospect pool to 300, improve her prospect qualification process, join a professional network, and publish two articles in two trade journals to position herself as an expert in the market. When you're clear about your priorities—for the year, the quarter, the month, the week—each day becomes a milestone on the path to achieving your long-term vision.

How well you articulate your priorities is a factor in accomplishing them. Like promises and requests (see Chapter 3), unless they are clear and specific, you have no shot at delivering them. To be potent, the statement of a priority should begin with an action verb, be given a timeframe, and be measurable—or at least stated such that it will be clear whether or not you delivered it. For example, "call potential clients" is not an effective priority. If you call one prospect, have you reached your goal? What if you called six prospects? Does it matter whether you actually reached them, or what you talked about when you called them? "Call potential clients" generates activity, not accomplishment. In contrast, "generate three requests for proposals this week" is clear. At the end of the week, there will be no question about whether you have delivered the priority or not. The following table gives other examples:

Activities	Priorities
Improve sales performance	Increase sales in each affiliate by at least 25% this year.
Make more money.	Get a 5% raise by March 31.
Have more fun.	Go dancing at least twice this month.
Be a better father.	Read to the children for a half-hour a day.
Increase speed-to-market.	Double speed-to-market to under 120 days this year.

If you develop priorities for or with a team of people, be sure that the team members are aligned on the top priority. Enormous power is available when everybody pulls in the same direction. To get aligned, make sure the team meets at the beginning of each priority cycle, for instance, on the first of each quarter and month, and at the start of each week, to review the past cycle's results, recognize accomplishments or lack thereof, see what's missing for success, and set priorities for the coming cycle. (If you want to hit the ground running, you might prefer to meet on the last weekday to set up the next week.) Begin each meeting by debriefing performance so that team members can learn from the past and share best practices (and the worst ones they would rather avoid next time around). Recognize each accomplishment and the people who were responsible for them, and find out what the success factors were. When a priority was not delivered, find out what went wrong or what kept the result from being produced; then remove the obstacle. Only when the debriefing is complete should you move on to create the priorities for the upcoming cycle. Especially in our Western activist culture, it's important to resist rushing into what's next. Don't go forward until there is a sense of completion about what has and what has not been achieved.

> **Tip:** When you are overwhelmed, chances are you are not focusing on your top priority.

One way to set priorities is to determine what you really do need to do yourself. To accomplish anything of size, delegation has been the key to the successes of leaders, starting with Moses, whose father-in-law Jethro (the first management consultant of record) advised him to build a structure of communication and delegation.

> The thing that you do is not good. You will surely become worn out—you as well as this people that is with you—for this matter is too hard for you, you will not be able to do it alone. Now heed my voice, I shall advise you, and may God be with you. You be a representative to God, and you convey the matters to God. You shall caution them regarding the decrees and the teachings, and you shall make known to them the path in which they should go and the deeds that they should do. And you shall discern from among the entire people, men of accomplishment, God-fearing people, men of truth, people who despise money, and you shall appoint them leaders of thousands, leaders of hundreds, leaders of fifties, and leaders of tens. They shall judge the people at all times, and they shall bring every major matter to you, and every minor matter they shall judge, and it will be eased for you, and they shall bear with you. If you do this thing—and God shall command you—then you will be able to endure, and this entire people, as well, shall arrive at its destination in peace.[168]

For many a leader of lesser caliber, Jethro's counsel would have been a license to arrogantly put himself above the people. Not so for the humble Moses.

Timothy Ferriss heads Brain-Quicken, a San Jose-based developer and distributor of sports nutrition products with wholesale customers around the world. In his own systematic process of self-emancipation, the first thing Ferriss did was recognize that "of more than 120 customers, a mere five were bringing in 95 percent of the revenue. In the next 24 hours, I made several simple but emotionally difficult decisions that changed my life forever." He put the unproductive majority of customers on passive mode. "If they ordered, great—let them fax in the order. If not, I would do absolutely no chasing: no phone calls, no e-mail, nothing." He also decided to avoid meetings unless they were about decisions. "If someone proposes that I sit down with him or 'set a time to talk on the phone,' I ask him to e-mail an agenda to define the purpose, and I set an end time. Decisions should take 30 minutes or less." To reduce his e-mail traffic, Ferriss "decided to e-mail permission to all customer-service supervisors to resolve any problem that took less than $100 to fix without contacting me." He outsourced customer service for order tracking and returns. To limit his e-mail obligation even further, he relied on outsourced personal assistants in India to manage his in-box (at $4 to $10 an hour).[169]

What worked for Moses can work for you, too: on your list of tasks to complete, designate each item as A, B, or C. An A is a task nobody else can do for you, such as designing your company strategy or getting a haircut. B tasks are those you would like to do, but need not do yourself. These might include delivering a report to your client or picking up a birthday present for your daughter. C are those you can delegate, such as managing accounts receivable or upgrading the company Web site. However, sometimes carrying out a seemingly small or menial action can have strategic value. It can make an important statement when an executive is not above going to the mailroom personally to get a priority package out in time. Mahatma Gandhi demonstrated this in 1930 by walking from his ashram 240 miles to the Indian Ocean, his bamboo staff in his hand, his back slightly bent, and his familiar loincloth around his hips; when he got to the sea three weeks later, he reached down and scooped up a piece of caked salt. With a grave and stern mien, he held his fist up to the thousands of spectators who had gathered, and opened it to expose the white crystals that the British occupiers of India had forbidden Indians to harvest. The great leader's menial action made salt a symbol for India's independence; within a week all India was in turmoil. The British responded with the most massive roundup in Indian history and swept people into jail by the thousands, including Gandhi, who managed to send a last message to his followers. "The honor of India," he said, "has been symbolized by a fistful of salt in the hand of a man of nonviolence. The fist which held the salt may be broken, but it will not yield up its salt."[170]

Tip: Few things have a greater effect on productivity—and reducing stress and focus-anxiety—than the following twin practice. First, begin each day with an accomplishment of size—never by answering your e-mails (except when cutting down your e-mail backlog *is* the top priority that week). "Don't speak on the telephone with anyone," the late Swedish film director Ingmar Bergman described his morning work, "get up early and eat breakfast, go for a walk, don't read the newspaper, don't speak on the telephone. Sit down at the desk."[171] Allow nothing else to get in your way until you've delivered that priority. Once that's done, you can turn to lesser tasks. Second, at the end of the day, before you leave the office, set up your next day: what accomplishment of size will you start tomorrow with?

Say "yes" to actions only if they're strategically important and high-leverage to you and your enterprise. Unless you learn to say no, you either burn out quickly or you're not in charge; you become a pinball of circumstances or the object of other people's agendas (which, we repeat, is the opposite of leadership). There's nothing negative about saying no, quite the opposite: The freedom to turn down an invitation, a request or an opportunity can be an act of responsibility and integrity. Indeed, without giving yourself permission to say no, you're not truly free to say yes. We all tend to have commitments that are not truly our own; they may be obligations imposed on us, like paying taxes, or they may be left over from choices that were once right but are no longer necessary, like weekly staff meetings for pure exchange of information. Especially in large corporations, politics and peer pressure can produce a powerful urge to please others; but you have to be true to yourself even there.

One of the CEO's clients, a top executive at a multinational oil and gas company, realized in an early coaching session that most of his day-to-day actions were reactive: "I am never clear what my priorities are and what the agendas of others are. I am not setting priorities enough; I don't make clear in the firm where I stand." A few months later he had developed the discipline to say no: "I don't let myself be pushed around because I now work from long-term goals and priorities." If you can integrate the different strands of your life into one powerful mission that you single mindedly pursue, instead of trying to hold together divergent commitments that pull you in many directions, everything you do serves one purpose. And if it doesn't, don't do it.

Tool 4.2
Weeding Out

Ten years after undergoing an operation for throat cancer, the sociologist Robert K. Merton issued his "Self-Emancipation Proclamation." In it, he wrote, "I hereby declare that I shall not again agree to write, revise or edit a book; deliver a public lecture; contribute to a symposium ...." This went on for a page.[172] The CEO has a similar practice. He keeps a list of all projects he is no longer committed to. He maintains the list in his PDA so he can review it on the subway or when waiting in lines at airports (or, quite frankly, in the bathroom, one of the few remaining places where stillness and uninterrupted thinking can happen). This practice of letting go of tasks greatly simplifies life. The CEO also lists old thought patterns and attitudes he is ready to jettison, such as "I will be punished if I don't succeed" or "I must have X now." This practice is in the tradition of Rabbi Schneur Zalman of Liadi, the Alter Rebbe, who wrote in his principal work *Tanya* how to deal with negative or destructive thoughts: don't struggle with them, but simply acknowledge that they come from an outside power, your animal soul; then push them out and away.

Say yes to actions only if they're strategically important and high-leverage to you and your enterprise. Paradoxically, the freedom *not* to pursue something can give you the freedom to do it. The CEO once wrote in his "What I Won't Do" list that he would *not* write a book on strategy. Several years later, he reviewed the list and reversed himself. The choice to do so came not least from the permission he gave himself to cancel the commitment.

Of course, if you've declared a commitment to someone else, you can't just write it in a notebook to revoke it; you must inform those affected that they can no longer count on you for taking action. This gives your colleagues several options: They can try to change your mind and convince you to still take the action; they can choose to do it themselves; or they can find someone else to do it. It's not that you're against the task itself; you're just not the one to complete it. Your colleagues are free to act on what is important and high-leverage for *them*. That's liberating. You'll be amazed at the freedom this procedure will create in your life and work. As the poet Rainer Maria Rilke said, "If I don't manage to fly, someone else will. The spirit wants only that there be flying. As for who happens to do it, in that he has only a passing interest."

It is important to remember that making things happen is not up to you alone. So don't get stressed out. Why do people have stress? Because they believe they must be the makers of their own fate 100 percent of the time. Of course you cannot just leave it all up to some higher power; but you are not in charge of the stock market. Nobody is. You can offer your product to the customer, but you cannot force him or her to buy it. So don't have the hubris to think you are omnipotent, as Enron did; don't seek to control everything. The action is up to you, the ultimate accomplishment is not. There is a Yiddish saying: *"Man darf tan, nisht uftan"* (One must do, not accomplish). You can prepare the soil and water the plant, but the plant will need to grow by itself. When the Rabbi's late grandfather, Reb Aharon Leib, visited Rabbi Yosef Schneerson[173] in 1927, just before his Rebbe left Russia, he asked him for a blessing for joy from his children. The Rebbe responded that when a young man asks for a blessing, he must know that a blessing is like rain; one must first plow the soil and sow the seeds, and "if you will plow and you will sow, God will bless you with rains of blessings." Practice the art and science of letting, instead of making, things happen; see if you can attract and receive results instead of pushing for them. This is leadership at its finest—when things seem to happen effortlessly and with grace. Try it. Practice it. It's the essence of the Commandment to keep the Sabbath.

The Bottom Line

- Leaders, by definition, are in constant danger of being overwhelmed. Since they gravitate toward accountability and commitment, the world cries out for them to take on more and more. Since they tend to see opportunities where others see obstacles, they are constantly in danger of suffering from an "opportunity surplus." To stay powerful and self-determined, they must regularly step back, be still, and refocus.

- In a 24/7 world, the ancient institution of the Sabbath is one of the most ingenious solutions for stress management, the prevention of heart attack, and the adjustment of your compass as a leader.

- The hallmark of great leaders is that they have the courage to say no to low-priority demands. Those who say yes to all opportunities or demands are the opposite of leaders—they are slaves or victims who will burn out.

- Tools for simplifying life are: managing from priorities, weeding out, and listing what you will *not* do.

CHAPTER FIVE

Commandment V
Respect Your Parents:
Appreciation is Power

Open my eyes, O God, to the marvels that surround me.
Show me the wonder of each breath I take,
of every thought, word and movement.
Let me experience the miracles of the world I witness—
ever mindful and always appreciative of all that You have made.
—Rabbi Nachman of Breslov

The most remarkable thing about my mother is that for thirty years
she served the family nothing but leftovers.
The original meal has never been found.
—Calvin Trillin

THE FIFTH COMMANDMENT: *"Honor your father and mother so that your days may be lengthened upon the land which your God gives you."* Appreciation is one of the most effective leadership tools, but we take so much for granted—our parents, the people with whom we work and live, and the small details that make for large accomplishments. Whatever, and whoever, you appreciate gives you power. Appreciation is crucial in a world of highly mobile knowledge workers whose intellectual capital goes home with them every night (if they're not already working from home) and who will jump ship the moment they get the feeling that you don't care enough. This chapter will show you how to use appreciation strategically: how to empower people, how to appreciate the obstacles and even the enemies in your path, how to leverage details others might miss, and ultimately as a strategy for taking charge.

We all know the Commandment to honor your father and mother. But our beloved folks are also among the people who can get us riled up the most, probably for the very reason that we love them so much. Their criticisms (for example, "I pray that someday you will make enough money to send me flowers on Mother's Day," or "He is visiting us for only ten days," or "Can't you afford a better sweater by now?") can hit home like all-out assaults on our dignity, with enough force to reduce fully grown men and women (no matter what successes they've achieved elsewhere in life) to immature twelve-year-olds. Take the man who gave a toast and told a joke at his own twenty-fifth wedding anniversary. It doesn't matter what the joke was, just imagine one of those jokes at wedding anniversaries. OK, it was neither very funny nor very new, but the assembled family and friends still laughed heartily—except for the man's mother. Without missing a beat, she scolded him publicly before the assembled guests. "Not only was the joke bad," she snarled loudly, "but you messed up the whole speech."

It was a show-stopper. The merriment stopped abruptly, and a pregnant silence fell upon the room. The guests were shocked; all faces turned to the son. What would he do? Finally he looked directly at this mother and spoke: "Mother, you have always been the leader of our home, and I respect what you say." However livid he might have been inside, his mature response saved the wedding anniversary from ruin.

When you've become grateful to your parents for everything you are and have, and appreciate that you would literally not exist were it not for them, you grow up and mature into fuller leadership. The story goes that when Rabbi DovBer of Lubavitch (1773–1827, the son of the Alter Rebbe who was to become the Mittler Rebbe) was twelve years old, he heard the public reading of the Torah portion Ki Tavo about the Jews receiving ninety-eight different curses and fell violently ill. People came to his bedside and asked, "Why did you get sick?" The precocious youth could barely lift his head from the pillow. Finally he whispered, "Because I heard the ninety-eight curses." DovBer's visitors were nonplussed. "But you have heard these curses at this time of year for several years now, and you never got sick before." He answered, "Usually my father reads them. When my father reads them, I hear no curses, only blessings." To him, his beloved father's recitation of the Torah portion softened even the harshest blows.

DovBer may have been blinded by the unconditional admiration of a twelve-year-old for his seemingly infallible father, but that is not the point. The point is the power you get from respecting your parents, as well as others, all of your life. The German philosopher Martin Heidegger pointed to an intimate connection, both etymologically and essentially, between *thanking* and *thinking*[174]—when you are grateful, whether it is for your parents or your staff or the smallest details that make your life work, you do better thinking, make higher-quality decisions, and lead more effectively.

The Talmud includes a famous story about appreciation. Rabbi Akiva, a student of Nachum Ish Gamzu (*gam zu* means this too [is for the best]), liked to say, *Kol d'avid rachmana le'tov hu d'avid* (Whatever God does must be for good). Akiva once traveled with a donkey, a rooster, and a candle: the candle so he could study Torah at night, the rooster as his alarm clock to wake him up for Torah study, and the donkey to carry his possessions. He stopped in a small town for the night and tried to get lodging at an inn, but there was no room available; he went from house to house, but none of the townspeople would let him in. Rabbi Akiva said to himself, "Whatever God does must be for the good," walked into the neighboring woods with his animals and set up camp. All of a sudden, a strong wind kicked up and blew out his candle; Akiva was sitting in pitch black darkness. A few moments later, a lion came up from behind his tent and killed the donkey. What was left? The rooster. A ravenous cat appeared and devoured it. Rabbi Akiva was stuck. Most of us in his situation would have cursed our bad luck. But what did Akiva say? The same thing he always said, "Whatever God does must be for the good." He went to sleep with a smile on his face.

The next morning, Akiva awoke in the forest, shouldered his baggage and went back into town. It was utterly deserted, a ghost town; he couldn't find a soul. He later heard that a band of robbers had attacked that night, killing all the villagers and stealing their money. After the deed was done, the posse had made off into the forest. Akiva realized in a flash that if the villagers had given him lodging, he would be dead now. And if the robbers had seen his candle in the woods, or heard his rooster's crow or his donkey's bray, he would have met with the same fate as the townspeople.[175]

> **Tip:** Whatever is in front of you, whether it's a recalcitrant subordinate, a cut-throat competitor, or an unhappy customer who walks away, practice saying, "This too is for the best." What opportunity lies hidden here?

Unfortunately the power of appreciation is (surprise!) barely appreciated in management. Quite the opposite: familiarity seems to breed contempt. We tend to take for granted the people around us, our colleagues and our leaders. In fact, some say that just as the Inuit can distinguish between twenty-seven types of snow, Jews have a huge repertoire of insults—Yiddish words ranging from *schmuck* (idiot) to *khazer* (pig), *ganev* (swindler), *nebbish* (nerd, loser), *shlemiel* (retard), *yold* (yokel), *tuches lecker* (ass-kisser), *alter kacker* (old fart), *momzer* (bastard), *shlub* (coarse, unrefined person), *meshugena* (crazy person, freak), *faygala* (faggot), *shtick holtz* (a piece of wood with no personality), *schmendrik* (fool, jerk) to the four-letter word *putz* (idiot)[176]—but almost none for acknowledgment. Jews are far from alone. In 2002, the CEO was in Berlin when the German national soccer team reached the finals in the World Cup; but match after match on their march to the top, you barely heard a word of appreciation from the German so-called fans watching their team's championship performance. The highest compliment was, "Not bad, but they could have done better." This is not a climate in which players, or any people, for that matter, succeed. By contrast, the Brazilian fans, whose team won the World Cup, as well as the Turkish and Korean fans, whose teams made it to the semi-finals, were all ecstatic; in their eyes, their teams couldn't have done better.

We don't have to go to Germany to see how often we all nit-pick and criticize people instead of rejoicing in their successes. It seems to be human to see what's missing, pinpoint what's wrong, or think the grass is always greener on the other side. We are not-enough-machines. When was the last time you woke up in the morning and said to yourself, Last night I *did* have enough sleep? When was the last time you thought, I *do* have enough money? And to those few among us who do have enough time or money, our bodies or our spouses are not beautiful or young enough, we don't have enough friends, we don't have enough security, we don't get enough love; the list goes on. (By the way, are you far enough along with this book …?) One of the CEO's coaching clients, a senior executive, harbored such disparaging thoughts (about himself, his job, or the company's boss he hated reporting to) that he, unwittingly but incessantly, shot himself in the foot. He was unaware of the fundamental axiom: What you resist, persists. To help him break through this vicious cycle, the CEO asked him to build his muscle of appreciation. The assignment was to find something new to appreciate each day, and to tell a different person each day what was great about his life. This simple task transformed how the client perceived reality, and hence it transformed his reality. Funny how things change when you value them; they gain in value—in short, they *appreciate*. (If you don't buy it, try the exercise.) That's why observant Jews say eighteen blessings upon waking up each morning, starting with "I offer thanks to You, living and eternal King, for you have mercifully restored my soul within me; your faithfulness is great,"[177] since the soul ascends every night and it is not taken for granted that it will come back.

> **Tip:** Every day for one week, tell a different person what you appreciate about your life. Be specific.

There's a Crack in Everything

But aren't we naïve, and perhaps even delusional, if we gloss over the bad news and see everything in a positive light? To be fair, many things in our day-to-day lives *are* hard to appreciate: automated phone menus when you call customer service; too much paper; daily onslaughts of e-mails in your inbox that cry out to be answered, but won't matter in the least even a month from now; long and indecisive conference calls;

Business Books of the Year, especially the ones in which CEOs (often and even more annoyingly, their ghostwriters) expound on their own brilliance (OK, call it CEO envy).

Tool 5.1
Drain vs. Leading/Learning

This tool allows leaders to distinguish what they appreciate about their work/life from what they don't. Take a sheet of paper and draw a vertical line down the middle. On top of the left column, put the title Drain. These are all the things that drain your energy, the things you see as a burden, as an obligation, as clutter, as a necessary evil in your day-to-day life; in short, the stuff you just don't appreciate. Then, on top of the right column, insert Leading/Learning. These are the things that you love to do, that make you happily lose yourself like a child in a sandbox, that make you forget it's time for dinner. List at least ten items under each title, and be specific. For example, if you abhor weekly management meetings, put under Drain exactly what it is that you cannot stand about these meetings (for example, your colleagues talking for the hundredth time about thinking out of the box without ever doing so). But there might be one or two aspects you actually do appreciate about the meetings, things that are buried in them somewhere (for example, learning about best practices or stepping back to see the bigger picture). If you do this long enough, you may find many more things you appreciate than you have previously acknowledged. Again, what you appreciate gives you power. Following is a sample list:

Drain	Leading/Learning
Data entry	Being/working with people
Running the business	Working with clients
Hustling for sales	Coaching people

Drain	Leading/Learning
E-mail backlog	Writing
Admin	Media interviews
Correcting proposals	Research, learning, reading
Worrying about financial viability	Big picture/strategy

Once you have listed all items on both sides, see what changes you want to make: How can you maximize the leadership/ learning aspects of your life and minimize (or delegate, as noted in Chapter 4) the burdens and drains?

Sometimes it is difficult to continue to appreciate the world around us when we are surrounded by tragedy. Didn't God allow for the destruction of the World Trade Center on 9/11 and for the senseless deaths of 2,975 civilians (not counting the hijackers)? Didn't six million Jews perish under the Third Reich precisely because they kept hoping that everything was for the best instead of planning for the worst? Doesn't God let some 20,000 children die each day of hunger or hunger-related causes, the equivalent of 100 jumbo jets crashing? On a personal level, didn't God let the CEO's younger sister die at eighteen from a heroin overdose? Aren't tragedies like these terribly unfair? In the midst of such pain, appreciation seems almost impossible to practice; but every time the CEO did, it made him stronger. In fact it was precisely his sister's premature death that taught the CEO several powerful lessons: Honor your parents (which for the CEO, led to a much deeper relationship with them); don't take *anything* you have for granted; and love life and live in a way that makes a difference. On a more global scale, paradoxically, Israel might not exist today were it not for the Holocaust: without the global outrage at their annihilation by Hitler's henchmen in World War II, the Jews might never have received their own state. "There is a crack," the Leonard Cohen song "Anthem" goes, "a crack in everything / that's how the light gets in."

> **Tip:** Remember the worst thing that ever happened in your own life, personal or work-related. Then think about what lessons or opportunities this event made available. Imagine where you would be today had that trial not occurred.

God Is in the Details

A crucial facet of appreciation is to value the power of details; Judaism is full of the divine power hidden in them. It starts right at home. You may have the most beautiful *mezuzah* (a piece of parchment, usually in a decorative casing, inscribed with specified Hebrew verses from the Torah, beginning with the phrase, "Hear O Israel, the Lord your God, the Lord is one") on each doorpost of your home, studded with silver or gold or diamonds; but unless you attend to the details inside (for example making sure the text of the prayer is on a kosher scroll made from a piece of skin of a kosher animal, and every letter of the text is correct), the *mezuzah* is just a pretty adornment. Rabbi Yehoshua Segall, a trained *sofer* or Torah scribe, tells a joke about the American who invited a rabbi from Israel to inspect his *mezuzah* (a routine practice for observant Jews). The rabbi opened the case, found it empty, and asked why. "The instructions?" the owner shrugged. "They were in Hebrew. I didn't understand a word, so I threw them out." Just as the *mezuzah* will not protect a home without the prayer on a kosher scroll, the most inspiring vision for your business will come to naught unless you take care of the small, seemingly trivial, or symbolic things.

When Oscar winners Martin Scorsese and Robert De Niro worked on *The King of Comedy*, they did twenty-six takes to fine-tune one bit of dialogue, a shared obsessiveness that Scorsese himself would call "kind of excruciating" twenty years later.[178] Many managers think erroneously that such attention to details isn't worth it and that they should focus on the big things—that one must "pulverize mountains and shatter boulders, turn the world upside down," as Rabbi Menachem M. Schneerson put it.[179] They too-often feel that the menial tasks are beneath them, that it's enough to have a great business idea, that trivialities should be left to others, that, to quote two co-founders of an Australian start-up, "this product will sell itself." But that's precisely where things break down (the start-up went out of business). And that's why the Talmud warns, "Flay a carcass in the market-place, and accept your pay, and do not say, 'I am a great man and it is disgraceful to me.'"[180] No man should see himself as too important for the details, or leave them to others. Unless the details match the strategy, you have no prayer of accomplishment, or worse, you'll achieve the wrong outcome. Rabbi Schneur Zalman, the Alter Rebbe, insisted that every tiny action can change the entire world. "It is known that all the worlds, the exalted and the lowly, are dependent on the precise and meticulous performance of one single *mitzvah* [good deed]," he wrote. "Through the omission of one required detail they are invalidated, and the intellect departs."[181]

History can be seen as a sheer infinite chain of countless small acts, with no grand actions per se. Even when a head of state signs a treaty, that seemingly historical event consists of nothing more than putting a pen to paper and signing a name. It's simply the culmination of many other tiny actions that preceded it, each performed with full attention. In 1962, President John F. Kennedy's administration narrowly escaped a major disaster, and perhaps World War III, because his brother picked up on a detail everyone else had missed. During the last days of the Cuban Missile Crisis, there were many sleepless nights during which Kennedy and his strategists painstakingly analyzed the situation and thought through the pros and cons of each policy option, including a blockade of Cuba. After days of agonizing waiting, Russian Premier Nikita Khrushchev finally announced the withdrawal of Soviet missiles from Cuba. Kennedy's advisers sighed with relief. The commander-in-chief gave the order for the American ships to end the blockade and back off; utterly exhausted, he went to get some long overdue sleep. There was just one weak link the strategists failed to appreciate: the Navy's Standard Operating Procedures did not provide for Kennedy's order to be executed. There was no procedure for ending a blockade. Were it not for Attorney General Robert F. Kennedy's personal intervention, his brother's instruction would have gotten lost somewhere in the chain of command. To end the blockade, the attorney general, together with Defense Secretary Robert McNamara, got the commander of the already-positioned ships on the phone and personally ordered, in a screaming exchange, an override of the navy's SOPs and withdrawal of the U.S. warships. Had he not followed the presidential order down the hierarchy, the Soviet fleet commander might have interpreted that lack of withdrawal as a hostile act, and one tiny detail could have ignited another world war.

In fact, one detail could have saved John F. Kennedy's own life a year later. At 12:15 p.m. on that fateful Friday, November 22, 1963, in Dallas, several minutes before Kennedy's motorcade passed through Dealey Plaza, eighteen-year-old Arnold Rowland and his wife stood at the west entrance of the Dallas County Records Building. While waiting to catch a glimpse of the glamorous president and first lady, Rowland looked up at the School Book Depository Building 150 feet away and saw a man standing in one of the windows, his rifle sticking out in full view from the street below. Rowland later told Senators Arlen Specter and Gerald Ford of the Warren Commission: "I noticed on the sixth floor of the building that there was a man back from the window, not hanging out the window. He was standing and holding a rifle." Rowland could have alerted a policeman or a state trooper, but "then the thought came to us that it is a security agent. We had seen in the movies before where they have security men up in windows and places like that with rifles to watch the crowds, and we brushed it aside as that, at that time, and thought nothing else about it until after the event happened."[182] Were it not for this quirk, history might have turned out differently.

Four decades later, yet another detail, a tiny piece of styrofoam, caused NASA's space shuttle Columbia to blow up. On February 1, 2003, during its re-entry into the atmosphere, the Columbia was positioned over Texas en route to the Kennedy Space Center when it disintegrated, killing all seven crew members. Investigators later found that the insulating foam used to connect the shuttle's external tank to its orbiter had come off, damaging the left wing and letting superheated gases into the orbiter once it dropped into the atmosphere. The damage ran into the billions, not to speak of NASA's loss of credibility, and above all the lost lives. How could this happen? The short answer: in a world of quick and punchy sound-bites, budget cuts, and pressure to get the show on the road, senior NASA officials had been sloppy with the small stuff. NASA management meetings worked with greatly condensed briefings, sometimes boiling a detailed forty-slide engineering analysis down to a single slide. The potential impact of foam striking the orbiter was one of the details that had been glossed over and fallen by the wayside.

The lesson is that tiny factors can make the difference between life and death, and leaders must be in command of them. The same goes for earthly endeavors. In 2001, a critical-care specialist at Johns Hopkins Hospital named Peter Pronovost designed a checklist for his intensive care unit.[183] He didn't attempt to make the checklist cover everything; he designed it to tackle just one problem: line infections. On a sheet of plain paper, he plotted out the steps to take in order to avoid infections when putting a line in. Doctors are supposed to wash their hands with soap, clean the patient's skin with chlorhexidine antiseptic, put sterile drapes over the entire patient, wear a sterile mask, hat, gown, and gloves, and put a sterile dressing over the catheter site once the line is in. Check, check, check, check, check. These steps were no-brainers; they had been known and taught for years, and it seemed silly to make a checklist just for them. Still, Pronovost asked the nurses in his I.C.U. to observe the doctors for a month as they put lines into patients, and record how often they completed each step. The nurses found that with more than a third of patients, the doctors skipped at least one.

For a year, Pronovost and his colleagues kept monitoring what happened. The results were so dramatic that they weren't sure whether to believe them: the ten-day line-infection rate went from 11 percent to *zero*. They followed patients for fifteen more months. Only two line infections occurred during the entire period. In just one hospital, the checklist had prevented forty-three infections and eight deaths, and saved $2 million. Pronovost recruited more colleagues, and they made more checklists. In December 2006, they published their findings in *The New England Journal of Medicine*.[184] The typical intensive care unit had cut its quarterly infection rate to zero. Michigan's infection rates had fallen so low that its average I.C.U. outperformed 90 percent of I.C.U.s nationwide. In the initiative's first eighteen months, participating hospitals had saved an estimated $175 million and more than 1,500 lives—at a total program cost of $500,000.[185] That is a 35,000 percent return on investment. These successes had been sustained for almost four years—all because of a stupid little checklist.

Of course, in the process you can't lose sight of the big picture, but you must be on top of enough details to ensure their implementation, continuing toward realization of your vision. Take sports, for example. Michael Jordan's astonishing slam-dunks were a result of his quiet, systematic, and incessant practice of the minutiae—his extra shots at night when nobody was watching. And in business, Bill Gates was famous for his uncanny ability to put his finger on unresolved nuances when Microsoft executives presented innovations. This is how one vice president described how Gates worked:

> You may think you have everything totally prepared, and the one area you weren't quite sure about, somehow he just finds it right away, and asks you the one right question. He'll know intricate low-level details about a program, and you wonder, "How does he know that? He has no reason ever to get to that level!" Some piece of code, or some other technology Microsoft isn't even involved in. You just shake your head.[186]

By contrast, when Terry Semel left Warner Brothers in 2001 to become CEO of the Web giant Yahoo, he had a grand plan. But he dropped the ball on the intricacies of implementation. "Terry's a big-picture, 20,000-feet kind of guy," said one Silicon Valley insider who has worked with Yahoo. "But operational issues trump strategic issues at a certain point."[187] In 2006, Semel earned the dubious distinction of being the CEO who provided the least bang for the buck: he made $53.3 million personally while his company *lost* 32.9 percent of its value.[188] (Semel is history. In 2007 he was replaced by Jerry Yang.)[189] Strong CEOs, on the other hand, are stimulated by seemingly minor events in their market, events that might foretell a new trend and give them big ideas.

Moreover, follow-up on the details pays off handsomely. A study by Keilty, Goldsmith & Company of more than eight thousand leaders in Fortune 100 corporations found a direct correlation between follow-up and leadership effectiveness. If you watched the likes of Larry Bossidy (the former head of Allied Signal), Jack Welch (the former head of GE), or any other proven implementer in a meeting, you'd discover that they all did the same thing: Near the end of the meeting, they always grabbed a pen and started writing exactly who had agreed to do what and by when, and they reviewed every commitment before the meeting was officially over. Afterward, they often sent each participant a reminder. This is the kind of follow-through and appreciation of details that differentiate the weak from the powerful leaders.

The detail freak par excellence was Sanford I. Weill, the former master-builder of Citigroup. Unlike Jack Welch, he did not leave behind a lodestar for future managers. Unlike Warren Buffett, he had no special genius in finance. Yet it was Weill, the consummate pragmatist, who put together the first truly global financial firm of the twenty-first century, linking securities, banking, and insurance. Part of his secret was his obsession with details. He rose early. He paced the floors. He was a master at exploiting seemingly small opportunities. "Sandy is insecure fundamentally," said Jack Nusbaum, the attorney who handled many of Weill's early acquisitions. "It drives him to be a perfectionist—to be a master of every piece in the puzzle."[190] Just like young Sam Walton who personally tended his WalMart inventory, or Donald Trump's father Fred Trump, a real estate developer in the New York City boroughs infamous for picking up discarded nails at his construction sites, Weill grasped that success would ride on the particulars. "There was never any long-range plan," said Robert Lipp, a former Chemical bank executive who joined the nucleus that came to run Citigroup, "that's what we did when we sat down at lunch."[191]

Every Person Counts

To be sure, Weill's focus on all the details had drawbacks too. "Sandy is on overload—he has too many decisions to make," said one Salomon

Smith Barney banker who did not want to be mentioned by name, "and people are afraid to tell him the truth, which is what he always thrived on."[192] Weill also had shortcomings in other areas. He was known for dressing people down; he was both full of himself and almost constantly craving validation; and he famously bulldozed long-term partners out of the way lest they endanger his rise to the lonely top. This brings up another important facet of appreciation: treating every human being as the key to the future.

Before Moses became a leader, he was a shepherd. Why did God not appoint him to a more prestigious job, say a doctor or a banker? Because, the *Midrash* says, a man is not elevated to greatness without first being tested with seemingly petty matters. One day, a sheep was missing. Looking everywhere, Moses finally found it at a stream of water. He said to the sheep, "You must be weary," put it on his shoulder and walked back. God saw that Moses was concerned not only with big or profitable people or animals, but even with a small sheep; He decided, "Because you had mercy in leading the flock of a mortal, you will assuredly tend My flock, Israel."[193]

Tip: Awe and wonder are the beginning of wisdom.

Years later, when Moses led the Jews through the desert, they took a census of the number of people that had left Egypt under his leadership. It was the first time in human history that people were counted— and that each of them counted. Until then, Israel had been a collective nation; now, in the eyes of Moses, it became an aggregation of individuals, each with an individual soul and spirit. This revolutionary moment took place thousands of years before the eighteenth-century enlightenment (in modern times, the first time Britain conducted a census was in 1801) and the twentieth-century ascent of universal human rights. Without people seeing themselves as individuals with unique lives and personal will, rather than as mere subjects of a ruler, leadership would not be available to ordinary people today.[194]

Every person is created in God's image; when you look into the eyes of another human being, you see divine eyes. Whether you're coming in for an interview or to sell a client on a proposal, who are some of the most important people you have to win over? The receptionist. The executive assistant. The slide show operator. "Some companies feel a lot can be learned from how candidates treat receptionists," said Greg Gostanian of ClearRock, "particularly if they're rude, condescending, or arrogant."[195] The story goes that Rabbi Akiva (the same Akiva whose life was saved because he lost his donkey, rooster and candle) had a huge school with 24,000 students. But they all died, simply because they failed to treat each other with proper respect, looked at each other with the evil eye, and judged and doubted one another. After this crushing setback, Akiva started again from scratch. Now he selected seven new disciples: Rabbi Meir, Rabbi Judah, Rabbi Jose, Rabbi Simeon, Rabbi Elazar ben Shamua, Rabbi Eliezer ben Yacov, and Rabbi Yohanan, also known as "the Cobbler." Going back to the basics he urged them, "My sons, the previous students died only because they had 'bad eyes'—concentrate that you do not act similarly." The core group of seven heeded Akiva's call and appreciated one another so much that they were able to build a unity that ended up filling all of Israel with Torah.[196] Such is the power of perception, the evil eye, and the good eye.

There is a Jewish saying that when you don't understand another person's behavior, and if there are several ways to interpret it, you should always give it the most favorable interpretation. The twelfth-century rabbi and philosopher Maimonides reminds us:

> If there is a certain person and you do not know whether he is right-eous or wicked, and you see him doing or hear him saying something which may be interpreted either favorably or unfavorably, you must interpret it favorably, and do not impute any evil to him. But if a person is reputed to be a righteous man, always doing what is good, and he is committing a certain act which is obviously bad, but can be justified with extreme difficulty, then it is proper that you should judge it favorably, since there is at least a remote possibility that the act is a good one, and you are not permitted to suspect such a person of doing evil. It is in this connection that the sages said: "He who suspects worthy men will be smitten with disease."[197]

Despite our propensity to cast blame, we have no right to judge other human beings as long as there's even the slimmest chance that they might have acted in good faith. Maimonides hastens to add that such benefit of the doubt by no means applies to a clearly wicked person, say a Saddam Hussein:

> However, if there is a person notorious for his wicked ways, and you see him do an act which to all appearances seems to be good, but there is a remote possibility that it may be bad, it is proper to beware of him, and you are not obliged to assume that it is good, since there is a remote possibility that it may be bad. It is of such a person that Scripture says: "He that hates dissembles with his lips, but he lays up deceit within him; when he speaks fair, believe him not."[198]

But on the whole, "Who is honored?" asked *Ethics of the Fathers*, a compilation of wise sayings of the early rabbis written a millennium before Maimonides and very much a book on moral leadership. "He who honors others."[199] Rabbi Levi Yitzhak of Berdichev, one of the eighteenth century's outstanding rabbis, always saw the good in people. Once he and his congregants stepped out of the synagogue and saw a man in his *tallit* (prayer shawl) and *tefillin* (philacteries) in the middle of greasing the wheel of a wagon. Since Jews wear *tallit* and *tefillin* for prayer only, it was a most unusual sight indeed. Several congregants grumbled and glared with contempt at the man; he was obviously defiling the holy regalia. But Rabbi Levi said the opposite of what was on everybody's mind: "This man is so pious that he prays even while he is working."

Tip: Whatever action or behavior you acknowledge people for, they will likely keep doing. (Many parents know this: if they want a child to do something again, the best way is to say, "The way you did XYZ yesterday was really great." The child will likely lap up the compliment and do it again.) The same goes for your colleagues: Appreciation does not merely recognize their past performance, but points to their future.

Lack of appreciation, on the other hand, can lead people to do stupid things. Those who knew Andrew S. Fastow, the chief financial officer at the center of the Enron scandal, said they often got the feeling he had something to prove. "I think people respected what Andy did," said one former Enron executive who worked with him, "he just didn't think people respected it enough." Fastow had been the first high school student ever to sit on the New Jersey board of education. At Tufts, he had pressed college administrators to create a special major in Chinese studies just so he could put something unique in his resume. And at Enron, then one of the world's largest corporations, he was named CFO before he turned thirty-seven. But for all his lobbying and financial derring-do, Fastow never quite felt valued enough for his creativity and innovative ideas. In fact, two of his former colleagues said that he saw his loot from fake partnerships he'd come up with as an alternative form of compensation for all the work he'd done to manage Enron's books and make the company a Wall Street darling in the late 1990s. When Enron's stock was soaring in 1999 and 2000, Andy Fastow figured that no one had done more for Enron than Andy Fastow.[200] Of course there is no excuse for Fastow's behavior. It goes to show what criminal or pathological acts some people come up with to feed their bottomless hunger for approval. (Not to mention John Lennon's killer Mark David Chapman, suicide bombers, or Hitler.)

Even the infamous mobster John Gotti understood the art of showing appreciation. It may well have been his only redeeming skill. Aneisha Howard of Grand Rapids, Michigan, Gotti's pen pal for several months, relates that one spring day in 1999, she dashed off a note to the notorious mafia boss. Two months later, a letter arrived from an unusual return address: Gotti, #18261-053, P.O. Box 1000, Marion, Ill. Gotti had written back to encourage her (reminding her in capital letters to "THINK BIG"). "Judging from your letter, you have lots of energy, lots of ambition," he wrote in a note postmarked June 4, 1999. He went on to praise her for being "a very caring mother—very unique these days."[201] If even a mafia boss recognizes the power of appreciation, then we know it is a necessary, but not sufficient, condition of leadership. Another related one is anger management, the focus of the next chapter.

The Bottom Line

- What you can appreciate gives you power. No matter how bad it gets, keep looking for the blessing in disguise. Rather than wallowing in disappointment or obsessing over how things did not turn out according to plan, leaders see the opportunity in every moment. The more you can appreciate, the more invincible you are.

- The question is, how quickly can you recover from a mindset of "This is wrong" or "it should be different" or "I/you/they should have ...", and shift into a mindset of "This too is for the best"? That mindset is like a muscle you build in the gym through repeated practice.

- Effective leaders pay attention to details; they're the raw material of accomplishment. Contrary to popular opinion, leaders should sweat the small stuff.

- Appreciation of people is not merely the recognition of their past performance; it also points to their future. The more you can appreciate people and what they bring to the table, the more they will bring to the table.

CHAPTER SIX

Commandment VI
You Shall Not Kill:
Anger Management

A quick-tempered man does foolish things...
A hot tempered man stirs up dissension.
—Proverbs 14:17–18

Anger is only one letter short of danger.
—Anonymous

THE SIXTH COMMANDMENT: *"You shall not kill."* History is filled with leaders, from czars to kings to modern-day dictators, who killed to get their way. Many corporate leaders today still feel they have to use force, intimidation, or anger, if not as a modus operandi, then at least as a last resort, to make people do their bidding. But unchecked rage kills off leaders around you. In the twelfth century Maimonides said that if you get angry and embarrass someone, it is as if you killed the person. Unless you channel your wrath into positive action, you lead the way to destruction. This chapter will show you how to regulate your anger and other emotions and turn them into productive energy.

As shown in the previous chapter, performance can improve when leaders appreciate their people and what they contribute, beginning with their own parents. Though Jack Welch often praised his mother publicly, he learned to value other people only later in his career, after

121

he had been known to write many of them off. On becoming CEO of General Electric, he'd first earned the nickname Neutron Jack not only for ruthlessly cutting 100,000 out of 400,000 jobs between 1981 and 1985 alone (like a neutron bomb that kills scores of humans while leaving the buildings intact), but also for his penchant to fly into a rage toward subordinates. GE managers all too often came out of Welch's office in a state of dejection and fear after being harangued by him; and GE was famous for firing the "bottom ten percent," the low-performers, each year. True, management by wrath and fear can motivate people, and Welch's aggressive tough-guy approach drove GE to transform itself from a slow-moving behemoth in the early 1980s into a lean, mean fighting machine with interests from aircraft engines to lightbulbs to finance; he made it into what management experts regarded as a model corporation, and one of the most profitable in the world. Its 1999 revenues of over $110 billion earned Welch the title of America's most admired chief executive. But his aggressive style became a liability when he sought to crown his career by merging GE with Honeywell. In negotiations with the European Union competition authority, Welch's anger was one cause of the merger's failure, wrote Michael Bonsignore, the former chief of Honeywell. In particular, Bonsignore noted that Welch's wrathful behavior vis-à-vis the then EU competition commissioner Mario Monti "was a case study in how not to handle process and protocol."[202] In a two-day meeting in Brussels just after 9/11, Welch made a last-ditch appeal to Monti; but when he saw that his plea left the commissioner unmoved, he angrily accused Monti of acting as "judge, jury and prosecutor" and said Monti was "making up the rules as he goes along." He abruptly declared that he was leaving Brussels to work on his book. "That's good, Mr. Welch," Monti was quoted as saying with excruciating calm. "You can make this meeting your final chapter."[203] Of course the former GE chief's anger was not the only factor in losing the GE/Honeywell deal, but it certainly did not help. By controlling his own feelings, Monti held the upper hand.

While anger can spur people into immediate action, it is costly in the longer term. Lack of emotional discipline, Jim Collins found in his study *Good to Great*, was a key difference between short-term and lasting success. This was "a pattern we found in every unsustained comparison: a spectacular rise under a tyrannical disciplinarian, followed by an equally spectacular decline when the disciplinarian stepped away, leaving behind no enduring culture of discipline." A typical example is that of Rubbermaid under the helm of Stanley Gault, who was accused of being a tyrant and quipped in response, "Yes, but I'm a sincere tyrant." Gault's COO confirmed that "He gets livid." The result: Rubbermaid rose dramatically under Gault—it beat the market 3.6 to 1— but after he left, it lost 59 percent of its value relative to the market before being bought out by Newell.[204] GE's losses since Welch's departure are less dramatic but still significant: as of late 2006, its stock was down 14 percent while the S&P 500 was up 25 percent from the prior year. True, other factors played a role in GE's relative slowdown, such as a tougher regulatory environment or the simple fact that GE had matured and that mature businesses grow more slowly. But the question remains whether Welch's forceful and often heated leadership approach produced results while he was at GE and did not last in the culture after he left.

The Sixth Commandment, "Thou shalt not kill," translates into a key leadership competence: regulating your anger. For George Anderson, a psychotherapist who coaches Fortune 500 CEOs, university professors, and movie executives in anger management, "Controlling your anger and your emotion is a skill" that produces a complete transformation of the atmosphere when a leader learns it. "It's amazing to see the change in the entire work environment if someone at the top is able to do business in a calmer and more controlled manner."[205]

"Desk rage," the office equivalent of the well-established road rage and the more recent phenomenon of "air rage" (see chapter 10), on the other hand, exacts incalculable hidden costs. Studies have shown that employees spend up to 42 percent of their work time trying to resolve conflict—that's more than two workdays each week. Yelling and verbal abuse at work is experienced by 42 percent of American workers, one in every ten has worked in an environment where violence occurred, and 14 percent work in companies where rage has led to damaged equipment or machinery. A National Safe Workplace Institute study in 1993 estimated over 111,000 annual violent incidents and calculated that workplace violence costs some $4.2 billion each year; a more recent estimate put the costs of desk rage at between $6.4 billion and $36 billion in lost productivity, diminished image, insurance payments, and increased security.[206] There are no hard data for the direct relationship between anger and lost productivity, but according to Bureau of Justice statistics, employees miss over 175,000 days of paid work each year because of domestic violence. The issue is not confined to the United States. In fact, 66 percent of Fortune 500 senior executives said that addressing domestic violence would benefit the financial performance of their companies.[207]

Moses knew about anger management; he learned it the hard way. He was not above killing his enemies or detractors (as described in Chapter 1). When he was still a young prince living in the Egyptian palace, two fellow Jews, Datan and Abiram, ratted on him to the king. After he killed the Egyptian slave-driver, they reported him to the authorities, which led to a death sentence and forced him to flee the country.[208] Later, in the desert, the two men remained the bane of Moses' existence; they seized every chance to undermine his authority. They challenged the food security rules for the manna, the divine supply of food that was crucial to the Jews' survival in the desert; they deliberately left manna to rot; and they joined the rebellion of Korah, a Levite who was the son of Izhar and who mobilized 250 Israelite chieftains to rise up against Moses.[209] But Moses had the inner discipline to invite his intractable enemies to engage in a dialogue. When they ridiculed him and refused to come to him, he refused to take offense and humbly went to them.[210]

To be sure, controlling your anger does not mean swallowing it. Some cultures tend to twist rightful anger into sarcasm or passive-aggressive taunts, or they suppress it altogether. Take the Finns. "Self-control is very important in Finland," said Dr. Liisa Keltikangas-Jarvinen, a professor of psychology at the University of Helsinki. "You cannot show anger; it means you can't cope. If a person is very temperamental and alive, expresses emotions like anger and happiness, the person is seen as infantile." Turo Herala, a theater director with a yen for therapy, took it upon himself to bring "anger venting" classes to his compatriots. But there were few takers, leading him to conclude that "Anger in Finland is a bigger taboo than sex."[211]

Anger management does not mean you never get angry; it just means you regulate your emotions and have a choice about how you express them. There are alternatives to the type of knee-jerk reactions of the actor Alec Baldwin, who left an angry voice mail for his eleven-year-old daughter Ireland, calling her "a rude, thoughtless little pig." Here is an excerpt:

> I want you to know something, OK? I'm tired of playing this game with you. I'm leaving this message with you to tell you you have insulted me for the last time. You have insulted me. You don't have the brains or the decency as a human being. I don't give a [expletive] that you're 12 years old, or 11 years old, or that you're a child, or that your mother is a thoughtless pain in the a** who doesn't care about what you do as far as I'm concerned. You have humiliated me for the last time with this phone.
>
> So you'd better be ready Friday the 20th to meet with me. So I'm going to let you know just how I feel about what a rude little pig you really are. You are a rude, thoughtless little pig, OK?[212]

Baldwin later issued an apology and said he was "driven to the edge" by his bitter custody dispute with ex-wife Kim Basinger; but the damage was done.

Yes, sometimes you have to raise your voice, but only at yourself, to rouse yourself from a state of apathy or defeatism. Swiss tennis champion Roger Federer (who hails from Basel, the CEO's hometown) has become a master not only in tennis but also in anger regulation—and the latter might explain a lot of the former, since 90 percent of the game is said to be mental. Federer had won 48 of 49 matches since his U.S. Open victory in August 2004, but during the Nasdaq-100 Open finals at Key Biscayne in April 2005, he found himself in trouble. His rival, the young Spaniard Rafael Nadal, exploited almost every one of the top-ranked player's shots and won the first two sets, an almost impossible situation to get out of. In the third set, at the end of the ninth game, came the final straw: Federer missed a break-point opportunity. In a decidedly un-Swiss outburst he slammed his racket to the ground. "I was really angry, so I threw it out," Federer said later. "I was very disappointed. I was missing one opportunity after the other.

I really felt like I'm climbing uphill all the time, and I had an opportunity and I missed it again, and I just had enough. Who knows, maybe it did me good, and I kind of woke up." The decisive difference was that Federer did not get angry at others; he used his fury like a wake-up call to rouse himself — and then he went on to win the match.

Uncontrolled rage, on the other hand, is destructive. It may cloud your judgment, lead you to bad business decisions, make you enemies and lawsuits, or depress morale around you. Otherwise reasonable people can get into fistfights, as happened in early 2007 in Serbia, when two surgeons started an argument right in the operating room and abandoned the patient (who was under anesthesia and had no idea what was happening) to take it outside. An assistant, luckily at hand, had to complete the operation.[213]

Rabbi Isaac Luria, the sixteenth-century kabbalist known as the Ariz'al, taught that according to the Kabbalah, one who loses his or her temper and acts out of anger must fast for 151 days and repent.[214] While such severe punishment seems a bit excessive today, the ability to curb your anger in matters big and small is a leadership skill often overlooked. As long as things go smoothly, it's easy to act like a mature leader. The question is how you react when things seem to be going against you. You can either blow up to force others to your view, or you can channel your emotions into productive energy.

What if someone clearly sabotages your efforts; aren't you entitled to get angry? And isn't fury a great weapon for getting your way? Didn't Bill Gates, one of the great entrepreneurs of our time, use anger to his advantage? Yes, frequent shouting matches between Gates, Paul Allen, and other Microsoft co-founders are the stuff of Silicon Valley lore. (To be fair, similar spats took place at archrival Apple.) Vern Raburn, who in 1976 became one of Microsoft's first executives, likens Gates, Steve Ballmer, and other Microsoft founders to young stars of a hot rock 'n' roll band, lacking even the most basic human skills, and arguing over every drumbeat that went into a song. These entrepreneurs were brilliant, but too young for some aspects of business leadership, Raburn says. "How many people start companies before they can drink?"[215]

Their youthful volatility often brought Microsoft leaders to the brink of blows. Raburn still remembers a proposal he submitted on how Microsoft should package and ship hardware. It now seems insignificant, but at the time it was enough to inspire an all-day shouting match in Paul Allen's office, one that ended only because Raburn had twenty-six minutes to catch a flight, and the Microsoft record dash to the airport was twenty-four minutes." "Extreme debating," is how Raburn characterizes the early Microsoft culture. "The company wasn't big enough for a bunch of alpha males pissing each other off."

Although he has since learned to regulate his rage, Bill Gates is still not exactly known as a calibrated communicator. One journalist, who spent several months as a fly-on-the-wall at the company, wrote about how Gates "exploded in anger," leaving a "palpable nervousness in the room."[216] Not everybody's creative juices get flowing when they get yelled at; not to speak of employee loyalty. "It just got so frustrating," said Eric Engstrom, an eight-year Microsoft veteran who left the company in the late 1990s to co-found Chromium Communications. "You want to do innovative work, but you have to spend half your time defending your turf."[217]

Some managers think that venting their anger gives them power, gets people's attention, and makes people do their bidding. But these benefits are unreliable and short-lived at best, while the costs are self-evident and immediate. And by the time you've blown your fuse, it's too late; you've already betrayed weakness and impotence. In September 2005, Microsoft CEO Steve Ballmer reportedly vowed to "kill" Google in an expletive-laced, chair-throwing tirade when a senior engineer told him he was leaving the company for Google. In a sworn statement, Mark Lucovsky, who switched to Google in November 2004, recounted Ballmer's angry reaction when he told Ballmer he was going to join another company. "At some point in the conversation, Mr. Ballmer said: 'Just tell me it's not Google,'" Lucovsky said in his statement. Lucovsky replied yes, it was. "At that point, Mr. Ballmer picked up a chair and threw it across the room hitting a table in his office," Lucovsky recounted, adding that Ballmer then launched into a tirade about Google CEO Eric Schmidt. "I'm going to f***ing bury that guy, I have done it before, and I will do it again. I'm going to f***ing kill Google."

Schmidt, who had worked for Sun Microsystems and been the CEO of Novell, must have been secretly delighted when he read the news. By the time Ballmer calmed down, nothing good had come of his tantrum. Clearly Google had the upper hand in this particular battle for senior talent.[218]

Unchecked wrath often hurts the angry person more than it does its target. Psychologists have shown that anger easily leads to anxiety, guilt, depression, and social isolation. Not only that: When you're riled up, your heart rate can rise to 180 beats per minute, three times the normal pulse; your blood pressure may go up to 220/130, or at least above the normal rate of 120/80. Anger can lead to, and worsen, life-threatening medical conditions such as strokes, heart disease, ulcers, and cancer. (Some researchers have linked anger even to gum disease!) One study assigned a hostility measure to a group of physicians and then followed them for thirty years. Those who scored high on the hostility measure were five times more likely to have coronary heart disease than those who scored low. Another study found that unchecked anger even causes people to die sooner. Researchers assessed the hostility levels of groups of medical and law students and followed them to age fifty. In the low-hostility groups, 2 percent of the doctors and 4 percent of the lawyers had died by age fifty; in the high hostility group, 14 percent of the doctors and 20 percent of the lawyers had. In these two groups at least, people who are consistently angry are *five to seven times* more likely to die before the age of fifty than calmer people.[219]

Michael Eisner, Disney's ex-chairman, and Miramax co-founder Harvey Weinstein provide a prominent example of unmanaged anger. Eisner, who had forced Jeffrey Katzenberg to leave the company in 1994 after a bitter dispute, seemed to have found his match when Disney bought Miramax in 1993. For years, Eisner and Weinstein were locked in an ever-escalating, vicious exchange of both private off-the-record sniping and quasi-public salvos. Weinstein let it be known that he thought Eisner a soulless, tasteless, lying p***k. And Eisner made clear he thought Weinstein a profligate boor and a bully. Eisner publicly questioned Miramax's profitability and fought Weinstein bitterly over the distribution of Michael Moore's *Fahrenheit 9/11* (making Disney lose out on a cash cow); Weinstein, himself infamous for public screaming fits and putting reporters into headlocks, protested in an interview with *New York* magazine that his tantrums were simply a result of high blood-glucose levels in his body and were a thing of the past.

> I would just eat M&Ms all day, sweets, you know, for what I thought was energy, which is not energy at all, now that I'm off of it. And what happened was the glucose level would go from 50 to 250 in my case. It's not in everybody's case. Some people handle sweets better. And I would hit the adrenaline. So that's what caused these outbursts, you know. We had to find out through a specialized doctor. I had to go to a doctor. We found out I have adult-onset diabetes too as a result of this, so in the last year, I've lost 60 pounds eating a low-carbohydrate diet, you know, and exercise, and, um, in the last two, three years, as soon as I started to recognize the sugar thing, there have been no outbursts. There's been no anything at all. Zero. There's been nothing. Not a word to anybody.[220]

Weinstein does have a point about eating right, but the quote itself shows that he's not the calmest sugar-daddy, and all too willing to blame his angry outbursts on something else. As for Eisner, his bullying style and over-the-top anger tripped him: he made enemies who forced him to resign in September 2005. As Gandhi put it, "an eye for an eye will make the whole world blind."

It's no different in team sports. "Fury doesn't work in competition," said Phil Jackson, one of the most accomplished basketball coaches of our time (we met him in chapter 4), "at least not the way you usually see it invoked. What's more, it works even less well as the competition itself gets tougher. Anger is the real enemy in basketball, not your opponent." It's one thing to know this; it's quite another to practice it while somebody is yelling at you. In the 1991 playoffs against the 76ers, then Bulls star power forward Horace Grant was having trouble guarding Armon Gilliam and requested help with a double team. But Jackson insisted that Grant play his opponent straight-up. They started arguing, and Grant lost it. He shouted at Jackson, "I'm tired of being your whipping boy." Jackson realized that he had alienated Grant and had made a bad call that eventually cost them both the game.

Of course fury cannot be totally avoided. "In basketball you're dealing with anger at a very visceral level all the time," Jackson said. "You're always within a heartbeat of a fight. The players are much bigger and stronger now than they were twenty years ago, and intimidation is part of the game. You have to get into this warrior attitude where you do not lose control and erupt." And what if the opponent pushes you so hard you have no choice but to retaliate? Jackson says the key to being sucessful is to remember that "you *do* have a choice."[221]

From Prisoner to Prime Minister

One leader with ample reason to be enraged was Joseph. His father Jacob had twelve sons; but since Joseph was a handome lad and a child from his father's old age and his beloved wife Rachel, the Jewish patriarch loved him more than his eleven brothers—an all-too human injustice (a 2005 study in *Science Times* found that parents take better care of pretty children than of ugly ones).[219] It didn't help matters when Joseph told them about a dream he'd had: "Behold!—we were binding sheaves in the middle of the field, when, behold!—my sheaf arose and also remained standing; then behold!—your sheaves gathered around and bowed down to my sheaf." His brothers (really his older stepbrothers, since they were the sons of his stepmother Leah) said to him, "Would you then reign over us? Would you then dominate us?" And they hated him even more because of his dreams and his talk. People do crazy things when they are consumed with jealousy. The brothers schemed secretly about how they could remove Joseph from the scene; they conspired to kill him. When Joseph went to see them in the fields at Dothan, they said to one another, "Look! That dreamer is coming! So now, come and let us kill him, and throw him into one of the pits; and we will say, 'A wild beast devoured him.' Then we shall see what will become of his dreams."[223]

They threw Joseph into a pit with snakes and scorpions. Miraculously Joseph survived, but when merchants, or rather slave traders, came by, they pulled him out and sold him off for twenty pieces of silver. Seventeen years old, Joseph was taken to Egypt and brought to

Potiphar, the chief butcher in the pharaoh's government. His Egyptian master was pleased with Joseph; but his good looks got him in trouble again: Potiphar's wife cast a lustful eye on him. (Just like Cleopatra many generations later, she bathed herself in milk to make her skin smooth and fragrant. When she walked around the house barefoot, she would accidentally let the folds of her tunic fall open to reveal her breasts.) But Joseph diplomatically and steadfastly refused her attentions. One day, she couldn't take it anymore. She literally grabbed Joseph by his shirt and ripped it off his body. Embarrassed, he ran out of the house. The woman brought false charges against him, saying *he* had tried to seduce *her*. And as the minister's wife, she had clout with the court. A judge sentenced Joseph to ten years in prison. (Even in prison he was a natural leader: the warden placed all inmates in his custody.)

Meanwhile the Egyptian pharaoh had two strange dreams. In the first, seven gaunt and ugly cows devoured seven beautiful and robust cows. The pharaoh awoke, fell back asleep, and dreamt again. In this dream, seven good and healthy ears of grain were consumed by a stalk of seven thin ears. The pharaoh awoke in great agitation and sent for all the necromancers and wise men in Egypt to decode the two mysterious dreams. But no expert in the entire kingdom could explain it, no one, that is, until one of the pharaoh's cupbearers remembered Joseph and his core competence from prison: interpreting prophetic dreams. Desperate, the pharaoh summoned Joseph, who was rushed from the dungeon to the palace. The pharaoh told him, "I dreamt a dream, but no one can interpret it. Now I heard it said of you that you comprehend a dream to interpret it." Joseph told him that the two dreams were really one. Soon Egypt would experience an abundance of grain and food for seven years. But then, it would suffer a seven-year famine that would consume the land, a food shortage so severe that Egypt's people would soon forget there had ever been seven years of plenty.

Grateful and impressed with Joseph's brilliance, the pharaoh appointed him viceroy (the equivalent of a prime minister today) of Egypt, saying, "There can be no one so discerning and wise as you. You shall be in charge of my palace and by your command shall all my people be sustained; only by the throne shall I outrank you." And he added, "See! I have placed you in charge of all the land of Egypt."[224]

Seven years of plenty came and went; then a terrible famine struck the land. A visionary innovator, Joseph found a solution for storing food throughout those years of want, and Egypt was the region's only country whose population was spared. Many people traveled there to get food and learn from its best practices; Joseph's brothers decided to go too. They were granted an audience with the powerful viceroy, but since over twenty years had passed, they did not recognize him (they hadn't checked his Facebook profile). He asked probing questions about their past, and awed by his authority, they admitted they had once, decades earlier, wronged a younger brother. At first Joseph accused them of being spies, jailed them for three days, and insisted that Jacob's youngest be brought to Egypt, thus separating his younger brother Benjamin and Jacob's remaining son from his father. When Benjamin finally arrived, he secretly ordered a goblet placed in Benjamin's luggage, and after his brothers left the palace, sent his men after them to look for the "missing" goblet.[225] Finally, after causing his brothers to regret their actions, Joseph revealed his true identity. "I am Joseph," he said. "Is my father still alive?" Stunned, the brothers could not get a word out. He repeated, "I am Joseph your brother—it is me, whom you sold into Egypt." The brothers cringed—they feared he would put them to death. They prostrated themselves and begged for mercy. But Joseph lifted them up and said:

> And now, be not distressed, nor reproach yourselves for having sold me here, for it was to be a provider that God sent me ahead of you. This has been two of the hunger years in the midst of the land, and there are yet five years in which there shall be neither plowing nor harvest. Thus God has sent me ahead of you to insure your survival in the land and to sustain you for a momentous deliverance.[226]

Overwhelmed by Joseph's magnanimity, the brothers kissed him, their tears flowing freely. Ultimately, the whole family moved to Egypt, and after twenty-two years father and son were reunited.

When Jacob died another seventeen years later, the brothers were again seized by fear; now they worried that their stepbrother had only waited for this moment, with the family patriarch out of the picture, to finally take his rightful revenge. And they had every reason to be afraid. For twenty-two years he had not seen or spoken with his family. All those years, Joseph had had good reason to harbor bitterness. But he did not lose his cool; he stayed calm and collected and told his brothers, "Although you intended to harm me, God intended it for good: in order to accomplish—it is as clear as this day—that a vast people be kept alive."[227] Joseph applied the same principle that many generations later would help Rabbi Akiva and Rabbi Ish Gamzu tackle adversity: He knew that all the cards life dealt him were ultimately good, even when the goodness was hidden from him at the time.

Don't Lose It, Use It

Perhaps the leader who most embodied Joseph's anger management in modern time was Mahatma Gandhi. The late Indian industrialist Ramkrishna Bajaj, who as a young man had been Gandhi's accountant (and "Gandhi's coolie," as he wryly put it in the title of his memoirs) shortly before his death told the CEO a story about one of Gandhi's followers, Dr. Mahadev Desai, who had been a militant anarchist in India's underground movement and had known India's jails from the inside. But Desai came to embrace Gandhi's nonviolent ways; from 1942 onward, he served as Gandhi's assistant and for a while was in charge of answering all the letters that came to the independence leader. And there were heaps of letters. Since India had virtually no telephones and e-mail was still decades away, Gandhi received an enormous amount of snail mail, including hate mail. Fearing that the vengeful letters would only upset Gandhi and distract him from his nonviolent mission, Desai decided to shield his leader from all that negativity. He hid the negative letters and quietly answered them himself. But Gandhi caught wind that something was amiss. One day he gently prodded Desai, "I seem to be getting only nice letters lately. Where are the critical ones?" Blushing slightly, Desai admitted that he had kept the hateful correspondence from Gandhi. He would never forget Gandhi's answer until he died in 1993. "I need the negative let-

ters," the Mahatma said. "My critics are my best friends—they show
me what I have yet to learn."

Gandhi was in good company. Rabbi Shalom DovBer, the Fifth
Rebbe of Lubavitch (1860–1920), urged his followers to "cherish criticism, for it will place you on the true heights."[228] And one of the transcendent leaders of our time, Nelson Mandela, talked with Bill Moyers
in a 1991 interview about how he had managed his own feelings of rage
during his years of imprisonment at Robben Island, an environment
that would turn anyone into a wretch of hateful bitterness. How did
Mandela keep his hatred in check despite torture and blatant injustice?
He agreed that "there was a lot of cruelty on myself and my colleagues." But Mandela found common ground with his jailors:

> You must also understand that the wardens who worked with us are
> themselves workers, are themselves human beings, with problems,
> who are also exploited, the victims of the system. And one of our
> objectives was to ensure that we improved the relations between our-
> selves and these wardens, help them in their own problems. And in
> that way, you forget about anything that is negative, like hate. You are
> dealing with human beings and you want them to live in peace with
> his [sic] people. You want them also to go and spread the same mes-
> sage to their people as we want to spread to our own people. And in
> that situation it is very difficult to find room for hate.[229]

Three years later, when the CEO met Mandela at an award ceremony
honoring him with the Africa Prize for Leadership, then-President Clinton described the rich rewards of self-control demonstrated by the
newly elected South African president: "Perhaps his most remarkable
achievement was that he spent twenty-seven years in prison and came
out the freest of all people."

You might object that Joseph, Gandhi, and Mandela are transcendent leaders who must have had superhuman capabilities to control
their anger; but what about us normal mortals? You don't have to be
sold into slavery, get hate-mail, or spend decades in prison to be furious; at times it seems near impossible to ignore some small nuisance
that bothers you. A tiny razor cut when you shave in the morning can
be more upsetting than all the blood spilled by Al Qaeda (provided one

of your family members was not among the victims). In 2004, the Rabbi's mother bought his wife Shternie a hand-tailored suit for the bar mitzvah of their eldest son. At home, they inspected the new suit (remember the power of details, from Chapter 5) and lo and behold, they found a black mascara spot on the sleeve near the shoulder. They brought the stained suit back to the shop owner, who promised that his tailor would replace the whole sleeve (the least they could do for that kind of money). But that evening the shop owner called to say that since the bar mitzvah was to be on the Sabbath, the deadline was too tight. Instead Shternie should wear the suit to the bar mitzvah and bring it back afterward for them to finish the repair. They sent a driver with the garment bag, and Shternie put it in her closet.

Friday afternoon, Shternie was getting ready for the bar mitzvah and opened the garment bag. The skirt was missing. *Oy vey* (a Yiddish exclamation of dismay or exasperation, literally O pain)! At that moment, the Rabbi's heart almost stopped. He said to himself, "My wife is going to go crazy. She's going to be very mad. The whole weekend will be in the pits." (Yes, even Rabbis talk like that.) They called the store immediately, but no-one answered so close to the Sabbath. Facing a small crisis, they faxed a letter:

"EMERGENCY.
NEVER GOT SKIRT.
PLEASE SEND MY SKIRT.
—SHTERNIE."

Then they went to the synagogue before sunset to take some pictures (it's against Jewish law to take photos on the Sabbath), and on to services and the Sabbath dinner. All this time, the Rabbi was waiting for his wife to blow up, to lose control. She did not.

Very late that evening, after services and dinner, they came home to find the skirt hanging in front of the closet. They asked the babysitter what had happened; she explained that just before sunset, a car service had delivered it. A note was attached: "We are sorry for the inconvenience. We will, therefore, be happy to give you a free suit of your choice."

Every challenge in life, large and small, is a test of your self-control. Had Shternie got upset, the bar mitzvah guests would have felt uncomfortable, the Rabbi would have been upset too, and she still would not have had her suit for the bar mitzvah. Because she kept her cool, all the guests were happy, the Rabbi was happy, she still got to wear her new suit on Sabbath day, *and* she received a new suit free of charge.

> **Tip:** Don't lose it—use it. Stage actors have a ground rule that lets them dance or improvise with unforeseen events. For example, when a colleague forgets a line or fails to appear on stage, or when the prop is not there when they need it: Use It. The same is true for any field, including business. When things don't go as planned in your original script, you can always improvise and use whatever is happening as a new pathway to your goal. Say you were expecting twenty people at a presentation, but only one shows up; you could use what's happening by taking that one person out to lunch and treating him or her as a key leader. Unforeseen changes may seem upsetting because they don't fit our plans, but could actually be a window into something new and even better, as long as we can let go of our pre-existing pictures. And ultimately, without darkness, light could not exist. Light comes from darkness.

What can *you* do when anger surges within you? Rabbi Yosef Y. Schneerson, the Sixth Lubavitcher Rebbe, quoted his uncle as suggesting that when you become angry, you should wait at least sixty-one minutes until you can think clearly again.[230] But it's easy to say that when you are calm; once you are filled with righteous wrath, it is near impossible to stop.

Tool 6.1
Cool It with Your Boss[231]

A few years ago, the hoopster Latrell Sprewell flipped out and went for the neck of his boss. Sprewell throttled the much shorter and less well-muscled coach of the Golden State War-

riors, threatened to kill him, departed to cool off, did not succeed, returned, and delivered a straight blow to the senior official. It did not have to come to this. There are several strategies
you can muster before wrapping your fingers around the
offending windpipe and strangling a truculent boss.

You can discuss cordially that there must have been a misunderstanding and that the boss believes he has told you
something when, in fact, he did not. Tell the boss calmly, "I am
sorry if there is a misunderstanding between us. Let me tell
you what I heard you say, which—now this is kind of funny—
was just about the opposite of what you just told me you said."

You can appeal to the boss's humanity. Refuse to get worked
up. Never react emotionally to an accusation. Tell the boss in
an amicable way that you don't appreciate being yelled at.
Remember, talk about your experience of the boss's words,
rather than characterizing the boss in any way. For example, "I
want to do better, too, but when you say X, my experience is
that I feel unfairly accused, and it's hard for me to improve
when I feel so bad about myself."

You can talk to your boss's superior. For example, "I have
nothing against this guy, he is a terrific coach, but he is really
down on me lately. Do you see another way of dealing with his
anger?"

You can simply say nothing. Refuse to take part. Walk out
the door, or make conversation with your peers. And be sure
that the problem with your boss does not affect your performance. Show the boss that you are focused on the results and are
out there, doing the best for the company every day.

You can make a straightforward request. "Please stop getting
on my case—*right now.*"

And if none of these have any effect, as a last resort, go
ahead and choke him (or her); but before you do, know that
you will get fired, and maybe before that point, you'll realize
the job wasn't worth it after all.

If, for example, a customer throws a fit, responding in kind will only escalate the conflict. Instead, words like "I hear you—I'm here to help" might defuse the tension. Take a deep breath (or a walk if you can), and above all, avoid aggressive reactions like blaming, name-calling, or threatening.

Tool 6.2
Back to the Source of Anger

A more penetrating practice is to see whether you can remember—and then express in non-escalating language—the emotions that preceded your anger. We would do well to remember that some comments or situations are bound to reactivate our resentments or fears. Such feelings are practically inevitable; as human beings, we're prone to take things personally. The question is what we do with those thoughts and feelings when they do appear.

To go deeper, you could observe your reactions, rather than blindly acting them out. By becoming aware of how you react and not assuming that your every reaction is justified just because it's yours, you gain insight into your own patterns and perspective on what's occurring around you. (For example, you may have thoughts like: "Interesting—every time he mentions last year's lackluster performance, I feel like throttling him," or, "Every time she goes on a business trip, I think I should have been asked to go instead.") It is possible to observe your reactions as if they were the weather. Another way is to step back, see the big picture, and evaluate whether or not the current battle is actually worth fighting. You can create a context larger than whatever concerns your ego. Ask yourself, How important will this be a month or six months from now?

Going even deeper into your patterns, you can ask yourself, Why am I getting so mad here? Anger is a defense mechanism; according to the psychoanalyst Erich Fromm, "'benign' aggression is in the service of the survival of the individual and the species."[232] You feel threatened; it feels like your back is against the wall and the force of fury is the only way you can see to get what you want. (In fact you cannot see anything, and you barely remember what it was you wanted in the first place. It's as if some unseen force, like a storm, has taken hold of you from within and blinded you with its whipped-up dust. In those moments you're not in charge of yourself. German-speakers describe this state, roughly translated as "she's been bitten by the ape" or "the devil is riding him.") Ask yourself, How old is this emotion? When did it start? When in my life did I first feel this way? And what experience prompted my original anger then?

Tool 6.1 comes from psychodynamic theory. A more spiritual view is *hashgacha protis*,[233] divine providence. The key to anger management is to realize (as the *Zohar*, the classic kabbalistic commentary on the Torah, put it and as we've learned from Rabbi Ahiva) that everything in life—everything—happens for a reason and is ultimately good. This does not mean you should passively accept or condone everything that happens to you. If you see something go wrong, you have every right to change it. For example, you're waiting to get on a particular flight and have just been told by the ground staff with that broad flight-attendant smile, "I'm so sorry, but we cannot put you on this plane, sir. It's full." You're entitled to say, "Excuse me, I want to talk to your supervisor. I think I have a right to go on this flight. I want to go on this flight. I need to go on this flight." But if you get angry and vengeful, it is tantamount to losing faith, as the rabbi, physician, and global citizen Moses Maimonides (aka the RaMbaM, for Rabbi Moses ben Maimon), put it nine centuries ago.

> Anger ... is an extremely destructive trait, and it is fitting that one should distance one's self from it to the most extreme, and train himself not to get angry, even at something at which it is appropriate to be angry. If he wishes to make a point with his family or his commu-

nity, if he was a trustee, and he wishes to improve their ways, he should feign anger in front of them in order to impress them, but he should be in control of himself when he is feigning anger, for he should not truly be angry. The sages stated: Anyone who becomes angry is like one who practices idolatry."[234]

Why does the Rambam call anger idolatry? This brings up a fine point of Jewish law. Let's say a reckless driver hits your car: the crash has already been predestined. Even if, God forbid, someone kills a member of your family, the murder has been predestined.[235] Rabbi Schneur Zalman of Liadi wrote, "This unfortunate incident was already decreed in heaven, and God has many agents through which He acts."[236] And the Talmud backs him up: "God sends an evil person to do evil things and a good person to do good things." But if both the driver and the killer are mere tools of divine will, can you sue and seek a prison sentence for the driver? Are you entitled to punish the murderer? According to Jewish law, the answer is yes. You can punish the perpetrator for accepting the job of inflicting pain, for accepting the role, just not for the act itself, which was *hashgacha protis*. After all, nobody asked the perpetrator to take on this bad-faith mission. But acting in anger and rage is different from inflicting punishment; anger and rage indicate a loss of faith. According to Rabbi Schneur Zalman, "Faith in God and divine providence has left the individual who acts out of anger or rage." When you get angry, you are stuck with your pictures of how you think things should be instead of taking reality at face value; you have fallen prey to a false image, a mirage. In a sense, you have become just like the Israelites who danced around a golden calf. Anger is idolatry.

Divine Design or Random Chance?

The word "faith" brings up one of the eternal questions of human existence: Are events expressions of intelligent design, random chance, or human willpower? Had God really planned for Joseph to succeed? Was his luck mere coincidence? Or did he use his own talents to pull himself up by his own bootstraps? A true story from Germany illustrates the question. Caught up in the festive spirit of a New Year's Eve in Hamburg right after the fall of the Berlin Wall, a man decided to release a yellow balloon with a New Year's card to his long-lost friend somewhere in the German Democratic Republic, bearing his own address. The balloon disappeared into the cold, starry, windy sky; a strong west wind blew it east. Several thousand meters above, the air pressure sank and grounded the balloon. The next morning, New Year's Day, a home owner in East Germany found the balloon in his apple tree and became incensed over what he saw as yet another children's prank, until he saw the card and read it. The sender, who begged for "a call at all costs," turned out to be an old friend from his youth; the two had lost touch with each other forty years earlier when Germany was divided after World War II. Thanks to the yellow balloon, Wolfgang Steude from Hamburg and Uwe Kracht from Grömitz found each other again in early 2003.[237]

Is that chance or not? We could explain the highly unusual outcome as a causal chain of improbable events: Mr. Steude went to a New Year's Eve party that happened to offer yellow balloons; he got a little drunk and euphoric; feeling nostalgic, he remembered his old friend Uwe; on a whim, he released a balloon and attached a card to Uwe; the wind was just right; the air pressure fell just at the right time; the balloon landed in an apple tree in Grömitz; Mr. Kracht went outside on New Year's Day to marvel at his apple tree; and so forth. Or we could say that the probability is one in a billion that something like this could happen, and that therefore it must be a divinely inspired miracle. Even the physicist Albert Einstein, who sought to make all physical phenomena logically explicable, famously asserted, "He [i.e. God] does not play dice." And the French poet Anatole France wrote, "Chance is perhaps the pseudonym of God when he does not wish to sign his work."[238]

But even France said *perhaps*, so there is no final answer to our question. Ultimately, it comes down to a choice: Is it more useful to see the universe as random, or as divinely designed? (Of course there are those who refuse to choose, and instead take the best of both worlds. Rabbi Harold Kushner, who lost his fourteen-year-old son to progeria (from the Greek word for old age, an extremely rare genetic condition that causes greatly accelerated aging), writes in his book *When Bad Things Happen to Good People*:

> The world is mostly an orderly, predictable place, showing ample evidence of God's thoroughness and handiwork, but pockets of chaos remain. Most of the time, the events of the universe follow firm natural laws; but every now and then, things happen not contrary to those laws of nature but outside them. Things happen which could just as easily have happened differently.[239]

In a world growing ever more intricate and complex, assuming divine providence in everything that happens might be more empowering because the assumption permits you to make sense of life instead of whining about events you cannot control anyway. True or false, the assumption may also help you make more grounded choices. As Rabbi Menachem M. Schneerson wrote in a 1963 letter, "What can guarantee that people will behave in a righteous and just manner, if not for the belief in a greater power?"[240] Whatever you can embrace no longer angers you. Ricardo Levy, the founder of Catalytica, one of the pharmaceutical industry's biggest contract manufacturers of the anti-AIDS drug AZT and Sudafed, learned that listening to divine providence allowed him to make better business decisions. For twenty-five years Levy watched proudly as his brainchild grew from a tiny consulting firm started in his basement in New Providence, N.J., into a $750 million pharmaceutical and energy company with headquarters in Silicon Valley, a factory in Greenville, N.C., and 1,800 employees. Then Levy faced one of the most difficult decisions of his business career—whether to sell the company's biggest and most successful division. "I had never considered selling," said Levy, a reflective fifty-six-year-old chemical engineer. "An entrepreneur wants to keep the baby and take it all the way." To complicate matters, Levy took a strong dislike to the point man for the potential buyer, Dutch pharmaceuticals giant DSM. The man's style irritated him. He simply couldn't stand the guy.

That Levy ultimately chose to sell most of Catalytica is unremarkable, per se. But the way he made the decision is not a management tool taught in many business schools these days. When DSM's offer came to buy Catalytica's pharmaceuticals business, Levy had to contemplate several tough questions. Getting a fair price for investors was essential but not sufficient. How would selling affect his employees? What about his customers? Could Catalytica's combustion division, which DSM didn't want, survive on its own? And most importantly, what would he do with the rest of his life? Levy attacked all the questions logically; then he went deeper. "Those are subtle issues that don't fit into an Excel spreadsheet. It's not writing a list on the left and a list on the right," he said. "It's really more than anything a matter of feeling. The question is, feeling what? Really it's your compass. How your total psyche, how your intellectual and spiritual being interfaces with the issue."[241]

As he made up his mind to sell the company, Levy used meditation to overcome the hostility he felt toward his negotiating opponent at DSM. He tried to reach out "in a loving way" and found that his own kinder demeanor helped move the talks along. After all, the adversary was just a human being too. Catalytica sold its drug business to DSM in 2000; its combustion division became a stand-alone public company, with Levy as chairman.

> **Tip:** Remember that 99.9 percent of what happens in life is not an attack on you. A rainstorm, for example, is not personal, even if it ruins your golf game; to think otherwise smacks of arrogance. Most people, most of the time, are not out to make you miserable. They are so busy with their own lives that they have precious little time or energy left over to zero in on others. As Maimonides told us, "Anyone who lowers himself and thinks lightly of his person in these situations is [truly] a great person, worthy of honor ..."[242]

Tool 6.3
Institutionalizing Anger Management

Going beyond the individual to the organization, anger management can be institutionalized, and organizations that invest in programs to reduce hostility reap rich rewards. Years ago, a few U.S. Postal Service agents were so furious that they went berserk, adding the term "going postal" to the American vocabulary and making postal workers the frequent butt of workplace anger jokes. These violent incidents, while often deadly, were isolated. The real problem was an avalanche of complaints by angry, frustrated employees to the federal Equal Employment Opportunity Commission. By 1997, internal complaints about intimidation, sexual harassment, racial discrimination, and other management abuses at the U.S.P.S. reached the stunning number of 30,000 a year. Executives realized they needed to do something. The agency's mediation program, aptly named Redress (Resolve Employment Disputes, Reach Equitable Solutions Swiftly), produced an unprecedented breakthrough in anger management. From September 1998 through June 2000, 17,645 informal disputes were mediated; 80 percent of them were resolved. During the same time, formal complaints that had peaked at 14,000 in 1997 dropped by 30 percent. The attorneys who had started Redress out of a class-action lawsuit in 1994 estimated that the program had saved the agency millions of dollars in legal costs and improved productivity, to say nothing of gains in job satisfaction. "We have found that companies are very interested in transformative mediation," said one of the lawyers, Cynthia Hallberlin, "because of its promise to not just solve the problem at hand, but to help the parties communicate more effectively in the future."[243]

How did the postal service do this? Redress's success had a lot to do with helping employees regulate anger. One mediation case involved a postal supervisor and an employee, a white and a black woman, neither willing to back down in a dispute over the employee's repeated lateness. After yelling at each other for one and a half hours, the two became quiet. Elaine Kirsch, the outside mediator, took the opportunity to point out that the two had more in common than they might think. Once the supervisor and the employee returned to hammering out particular issues, suddenly one of them said words like, "You never lied. You always say what you mean." The ice was broken. It turned out that the employee was often late because she had trouble finding care for her asthmatic child. She agreed to call her supervisor when this happened, and the supervisor agreed to be more understanding.

Anger management is important to your "brand," your standing as a leader; a single outburst can inflict long-lasting reputation costs. But building sustainable "lead cred" requires something else, as we'll see in the next chapter.

The Bottom Line

- The ability to regulate your emotions is an integral part of self-determination, the hallmark of effective leaders. Acting out of anger is unhealthy and might lose you friends and allies. Unchecked anger even causes people to die sooner. Getting angry shows weakness; it is like losing faith in your destiny.

- Tools for managing your anger include taking time out (or a walk), avoiding language that escalates the issue, and revealing the emotions that were present before you hit the roof.

- Whether or not you have an explanation for whatever is happening to you, whatever happens to you must be for the best (whether true or not, this is an empowering attitude).

- Like the U.S. Postal Service, you can institutionalize anger management across your organization through mediation directed at diffusing conflicts.

- If you keep your cool, you might just end up as prime minister of Egypt.

CHAPTER SEVEN

Commandment VII
No Adultery: Walk Your Talk

The origin of all conflict between me and my fellow-men
is that I do not say what I mean, and I do not do what I say.
—Martin Buber

The illegal we do immediately, the unconstitutional takes a little longer.
—Henry Kissinger

THE SEVENTH COMMANDMENT: *"You shall not commit adultery."* Adultery can be anything from sleeping around to selling out on your principles. But your greatest power as a leader does not come from your authority, job title, popularity or resources; it comes from your integrity. The capacity to walk your talk—an unadulterated match of your words and your deeds—is quite possibly the chief capital of leaders. In a complex world of cyberspace, global markets, and virtual organizations, the temptation to lose your integrity is everywhere; you can get away with cheating, lying or corruption. Judaism is a comprehensive system of ethical decision-making that allows you to see the difference between right and wrong. In this chapter, you will learn how to tackle ethical dilemmas by getting your value priorities clear.

The Bible tells the story of Judah (one of Joseph's brothers), who had a stunningly gorgeous daughter-in-law named Tamar. Twice widowed, she had her share of tragedy. Jewish law mandated that when a husband died childless, his surviving wife married his brother to make sure

147

the family line survived;[244] so when Tamar's first husband Er died, her brother-in-law Onan wed her. But whenever Tamar and he slept together, Onan "spilled his seed on the ground" to avoid impregnating her. Presumably for this sin of onanism (which came to be named after him), Onan too died. Now Tamar was to marry Judah's third son She-lah who was next in line, but Judah was filled with the superstitious fear that Tamar was somehow cursed, that there was a connection between her and the deaths of his two sons. Under the pretext that Shelah was still an adolescent and too young for marriage, he sent Tamar away to live alone as a widow and wait for Shelah to grow to manhood. A long time went by, Shelah was now a man, yet Judah kept withholding his approval. Tamar found herself a pariah; what was she to do? She took charge of her life and worked with what she had. When she heard one day that Judah was going to Timnah for a sheepshearing, she sat at the roadside and waited for him to come by. As she expected, he mistook her for a prostitute. (Before receiving the Torah in the year 2448, the Israelites permitted prostitution.) Since he himself was now a widower who had ended the period of mourning his wife, he suc-cumbed to his desire; he approached the exceptionally beautiful young woman on the street and asked for her services. She asked what he was willing to pay; he said he wanted to send her a kid from his flocks. Tamar demanded his signet ring, cloak, and staff as collateral. Later, when he sent his friend to pay her with the animal, the mysterious woman was gone. Judah had no idea that he had bedded Tamar. Three months went by, and Tamar was visibly pregnant. Judah himself con-demned her to death for adultery. But rather than embarrass her promi-nent father-in-law in public, she silently faced the ultimate punishment. As Tamar was led to her execution, she sent Judah his belongings with a note: "I am with child by the man to whom these belong. ...Examine these. Whose signet ring and cloak are these?" At the last moment Judah realized the unthinkable, shameful reality: he himself was the father. He publicly, and courageously, confessed his error and declared, "She has been more righteous than I."[245]

Judah was not the first man to succumb to temptation, which is as old as humankind. God asked Adam, "Where art thou?" and Adam hid himself in shame. From Adam and Eve's lies about eating from the tree of knowledge to the Israelites dancing around a golden calf, stories of sin and temptation can be found throughout the Torah. No wonder the sages warned in the Talmud, "The greater the person, the greater his evil inclination."[246] Even King David, one of the great Jewish leaders of all time, knew that, like the rest of us, he had a darker side. The once courageous slayer of Goliath had become a callous ruler who sent others to war, stayed behind in comfortable Jerusalem, took a stroll at sunset on his rooftop, secretly watched the beautiful Bath-sheba take a bath, summoned her to the palace, and had sex with her. After she sent him a message that she had conceived, he summoned her husband Uriah the Hittite and got him drunk. The next morning he wrote a letter to his army commander at the front with a simple instruction: "Place Uriah directly in front of the fierce fighting; then withdraw from behind him so that he shall be struck and die."[247] It was a contract killing, and he sealed the letter and sent it with Uriah, making Uriah the messenger of his own assassination. In less than a month David had become both an adulterer and a murderer.

In our own time, some of the greatest leaders had great evil inclinations and could not help cheating. Sorry to rain on anybody's parade, but Martin Luther King, Jr. and John F. Kennedy were transcendent leaders of the twentieth century whose adulterous affairs are well-documented and need no elaboration here.[248] What does need elaboration is how a more recent leader, former New York Governor Eliot Spitzer, could have fallen so hard so fast. The brainy kid who graduated from Princeton and Harvard Law School, the ambitious Spitzer rose to national prominence as an avenging state attorney general who hunted down Wall Street malefactors, exploiters of immigrant workers, and mobsters with moralistic fervor. Everywhere the self-styled defender of the American investor found "betrayals of the public trust" that he called "shocking" and "criminal." In 2007, Spitzer swept into office pledging to usher in a new era of clean government; a year later, in March 2008, two days after having been linked to a prostitution ring, he announced his resignation. The stunning development came after authorities and court documents showed that Spitzer, a father of three teenage girls, had been caught on tape arranging a liaison with a high-end call girl, and may have spent as much as $80,000 on prostitutes.

Ironically, one of the industries Spitzer had aggressively prosecuted had been prostitution services.

Spitzer's meteoric rise and fall had almost Shakespearean dimensions; but he is far from alone. Senator David Vitter patronized a professional prostitute called the D.C. Madam while branding himself a defender of traditional marriage. Congressman Mark Foley crusaded for tough laws against those who used the Web to exploit children while he himself went online to engage in sexually explicit exchanges with underage congressional pages. Extramarital trysts are quite commonplace; to prove that spouses lied about their infidelity, many divorce lawyers now use the E-Zpass electronic toll-collection system operating in twelve states in the Northeast and Midwest. "It's an easy way to show you took the off-ramp to adultery," said divorce lawyer Jacalyn Barnett.[249] Adulterers in Europe have it easier: In 2008, Italy's highest court ruled that Italians cannot be punished for lying to police about their love affairs. The case in question: A 48-year-old woman had lent her mobile phone to her secret lover, who then used it to call her estranged husband and verbally insult him. The woman was convicted by a lower court for having hidden the fact from the police investigating the abusive calls that the caller was her lover. But the Italian Supreme Court disagreed. "Having a lover is a circumstance that damages the honor of a person," the court determined; bending the truth in hiding that circumstance was evidently a kind of self-defense.[250]

French adulterers can now enlist professional help in cheating on their spouses. Alibila, a company in Paris founded by former private investigator Regine Mourizard, provides clients with convincing cover stories for their affairs, from calling their homes with fake emergencies to sending invites to imaginary out-of-town events. For 19 euros customers get a simple telephone call and twelve hours of cover; for a premium the company will also arrange for hotel rooms and romantic gifts for the mistress, print out fake receipts for nonexistent restaurants, provide merchandise from fake conferences, fabricate bills, and send postcards from places the customer is supposed to have been.[251]

Schemes and Swindles in All Walks of Life

Just like adultery, corruption (officials seeking personal gain, also called rent-seeking in economics) has been around ever since the advent of money, if not before. The first-century Roman emperor Vespasian said, somewhat crudely, that *pecunia non olet* (money doesn't smell) when he leveled an outrageous tax on public toilets. Many centuries later, in 1920, Charles Ponzi came up with the Securities Exchange Company, promising ordinary people extraordinary windfalls. For several months that year, Boston was the site of an astonishing daily ritual: Every morning, hundreds of people, their numbers swelling week by week, lined up in front of Ponzi's office, many with their entire life savings in their pockets. They handed over their greenbacks to tellers behind old-fashioned caged windows, their bills piling up so fast that when the drawers were filled with them, they would be tossed into wire baskets. In return, each investor received a small, ornate certificate pledging a 50-percent return in 45 days. Ponzi, an Italian immigrant, opened for business in 1919; in February 1920, he took in $5,290; in April, more than $140,000; in May, more than $440,000; in June, more than $2.5 million; and in July, nearly $6.5 million—this at a time when the president of Harvard earned $6,000 a year. To this day, Ponzi's name is synonymous with swindle.[252] It took leadership—charisma, cleverness, and charm, coupled with the creativity needed for a complicated market manipulation—to come up with a brazen, gargantuan rip-off like the Ponzi Scheme that would make millions for the man who conjured it up while robbing 30,000 people of their livelihood. Of course it was bad leadership; the question is always, what is leadership in service of? In this case, it was in behalf of a crime.

The schemes continue today, perhaps more so given the complexity of global markets and the anonymity of cyberspace, which offer even more loopholes for those who would exploit them for a fast buck. At various times over the past years, on any given day, there would be in the newspaper not one but several stories of cheating, corruption, and shady dealings. All through 2001 and 2002, the business sections reported on the machinations of Kenneth Lay, Jeffrey Skilling, and Andrew Fastow at Enron. But they were only the straw that broke the

camel's back. Daniel H. Bayly got a prison sentence for his role in Merrill
Lynch's purchase of three Nigerian barges from Enron. In Germany,
Heinrich von Pierer, chairman of the electronics giant Siemens, faced
massive pressure to resign during a bribery scandal in 2007 because of
allegations that the company gave $13 billion to foreign governments
to obtain contracts. The German car manufacturer Opel was riven by a
culture of corruption; entire departments had accepted secret bribes by
suppliers, from computers to trips to vacation homes. In 2005, Samuel
Israel III and Daniel Marino, co-founders of Bayou Group, a $450 mil-
lion hedge fund, pled guilty to fraud charges, essentially admitting that
their investors' millions had been thrown away in a failed business
while enriching the founders. Two months later, Paul E. Johnson, a former Wall Street analyst, was found liable by a federal jury of violating
federal securities laws by misleading investors with his stock research.
(Johnson was a former colleague of the CEO at Columbia University;
he had taught securities analysis since 1992. Ironically, at the time of
his conviction, his business school syllabus was on value investing.
Well, at least he wasn't teaching business ethics.)

Other so-called business leaders get away without accountability for
results. Their compensation packages are no longer tied to company
productivity, and they don't pay the price for failing. In *Pay Without
Performance*, two researchers at Harvard and Cornell found that since
the early 1990s, the pay of top executives has risen about twice as fast
as the market value of stocks, and much faster than corporate income.
In 2004 alone, Maurice "Hank" Greenberg earned $34.1 million while
AIG's stock *lost* value and performed at 11.4 percent below the S&P
500. In 2007, Charles Prince collected a similarly huge pay package of
$29.5 million after Citigroup announced it had to write off $11 billion
in bad mortgage debt. And when Stanley O'Neal retired from Merrill
Lynch in 2007, he walked away with $159 million after Merrill wrote off
$7.9 billion in mortgage-related debt.

Business is not alone with its excesses and ethical lapses. In acade-
mia, the South Korean scientist Dr. Hwang Woo Suk was disgraced for
having fabricated stem-cell research, leaving many scientists to wonder
how he could have risen so fast, deceived so many, including leading
scientific journals, and fallen so hard. The student-loan industry came

under a cloud when college financial-aid personnel (including some at Columbia University) accepted money to steer business to certain lenders. (In a settlement with the New York State Attorney General's office, Columbia agreed to let its financial aid office be monitored for five years, and to pay $1.125 million to a national financial aid education fund.) Given these corrupt role models, it is hardly surprising that students themselves are not above cheating: A Pew survey found that 46 percent of teenagers with online profiles say their postings contain at least some false information; of those, 8 percent said their profiles were "mostly or entirely false."²⁵³ On paper, kids are getting the message that lying is wrong: In surveys, 98 percent said that trust and honesty are essential in a personal relationship. But Dr. Nancy Darling, then at Penn State University, interviewed teens and found that 98 percent of them lied to their parents about topics like what they spent their allowances on, whether they had started dating, and what clothes they put on away from home. They lied about what movie they went to, and whom they went with. They lied about hanging out with friends their parents disapproved of, about their alcohol and drug use, and about whether they rode in cars driven by drunken teens.²⁵⁴ If 98 percent say honesty is essential, and 98 percent lie, it does not bode well for the next generation of leaders.

Back to politics: In the last five years, more than one hundred state and local officials in New Jersey were convicted of corruption charges. The widow of the late Palestinian leader Yasser Arafat, Suha, received more than $7 million in secret payments between 2002 and 2003 alone, money meant for the Palestinian people who were left without basic government services. Former Israeli prime minister Ariel Sharon's son Omri pleaded guilty to falsifying documents and perjury for setting up fictitious companies to hide illegal contributions to his father's 1999 election campaign, and went to jail for nine months (the judge reportedly wrote in the ruling, "This is a swamp of political corruption and it must be dried up").²⁵⁵ Zheng Xiaoyu, the first head of China's State Food and Drug Administration, who had lobbied for creating the agency to curb corporate corruption, was convicted of accepting gifts and bribes—a car, a villa, furniture, $300,000 in cash, and corporate stock, all in all $850,000 for him and those members of his family who were in on it—from eight drug companies that sought special favors; he was executed on July 10, 2007.[256]

The list could be much longer, but the point is clear. Leaders of all stripes have paid lip service to laws or ethics standards, much like adulterers who insist they are faithful while quietly cheating. Walking your talk sounds straightforward, but it is one of the hardest things to do in life and in business, especially for leaders, who tend to live in a fishbowl and whom the public or the media hold accountable for their own transgressions as well as those of others under their watch.

Beyond the breach of laws and ethical standards, it is hard to match words and deeds. People of all stripes, from politicians eager for votes to businessmen anxious to make a buck and UN officials wanting bigger budgets, make noble promises but all too often fall short in the implementation. Donor countries pledge billions of dollars to Darfur, followed by a trickle of cash. Politicians make grand campaign promises, only to switch policies the moment they're elected, or worse, to fork over money to their cronies or relatives. It is akin to New Year's resolutions to finally use that gym membership and lose weight, only to cave in a few weeks later. It seems like a pandemic. The 2007 subprime mortgage crisis that turned into a full-blown economic tsunami in 2008 resulted, at least in part, from lenders giving loans to people who lied about their income levels on their mortgage applications. In the decade since 1998, more than seven million borrowers had bought homes with subprime loans; by the end of 2007, one million of them had defaulted. We know how to travel safely to and from the moon; we know the innermost secrets of the human DNA; yet we know next to nothing about living up to our word (or holding others accountable for theirs).

In this context, leadership is a dual challenge. The Hebrew word *melech* (king) is composed of the word-roots *mal* (speaking) and *lech* (walking); and so leadership is about speaking to and inspiring people to get to a place they would not reach on their own. But there is another dimension of *melech*: leaders must match their talk (*mel*) and their walk (*lech*). Maimonides defined a rabbi not as someone who knows a lot, but as someone who lives what he or she knows. Much of Judaism is based on oral law; reading about it is not enough. You are supposed to live it and *be* it. (Unlike the clerics of some other religions, rabbis must get married and have children—to walk their talk and tackle life's challenges not from the ivory tower of ideas but in the action of living.)

Wanting to be good is not enough either. "The crisis of ethics," wrote the philosopher Abraham Joshua Heschel, "has its root ... in the view that the essence of the good is in the good intention."[257] In Jewish thought, it is not the theory or the intention that counts (after all, the road to hell is paved with good intentions); it is the action—the supreme virtue and best teacher. Jewish teachings are based on the premise that you cannot monitor what's going on in someone's head, so you will never truly know whether someone is being honest or just pretending. But what you *can* monitor is people's actions. We cannot know if someone else is really sincere about a fervent prayer, but what we do know, because we can monitor it objectively, is whether the person observes Jewish laws and practices. Action is the chief value; in the words of Heschel, "The deed is the source of holiness."[258] You can't merely tell your staff (or your children, for that matter) about doing the right thing; you have to demonstrate it and lead by example.

The Power of Coming Clean

The French existentialist Jean-Paul Sartre and the novelist Simone de Beauvoir sought to walk the talk through what they called "transparency." When they met in 1929 as rebellious students in Paris, they started their relationship with a pact that said, in so many words, that they would be unfaithful to each other. They would have "contingent" relationships while preserving their "essential" alliance based on radical honesty. They would tell each other everything, and they would do everything.

As soon as de Beauvoir took her first teaching post in 1932, a "harem" (Sartre's term) of female students turned up in her bedroom. Sartre tried seducing de Beauvoir's favorite, twenty-one-year-old waifish Olga; he failed resoundingly. He then went for Olga's sister Wanda, who responded to his first kiss by running to the bathroom to vomit.

In short, Sartre and de Beauvoir did not live up to their own "transparency" principle. Instead, they came to spin elaborate webs of lies to keep up their escapades. When Sartre finally succeeded in seducing Wanda, he invented the most elaborate stories to maintain the fiction of his exclusive commitment to Wanda, and to keep Wanda from knowing that he still bedded de Beauvoir and, over time, a host of other women. In World War II, when Sartre was on leave from a meteorological unit stationed in Alsace, he made his comrades send Wanda a daily letter from the war zone, so she would not realize that he was actually in a hotel around the corner, with de Beauvoir.[259]

It was games like these that prompted Heschel to ask the essential question: "How am I going to keep myself clean? The most important problem which a human being must face daily is how to maintain one's integrity in a world where power, success, and money are valued above all else? How to remain clean amid the mud of falsehood and malice that soil our society?"[260] Heschel's contemporary Martin Buber answered, "There is no way out but the crucial realization: Everything depends on myself, and the crucial decision: I will straighten myself out."[261]

The first step when you have lied or cheated is to come clean. Unless you first acknowledge your errors, you cannot redeem yourself. When King David sinned by taking Bath-sheba as his wife and having Uriah killed, he saved himself only by repenting immediately and declaring unequivocally, "I have sinned to the Lord."

The Hebrew word *emet* (truth) is spelled *aleph-mem-tav*—the first, middle, and final letters of the Hebrew alphabet. According to Hasidic thought, something must be true beginning, middle, and end; partially true is not true. To say the least, owning up to the truth is neither popular nor convenient. Most leaders, from Martha Stewart to Maurice Greenberg, issue denials of any wrongdoing and don't even bother to do the denying themselves; they have their spokespeople do the dirty work for them. But most people know anyway. As Sir Francis Bacon is supposed to have said, "He doth like the ape, that the higher he clymbes, the more he shewes his ars." Martha Stewart had made a mistake by selling ImClone shares. She could have simply admitted her bad judgment and paid the $50,000 fine; but by stubbornly insisting on her innocence, she ran up millions in legal fees and ended up in jail (even if it was a comfortable one in her case).

Former governor Spitzer, to his credit, did own up to the truth; when he announced his resignation in March 2008, he managed to close, without going into the details, the gulf between his words and deeds:

> In the past few days I have begun to atone for my private failings with my wife, Silda, my children, and my entire family. The remorse I feel will always be with me. Words cannot describe how grateful I am for the love and compassion they have shown me.
>
> From those to whom much is given, much is expected. I have been given much: the love of my family, the faith and trust of the people of New York, and the chance to lead this state. I am deeply sorry that I did not live up to what was expected of me.
>
> To every New Yorker, and to all those who believed in what I tried to stand for, I sincerely apologize.
>
> I look at my time as governor with a sense of what might have been, but I also know that as a public servant I, and the remarkable people with whom I worked, have accomplished a great deal. There is much more to be done, and I cannot allow my private failings to disrupt the people's work.
>
> Over the course of my public life, I have insisted, I believe correctly, that people, regardless of their position or power, take responsibility for their conduct. I can and will ask no less of myself.[262]

Another valiant exception to the usual protestations of innocence is Richard James Roach. No one prosecuted more zealously the war on drugs in the Texas Panhandle's five counties overrun with methamphetamines than the blustery and hot-tempered Republican district attorney. In his successful run for office in 2000, Roach had made drugs his signature issue and vowed a crackdown: "I think it's quite clear that the good citizens of this district are fed up with drugs."[263] Soon he had wrung harsh sentences from juries: 36 years, 38 years, 40, 60, 75— and in one case 99. During an earlier race in 1996, he had told a local newspaper that "it's kind of hard to fight drugs when you've got dirty law-enforcement." He had neglected to mention that the dirty law-enforcement included the $101,000-a-year prosecutor himself. One morning in January 2005, the good citizens of Roach's district witnessed a shocking event: FBI agents clapped Rick Roach into handcuffs

in the Gray County courthouse. It turned out that even as he'd hounded
drug offenders into jail, Roach had sunk into his own hell of drug addiction. By his account, he had stolen methamphetamine and other drugs
from police seizures to cope with depression and sexual impotence. He
was brought down, in a chain of events that Roach said "makes
absolutely no sense," when he injected himself with methamphetamine
in the presence of his office secretary, who was secretly working with
the FBI and the DEA and was wired with a hidden recorder.

Nelson Mandela once said that "I am not a saint, unless the definition of a saint is a sinner who keeps on trying." If Mandela is no saint,
then it's safe to say that Roach or Spitzer aren't either; but what makes
them courageous leaders is that they did not try to swindle or buy
themselves out of the predicament they had brought on themselves.
"There's no excuse," Roach said later, with a frankness that has become
rare. "I've gotten what I deserve." He and Spitzer knew that by closing
the gap between words and deeds, publicly if necessary, they were putting themselves on the road to redemption and gaining the kind of
power they could never have gotten from a corner office, a title, popularity, or money: in a word, integrity.

What Is Integrity?

Integrity is, most simply, the congruence between what you say and
do, in great and small things. If I say I will have the report to you by
5:00 o'clock, you'll have it on your desk by no later than 5:00 p.m.,
and if I see that I can't keep my word, I will still honor my word by calling you ahead of time, letting you know it will be late, and making a
new commitment. That's integrity: making your word count.

> **Tip:** Because Judaism treats the making and keeping of
> commitments very seriously—whether or not you say "I
> promise" or "I swear," not being true to your word is itself a
> sin—it offers a disclaimer: whenever Jews make a promise,
> they may say *bli neder* (without a formal commitment).

Integrity is something nobody can take away from you; even if people take all your property, and even if, God forbid, they cut off one of your limbs, your integrity stays with you. (We learn from observing a Stephen Hawking or a Christopher Reeves that you don't need command of your body to be a great leader.) Courageous integrity is the capital of leaders.

The Insider with Russell Crowe and Al Pacino shows the power of that capital. The film tells the story of a high-salaried senior manager at the Brown & Williamson tobacco company in Louisville, Kentucky, who was fired when the company suspected him of telling the truth about the company's knowledge of nicotine and its effects. Jeffrey S. Wigand "had all the trappings of a successful corporate executive"; then, in March 1993, in the blink of an eye, he went from $300,000 a year plus stock options to a high-school teacher's salary of $30,000. He attributed his dismissal to having resisted his employer's use of a potentially dangerous tobacco additive; he had been warned to abide by the company's confidentiality agreement or face lawsuits and the potential loss of his family's medical benefits. He claims he even received anonymous death threats. His marriage fell apart when his wife couldn't deal with the pressure. After being fired, Wigand formed his own foundation, Smoke-Free Kids, to teach children about the dangers of tobacco. The foundation has a staff of one: him. But he got one thing out of the ordeal: he can look straight in the mirror without averting his eyes. "I am at peace with myself. I have a good name now. It's a very good name and I protect it very much." He added: "My name stands for integrity. I can't describe to you what it is like to have that feeling."[264]

One of the great teachers of integrity was Mahatma Gandhi, and he taught it by his personal example. One story about Gandhi involves a woman and her young son who traveled for many days—by train, by rickshaw, by bus, and on foot—to see him. As they stood before Gandhi, the woman begged, "Please, Mahatma. Tell my son to stop eating sugar." Gandhi was silent. Then he said, "Bring your son back in two weeks." The woman was puzzled, but she thanked Gandhi and said that she would do as he asked. She and her son traveled all the way back to their village, and two weeks later they undertook the entire trip again. When the pair stood before him again, Gandhi looked the youngster in the eye and said, "Stop eating sugar." Grateful but bewildered, the woman asked, "Why did you tell me to bring him back? You could have told him the same thing two weeks ago." Gandhi replied, "Two weeks ago, *I* was eating sugar."

When Integrity Clashes with the Bottom Line

Walking your talk is never easy, but it is simple when the choice is between right and wrong. Ever since the Ten Commandments, most humans know that it is wrong to steal or kill. Though we are tempted to do bad things, we know which course of action is good and which is bad. The eighteenth-century Italian Rabbi Moshe Chaim Luzzatto suggested in his *Path of the Just* that we should make a list of what is good and what is bad:

> One who wishes to watch over himself must take two things into consideration. First he must consider what constitutes the true good that a person should choose and the true evil that he should flee from; and second, he must consider his actions, to discover whether they appertain to the category of good or to that of evil. ... When there is a question of performing a specific action, he should do nothing before he weighs the action in the scale of the aforementioned understanding.[265]

So far so good. But what happens if you find yourself in a situation where you have to choose between two equally valid courses of action? There's a difference between a temptation (a right-vs.-wrong decision) and an ethical dilemma (a right-vs.-right decision). Today, leaders often face not mere temptations, but ethical dilemmas: "right-vs.-right" decisions where the better and the worse option are difficult to distinguish, and shades of "right" action hard to decipher.

William Clay Ford, Jr. is a case in point. Before he was named chairman of the Ford Motor Company in 1998 at the ripe young age of forty and then chief executive at forty-three, Ford made a point of joining the environmental camp: "Nature is where my heart is."[266] It wasn't just the old burled-maple desk that had belonged to his grandfather Edsel.

Bill Ford's office was 100 percent green, from the ceiling to the paneling to the paint. The wood came from sustainable forests. The leather on the office chairs was tanned in a non-chemical process. The upholstery, the curtains, and the carpet were compostable, almost edible.

Ford believed that a great company is not just profitable but also "makes the world a better place." When he took the company's reins in 2001, he had ambitious plans: he wanted to make Ford a worker-friendly company, satisfy shareholder's expectations, and build environmentally friendly cars. Driven by the triple goal of making it an economically, environmentally, and socially sustainable company, he thought he could combine Ford's success with his own principles. But the three priorities came into conflict—an ethical dilemma. Ford's flagship car, the Explorer, a gas-guzzling S.U.V. as well as a car for outdoorsy types, embodied the paradox Bill Ford found himself in. He loved nature, but he felt loyal to Ford's workers and to the family legacy. Plus, the Explorer was a big money-maker.

This clash of his principles led Ford to make decisions as chairman and CEO that bitterly disappointed the environmental community. It was inevitable. And the pundits were right on hand. "Bill Ford," Saul Rubin, an analyst at UBS (then UBS Warburg) put it, "is going to have to give up on his ambitions to create an environmentally friendly company. They need to focus all of their resources on becoming competitive again."[267] In other words: making green versus talking green. Is that the right answer? Only William Ford can decide when he lies awake at night and considers his core values and his legacy. And that's easier said than done.

Like Ford, leaders today face greater complexity than ever before in human history. Among other things, this means they must often juggle conflicting value-systems. What do you do when you have two equally valid core values that clash with each other? What do you do if you live in a slum in Mumbai, and to ensure your family's survival (the Sixth Commandment not to kill may include protecting others from getting killed) you must steal money (violating the Eighth Commandment not to steal)? What do you do if your shareholders clamor for relentless growth, and your CFO has found a legal way to hide some losses that might push the stock price down if the public knew about them? What if one of your direct reports is a high-potential leader with great promise who has a penchant to bend the rules? What do you do if you're a toy company whose war games are in huge demand from children, but might turn these children into war-mongers or ADD-ridden computer addicts?

Tool 7.1
The Four Ethical Dilemmas

When you face a right-vs.-right decision, you come face to face with an underlying ethical conflict. Ethical dilemmas come in four types.

Individual vs. Group.

Imagine you're an American junior officer fighting in World War II in Europe. You've been captured by the German army and thrown into a solitary prison cell. The door opens, and a guard pushes another prisoner into your cell. He turns out to be a senior U.S. officer. As soon as the two of you are alone, he tells you he knows some highly classified military secrets, and he's sure he will blurt them out if the Germans torture him in the morning. To prevent himself from jeopardizing the war effort, he asks you to strangle him. What do you do, kill him to help win the war, or uphold the sanctity of life?

A modern version of the individual-vs.-group dilemma is the question whether you are entitled to torture a suspected terrorist in order to extract intelligence that might prevent a terrorist attack and save the lives of thousands of people. On the one hand, torture to get someone to talk is an ancient tool of political oppression that hardly befits a modern democracy, it is expressly forbidden by the Geneva Convention, and civilized people the world over recoil from deliberately inflicting cruelty on anybody. On the other, a suspected enemy combatant may have information that could prevent the killing of people; the interrogation of Abu Zubaydah, for example, said to be in solitary confinement somewhere in Pakistan, yielded intelligence that helped foil a plot to detonate a radioactive bomb in the United States.[268]

One of many examples in the business world is Google. The company, founded by Sergey Brin and Larry Page, operates along two core values. One is its mission "to organize the world's information and make it universally accessible and useful." This is a group value: Google provides a public good. (As an aside, without Google, the CEO's Ph.D. dissertation would have taken three years longer, not to speak of this book.) It's expressed in low-key and targeted advertising. For example, Google strictly separated out so-called sponsored search results and gave up untold millions of dollars in revenue by keeping its home page ad-free. On search results pages, ads are discreetly placed on the right side of the Google screen and don't bother you unless you're looking. If you click on a company's link, that company pays; if you don't, it doesn't.

The other principle is "Do no evil," which Brin and Page took so seriously that they included it in a Securities and Exchange Commission filing. When Google went public, Brin and Page insisted on a Dutch auction so that even small-time investors could participate and Wall Street would not control its IPO. Google has long presented itself as the anti-Microsoft; a company that digerati can see as a force of good in the world of technology.

But as Google became a dominant force, its two core principles came into conflict with each other. The company aggressively collected information on users' activities online. It stored people's search data, possibly forever, and put cookies on their computers that made it possible to track those searches in a personally identifiable way. The cookies will not expire until 2038. Google's Gmail system scans the content of e-mail messages so that relevant ads can be posted. The company's written privacy policy reserved the right to pool what it learns about users from their searches with what it learns from their e-mail messages (though Google said it would not do that) and warned that users' personal information may be processed on computers located in other countries.[269] In March 2007, Google claimed on its own blog that it would anonymize all server logs after 18-24 months.[270] But what happens if under the U.S. Patriot Act, the government can gain access to Google's data storehouse simply by presenting a valid warrant or subpoena, and if, under the same Act, Google is barred from telling users when it hands over their e-mail messages or search histories?

Although the exact same thing happened with telecoms surrendering data to governments, this is speculation. But Google has already come under attack for allowing China's government to censor its content. Its "Do no evil" motto was pitted against its principle of making information universally accessible when the company faced the choice of either operating in China and thereby helping the government curb its citizens' freedoms, or staying out and keeping information beyond the reach of Chinese citizens altogether. As it expands, Google may have to increasingly take actions that benefit its own (individual) growth at the expense of the universal (group) human rights of consumers.

Truth vs. Loyalty.

Let's say you're in a meeting with your boss, who tells you that the firm unfortunately has to fire your colleague, who happens to be a good friend of yours. Your superior swears you to secrecy because he wants to be the first one to break the news to your friend. As soon as you leave the boss's office, your friend comes up to you and asks, "So what did he say? Will I get fired?" What do you do, tell your friend the truth, or be loyal to your boss?

While his brother Aaron believed there are times when you should bend the truth for the sake of peace, Moses was known for never bending the truth. There are leaders today who deal with the truth vs. loyalty dilemma by choosing truth over loyalty and staking their whole reputation on their commitment to truth. Warren Buffett is one of them. His Berkshire Hathaway owner's manual of thirteen broad managerial operating principles said it clearly: "We also believe candor benefits us as managers: The C.E.O. who misleads others in public may eventually mislead himself in private."[271] On January 6, 2005, the same day that then New York Attorney General Elliot Spitzer's office issued a subpoena to Berkshire and General Re as part of his investigation into insurance improprieties, Buffett sent a memo to all of his managers and board. "The current investigation of the insurance industry underscores the importance of the message that I regularly send to you in my (more or less) biannual memo. Berkshire can afford to lose money, even lots of money; it can't afford to lose reputation, even a shred of reputation," Buffett wrote. "You and I are the guardians of that reputation. And in the long run we will have whatever reputation we deserve. There is plenty of money to be made in the center of the court. There is no need to play around the edges," he added. "I trust you to make these calls yourself. But if at any time you want to check your thinking against mine, just pick up the phone." Buffett insisted that "a small chance of distress or disgrace cannot, in our view, be offset by a large chance of extra returns."[272] If only then-chairman Marcel Ospel of UBS, then-CEO James Cayne, and other business leaders had shown such restraint before the subprime mortgage crisis.

Long-term vs. Short-term.

It's one thing to have a beautiful mission statement (Johnson & Johnson calls it "Our Credo"), but what happens when your core values conflict with your raison d'être to return a profit to shareholders? Say you are Johnson & Johnson and your baby oil is a blockbuster, but you find out that consumers use it as sun lotion, which makes it highly carcinogenic? What do you do, keep the product on the market and keep making a hefty profit, or take it off the market and forego short-term profits in favor of your long-term credibility and brand image? You could claim with some justification that consumers should know better, and that deleterious side-effects of the baby oil are not your problem if consumers use it for purposes other than those on the product label. But that's not what J&J did. Its Credo, created in 1943 by Robert Wood Johnson who guided the company from a small, family-owned business to a global enterprise with 116,200 employees, begins with the pledge: "We believe our first responsibility is to the doctors, nurses and patients, to mothers and all others who use our products and services. In meeting their needs everything we do must be of high quality."[273] The Credo became a Harvard Business School case study; more importantly, J&J lived by it. The company recalled the baby oil voluntarily, opting for its long-term reputation instead of short-term sales growth.

In 1982, J&J faced another challenge to its Credo when seven people died because of a tampering incident with its flagship product Tylenol. Rather than passing the buck or making excuses, it voluntarily recalled every single package. By putting its long-term reputation above short-term profits, it helped build Tylenol and its own name as trusted brands in the U.S. market. The incident became a famous case study in corporate social responsibility.[274] (Twenty years later, J&J's response to problems with acetaminophen, the active ingredient in Tylenol, was less stellar. More than fifty-five million Americans use Tylenol each year, and there are 56,000 emergency-room visits because of acetaminophen, and a hundred deaths, according to the U.S. Food and Drug Administration. When an FDA advisory panel decided after twenty-five years of study that acetaminophen should carry an explicit warning about potential liver damage, the company faced up to these problems only grudgingly and vaguely.)[275]

Source Perrier faced a similar crisis in 1990 when U.S. regulators charged that Perrier's bottled water was contaminated with benzene, a poisonous liquid. But Perrier dealt with the issue less wisely than J&J had with its Tylenol tampering. Instead of taking charge of the incident, Perrier officials claimed the contamination was an isolated incident, decided it was not urgent to alert consumers worldwide, and recalled only a portion of Perrier bottles in North America. That piece-meal response didn't go down well with Dutch and Danish officials when they found benzene in Perrier bottled water in Europe. In response, the company suddenly reversed itself; it announced a worldwide recall, but at the same time claimed that benzene was naturally present in carbon dioxide, the gas created by sparkling water that was normally filtered out before bottling.[276] Since Perrier didn't explain why the benzene had not been filtered in this case, the explanation sounded like a cover-up. The price for this lame-duck response was high. In 1989, Perrier had been one of the leading imported water companies with 6 percent share of the U.S. bottled water market. The company's botched response to the crisis damaged its reputation, and the FDA required Perrier to drop the words "Naturally Sparkling" from its label. Fifteen years later, Perrier was still struggling to re-join the best-selling bottled waters in the United States.

Justice vs. Mercy.

Say you are a college basketball coach and have made it clear to the team that any players who don't show up for practice won't play in the championship game this weekend. Three players missed practice last night, and they're precisely the three players you most need to win the game. Do you make them sit out the game on the bench for the sake of justice, and almost certainly lose, or do you let them play, violate your own rules, and lose your credibility with the team (who will come to practice in the future if your word doesn't count)?

Again, there is no easy answer with any of these examples; they are not called dilemmas for nothing. The solution depends on how you rank-order your values. You can also see that the four ethical dilemmas are not entirely separate and can overlap. For example, you could frame Perrier's long-term vs. short-term dilemma as an individual vs. group dilemma, or the basketball coach's justice vs. mercy dilemma as a case of short-term vs. long-term (victory now vs. future practice sessions). The important thing is to learn to step back from the action long enough to see eye-to-eye with your own value system, find out which of your underlying values are clashing, and decide what is really most important.

Tip: *Ethics of Our Fathers* recommends that you "make for yourself a mentor" who cares about you, yet is objective enough to help you make these types of decisions.

Institutionalizing Integrity

A mission statement like Johnson & Johnson's is a good vehicle for building a shared understanding of core values across the organization, but no matter how inspiring, a mission does not a culture make (forgive the Churchillian word sequence). The question is, what do you, and your managers and front-line people, do when the rubber meets the road? Can you live up to your stated beliefs, or will you jettison your principles in the heat of the action?

In 2002, CEO Steven A Ballmer sent a 2,674-word message to Microsoft's 50,000 employees worldwide. The message was about values like integrity, honesty, and accountability. Ballmer wrote that "starting with the upcoming August review, every employee will have a formal discussion of how they are doing on values with their managers." Nice try, but how do you enforce this? There are several things Ballmer could do.

One good question to ask, said Linda Klebe Trevino, a professor of organizational behavior at Pennsylvania State University, is "what happens to top performers who *don't* live by those values?"[277] If you are serious about values, you have to rig the incentives so that people live them (and rig them against people who don't). Second, whenever you hire new people, in job postings and interviews, stress values like honesty and walking your talk. Have not only your human resources department, but your company's role models, interview key candidates. If the best people in the firm demonstrate that integrity matters to them, new people will notice and emulate them. Be a leader in the business community and set yourself apart from the pack that stops at mere legal compliance. Voluntarily adopt some of the corporate governance proposals floating around, such as, for example, rotating your outside auditors every few years, having only outside directors sit on the company's compensation and audit committees, and treating all stock options as expenses in your financial statement. Above all, remember that integrity, like all other values, either trickles down from the top, or "the fish stinks from the head," as Swiss Consulting Group advisor Nicholas Wolfson likes to put it. If you want to instill certain values, start by acting the way you'd like your work force to act.

In all of this, there is a caveat: Don't be so obsessed with your own integrity that you forget about the world around you. Rabbi Chaim of Zans (now Sacz in Western Galicia) married his son to the daughter of Rabbi Eliezer. The day after the wedding, he visited the bride's father and told him: "Now that we are related I feel close to you and can tell you what is eating at my heart. Look, my hair and beard have gone white, and I have not yet atoned!"

"O my friend," replied Rabbi Eliezer, "you are thinking only of yourself. How about forgetting yourself and thinking of the world?"[278] Instead of wasting precious energy by torturing yourself with what you have done wrong, apply this energy to the future and to making the difference you're destined to make. That's what the next chapter is about.

The Bottom Line

- Corruption has been around ever since there has been money, if not longer. (That doesn't mean money is bad; it just means people get a little weak-kneed around it.) You need a moral compass: what is wrong is wrong, period.

- How do you build real power as a leader? Not through your job title, your wealth, or your authority, but through integrity—defined as honoring your word and leading by example. Close the gap between word and deed, and between tomorrow's vision and today's action (for example, Oprah's Harpo managers at all levels start their meetings with "Here's my intention ..."

- If you've done something that most people would consider ethically wrong were it broadcast on TV, the first step is honesty: say what you did and come clean.

- Leaders must be competent in dealing not only with temptations (right-vs.-wrong decisions) but with ethical dilemmas: right-vs.-right decisions. The four ethical dilemmas are individual vs. group, long-term vs. short-term, truth vs. loyalty, and justice vs. mercy. When you face an ethical dilemma, it is time to step back and prioritize your core values.

CHAPTER EIGHT

Commandment VIII
Don't Steal:
The Business of Giving Back

We make a living by what we get, but we make a life by what we give.
—Winston Churchill

Who is rich? He that is content. Who is that? Nobody.
—Benjamin Franklin

THE EIGHTH COMMANDMENT: *"You shall not steal."* The prohibition against stealing seems trivial: of course, everybody knows that—so what? But if you can break the myth that underlies stealing, the myth of Not Enough, you can be a true leader who contributes to others. Leadership is not about you; it's about everyone else. If you stop focusing on what you don't have and don't really need, you can start leveraging what you do have. Giving is the heart of leadership that integrates all Commandments.

We all know that stealing is wrong. But what if the money we jealously and fearfully hold on to is tantamount to stolen money? The nineteenth-century French anarchist Pierre-Joseph Proudhon said that property is stealing;[279] but you don't have to be a socialist revolutionary to see the whole idea of personal property as a Western invention. In Japan for example, people are generally not seen as wealthy when they hoard a lot of money; wealth is not a function of how much money you *have*, but of how much *flows through you*.

Thousands of years before Winston Churchill acknowledged the power of giving in making a life, the first Jew, Abraham, knew about generosity. Abraham welcomed all who came to him in an ancient example of *mi casa es su casa*; his tent was open on all four sides. God said of Abraham, "I have loved him because he commands and connects his children and his household to me that they keep *tzedakah* [charity] and justice."[280]

The power of *tzedakah* is so great that it can raise an individual to a higher level. Once three guests paid Abraham a visit; it soon became clear they were angels. "And behold! Three men were standing over him." But as soon as Abraham had invited them into his home and given them food and drink, the Torah says the opposite: Now "he stood over them."[281] Rabbi Menachem M. Schneerson wrote that generosity "embodies the superiority of the human soul over the angels, for this ascent is greatest through an act of goodness—extending a favor to another, a material favor in general, a spiritual favor in particular."[282] Before Abraham's *mitzvah* (good deed, literally "command"), the three angels had been greater, but his act of charity raised him to new heights of leadership.

Standing on his father's shoulders, Abraham's son Isaac came up with the notion of tithing—giving one-tenth of his possessions to the poor—"and in that year he reaped a hundredfold"; Abraham's grandson Jacob continued the practice. Originally, tithes were designated for the priests, the descendants of Aron, who did not own or inherit land, but eventually the custom became to tithe for the poor in general.[283] Ever since, Jews have known and practiced *tzedakah*; they knew that *aser te'aser bishvil she'tisasher* (you shall tithe to be rich).

Hasidic thought goes beyond charity or tithing. Your "possessions" are not really yours; they are entrusted to you—on loan to you—for the duration of your life, if that. When you give away 10 percent of your earnings, these assets didn't belong to you in the first place—they were already the property of the poor, even while you "had" them. The U.S. steel baron Andrew Carnegie, who helped launch the age of institutional philanthropy in the late nineteenth century (and whom we met in Chapter 4), knew this instinctively. Carnegie used to say that the business elite had a moral obligation to give back to the capitalist system: "The man who dies thus rich dies disgraced."[284] When Carnegie died in 1919, he had given away $350 million, or $7 billion in today's dollars. The money helped build 2,500 public libraries and raised the country's literacy rate. When Queen Victoria asked the fabulously wealthy banker Sir Moses Montefiore (Nathan Rothschild's brother-in-law), "How much money do you have?" Montefiore, who had retired from banking in 1824 to devote his life to diplomacy on behalf of the Jewish community worldwide, told the queen it would take him a few days of accounting before he could give her a good number. When he finally told her, "Your majesty, I have 300,000 pounds," the queen grew quite irritated. "That is impossible," she protested, suspecting that the banker sought to hide his enormous wealth, not least to evade taxes. "Everyone knows that you have much more." He smiled: "No, I don't. None of that money belongs to me. Only the money I gave to charity is truly mine—and that is 300,000 pounds."[285] Montefiore was not trying to be clever or evasive; he simply knew that any other assets he held were only temporary and subject to confiscation or loss. This could happen to anyone today: In March 2007, James E. Cayne, the former CEO of Bear Stearns, whose stake in the company had been over $1 billion only a year earlier, disclosed that he had sold all his shares for $61 million.)

Those who think more money will bring them more happiness are mistaken. On March 15, 1996, at age 40, the entrepreneur Howard Jonas made $100 million. "That was the day my company, IDT, one of the world's largest Internet and alternative telecommunications providers, went public. As IDT's founder, president, and majority shareholder, I was instantly rich beyond my wildest dreams. People ask me if this was the greatest moment in my business life. It wasn't."[286] The German writer Erich Kaestner, whose books were burned by the Nazis, wrote that money is not the main thing; it is the most important secondary thing. The famous sage and scholar Hillel, in *The Ethics of Our Fathers*[287] suggested some two thousand years ago that *Marbe nichosim, marbe da'aga,* translated as "the more possessions, the more anxiety." That doesn't mean we should not aspire to wealth; money is opportunity; it is a powerful vehicle for making things happen. The story goes that when Mordecai Deitsch, the late founder of Deitsch Plastic, wanted to retire to study Torah, Rabbi Schneerson counseled against it. Why not? Wasn't the study of Torah the highest service? The way Mr. Deitsch's grandson tells it, the Rebbe answered with a counter-question: "Do you think you serve God more by studying as a single human being," he asked, "or by funding two thousand children to study Torah?"

Not all of us are as generous as Deitsch; one poor man became rich and promptly became a miser. He stopped inviting people to his home, which had become so fancy that he did not want the poor to soil it. He worked so hard that he had no time for people anymore. Once his Rebbe came to visit him. He walked on the heavy rug. He saw the costly paintings. He looked at the expensive new furniture and at the drapes made from the finest, softest velvet. Then he noticed the gorgeous mirror. He looked at its shiny gold frame. It was the biggest mirror he had ever seen.

"Quite a change, is it not?" the rich man said with a pleased smile on his face. "That mirror is my favorite treasure. Of all the lovely things I own, I like my mirror the best. It cost a great deal of money, but it was worth it. It is truly a masterpiece, a work of art, is it not?" he said and turned to the Rebbe.

"Yes," the Rebbe answered. "Quite a change. Quite a change." He said this softly. Suddenly, he said, "Come here," and asked the wealthy man to walk over to the window. He pushed aside the drapes and told the man to look out into the street. Since it was a small town, the man knew almost all the people walking past his house.

"It is strange, is it not?" the Rebbe mused. "A mirror and a window are both made of glass and yet they are very different."

"That is true," the man said. "A mirror and a window are both made from glass. The window is transparent. Light can pass through it. You can see everything on the other side. The mirror, on the other hand, is coated with silver on one side. The rays of light cannot pass through, and therefore a mirror can only reflect what is in front of it."

"I see," said the Rebbe and nodded his head. "The plain glass is clear through and through, allowing you to see others and their lives. But when it is coated with silver, then you can see only yourself. What a change, isn't it?"

Suddenly it dawned upon the wealthy man how stingy he had become, and his eyes filled with tears.[288]

Out of the Transaction Mindset

As Proverbs puts it, "The one who is gracious to the poor lends to God, and God will repay him for his good deed."[289] He becomes God's creditor. In fact, the Torah promises that "your kindness will be preserved for two thousand generations."[290] But tzedakah is much more than charity; literally it means righteousness or right action. Holding on to your possessions is wrong; giving is right. It is said to be the only mitzvah or good deed for which you use all 613 limbs (the number according to kabbalistic tradition, one physical channel for each of the Torah's commandments) since you worked hard for it with every fiber of your body, not only your brain or your fingers. And since tzedakah includes all other mitzvot (good deeds) and Commandments, the Jerusalem Talmud calls it simply "the Commandment."[291] The concept points to the fundamental difference between transactional and transformational leadership. Transactional leadership involves a deal: I give you x salary and y stock options and z other perks, and in return I expect you to deliver results. While this traditional model still has its uses, it falls short today when highly-mobile knowledge workers are looking for much more than just money. Transformational leaders, on the other hand—Gandhi, King, Mandela—offered their followers not a transaction but a vision. Churchill promised his compatriots not stock options but "blood, sweat, and tears" for joining the fight against the Nazi aggressors. Rabbi Menachem M. Scheerson asked his followers, "the Rebbe's army," to build a world of peace and harmony. And the great business leaders of today are about much more than money; people join Microsoft, Apple, Google, or Genentech to make a difference and give it everything they've got.

The same goes for *tzedakah*: it is not a deal. If you want to become wealthy, tithe to charity, but don't do it as a quid pro quo. Some of us make a deal with God, for example, "If you save my brother, I will give a million dollars to charity." Then the miracle happens: the brother gets better, and now we tell ourselves, "I really didn't mean a million, I only meant $500,000." Then we find out we have only $100,000. Finally we decide we didn't mean to pledge dollars but yen. Perhaps this is an exaggeration, but the transactional mindset is deeply embedded in our culture.

Someone once wrote a letter to Rabbi Schneerson explaining that he needed God to intervene on his behalf. He told the Rebbe that if God gave him what he asked, he would give a lot of money to charity. The Rebbe responded that you don't make deals with God; God doesn't work that way. First you have to take action and make that big contribution, and *then* you say humbly, "God, I request that you help me."

Tzedakah means rightful action—you give because it is the right thing to do, not to get recognition or fame. The Torah reminds us: "When you cut down your harvest in your field and have forgotten a sheaf in the field, you shall not go again to fetch it; it shall be for the stranger, for the orphan, and for the widow."[292] You leave your forgotten sheaf in the field and wait for the poor to pick it up because not being known for your giving is a higher level of *tzedakah*; and it's less embarrassing and more dignified for the recipient if he or she can get your gift without being seen. Jamnalal Bajaj, the father of Ramkrishna Bajaj (see Chapter 6) and one of India's first industrialists, was a principal financier of Gandhi's movement to free India. Without his money, India might still be under British rule today. And yet Bajaj's name is not in the history books, Gandhi's is. This level of *tzedakah* requires the deepest humility: you get no credit. You have to be willing never to be known for your contribution, nor to get your name on a plaque in a hospital wing or university library.

Some leaders today go beyond transactional giving or even tithing. Michael Bloomberg, the wildly successful entrepreneur and mayor of New York City, gives away half his profits each year. Bill and Melinda Gates had endowed their foundation with some $30 billion by July 2004, and the next year Gates announced that he would give away 90 percent of his fortune, valued at about $50 billion. The Gates Foundation is set up to combat AIDS, tuberculosis, malaria, and other health challenges that affect the poorest of the poor in developing countries; it also funds programs to reduce the high school dropout rate in the

United States. In the summer of 2006, Warren Buffett announced that he would give 85 percent of his fortune to the Gates Foundation, some $3 billion a year. Buffett never imagined that he would give his wealth away while he was still alive; he had always expected that after his death, his wife would manage the philanthropy. But when she died before him, he started talking with Gates, a close friend whom Buffett had long considered one of the best strategists he knew, about making a difference with his money.

Some think that only immensely wealthy business leaders, not the rest of us, can part with their money; after all, if the Gateses give away 90 percent of their wealth, that still leaves them with a comfortable $5 billion, and likely more. But you don't have to be rich to give. In 1995, a Mississippi washerwoman named Oseola McCarty decided to give away most of her life savings. She said there was nothing in particular she wanted to buy, and no particular place she wanted to go. She had made a small fortune by doing laundry and ironing, dollar for dollar. She wanted no monuments in her name. But her gift of $150,000 to help complete strangers get a college education at the University of Southern Mississippi in Hattiesburg would bring her worldwide attention, not least from Ted Turner, a multibillionaire. After hearing of her gift, Turner gave away a billion dollars, saying: "If that little woman can give away everything she has, then I can give a billion."[293]

After McCarty made her pledge to the university, she enjoyed a level of fame and luxuries she had thought impossible. For the first time in her life she would fly in a plane, be honored by the United Nations, and shake hands with then President Bill Clinton. She had never stayed in a hotel, so before checking out she couldn't help herself: She made the bed.

Needless to say, people like McCarty are exceptions to the rule. We live in a culture that encourages hoarding money. L. Dennis Kozlowski, the former CEO of Tyco International, is perhaps the most egregious example. As if the tens of millions of dollars in pay Kozlowski took home had not been enough, he persuaded his board to give him hundreds of millions more in stocks and perks. He was so hungry for cash that rather than waiving his fee to sit on his own board, as most executives do, he insisted on being paid $75,000 a year for that, too.

Making a Difference as a Core Competence

Giving back, on the other hand, need not be a luxury or an after-thought; it can be a business strategy. In January 2007, the Timberland Company, which sells outdoor-themed clothes, shoes, and accessories, was named by *Fortune* as one of the hundred best companies to work for. Why? For Jeffrey Swartz, the CEO, doing well and doing good are inextricably linked. His grandfather Nathan Swartz, an immigrant, had begun as an apprentice stitcher in Boston. In 1952, he bought half of a shoemaking company; three years later he bought the other half and invited his sons to join him. In 1973, they created the Timberland name and made it into a global brand. By the early 1990s, Jeffrey had taken over the company's reins from the second generation. Then, one day, a young man came to his office. "Alan Khazei, a Harvard Law School graduate, sat across from me and said: 'You know, you make boots, and you think that that's the objective of your life. You think shareholder value and creating wealth for you and your children—you think *that's* what it's about.' He went on: 'I on the other hand spend my life trying to redeem the world around me. I'm about transforma-tion of self and the galvanizing of community. I'm building the beloved community that Dr. King spoke about, and my gift to you today is to show you how the two can be linked.'

"I'm a good salesman, Swartz recalled, "so I'm open to a new pitch. He gave me one. He said, 'All you have to do is give me half a day. Come serve with us. Come serve with the 17- to 23-year-old young people who give up a year of their life to do service. I'll show you how by serving others you can be transformed yourself.'"

Despite his hectic schedule (four hours is a good night's sleep), Swartz made a leap. He and nine Timberland employees went with Khazei and gave a day of service. They painted walls and renovated a drug rehab center for young people. Indeed, he experienced the trans-formation Khazei had promised. On that day, Swartz recounted, "I thought to myself: Aha! The third generation now has a purpose. My grandfather invented a boot, and my dad invented a brand." What if his generation's purpose was making a difference? "What if we talk about community building as a business strategy, for separating us from people we compete with?"[294]

They did. They called it the Path of Service and involved the staff at Timberland. For a sales meeting in Florida, "We brought in the sales force, who all brought their golf bags and their tennis rackets—but we didn't do golf. Instead, we climbed into school buses" for a day of service, "and the transformation of our staff was unbelievable." By 2000, all six thousand Timberland employees each performed forty hours of community service annually (paid by the company); five years later, Timberland's Serv-a-palooza hosted 170 service projects in twenty-seven countries and contributed 45,000 volunteer work hours. "Now, is that the job of a boot company?" Swartz asked. "Absolutely."

The Timberland CEO understood that *la'asok be'divrei Torah* (immersing oneself in the sayings of Torah), the blessing Jews say once a day, means not just that. Since the verb *la'asok* (to busy oneself, to engage) has the same root as *ish asakim* (businessman), it also means the business of Torah. It's not just when you're sitting with a Bible in front of you; as a businessperson, whether you hire someone or work with a customer, you're immersed in living the Bible all day long. "Every phone call is the business of Torah," Swartz says, because it's the business of uplifting another human being. "No one believes in this more than we do," he adds, "and that is our competitive advantage." The numbers proved him right: from 2000 to 2005, his company saw sales grow at a compound annual rate of 9.7 percent and earnings per share by 20 percent. Its stock price rose 64 percent over the same period. And it's all built on Timberland's culture: "Boots, Brand, Belief."[295]

Timberland is part of a trend that builds on the integration of doing well while doing good. If the first, second, and third sectors of our economy are the private, public, and nonprofit sectors, the most innovative corporate models are now in what has come to be called the fourth sector: state-of-the-art organizations set up as a mix of making profits and making a difference. "There's a big movement out there that is not yet recognized as a movement," said R. Todd Johnson, a San Francisco lawyer working on an online wiki for what he calls "for-bene-

,

fit corporations."[296] Making a difference used to be the exclusive domain of idealistic do-gooders. Now it makes commercial sense; investors see the ROI and are flocking to the business model. Even among major investment funds, perceptions of profit and value are changing: for example, the California State Teachers' Retirement System, a $162 billion pension fund, has taken a hard look at insurance companies and decided that they were not paying enough attention to climate change and hence were a riskier investment than in the past. Why? "There are many motivations for this," said Abby Joseph Cohen, Goldman Sachs' influential chief U.S. investment portfolio strategist. "Companies are taking a broader view that allows them to see that a cost today may reduce future liabilities, and the reduction of those future liabilities in turn has a positive impact on their cost of capital."[297] In other words: making a difference is good for making money. And giving back is a competitive advantage not only for firms, but also for individual leaders who want to leverage their careers and build wealth. This is evident in what might be called the Raul Julia Model.

Tool 8.1
The Raul Julia Model—Investing from the Future

Jewish thought differentiates between four types of donors. The first type is one who wishes to give himself but wants others not to give; he begrudges others. The second type thinks others should give but he should not give; he begrudges himself. The third type feels that both he and others should give; he is pious. The fourth and final type thinks neither he nor others should give. He is called wicked.[298]

The 2004 tsunami changed all that. After the world witnessed the devastation of millions of lives in several Asian countries, countless people the world over became type-three donors: they responded with unprecedented generosity and charity in a worldwide outpouring of human empathy. But what if we opened our hearts and pocketbooks not only in reaction to a crisis? What if we invested in the future, standing in the future?

One person who embodied this way of giving was the late actor and activist Raul Julia, who is known for films such as *Kiss of the Spider Woman*, *Presumed Innocent*, *The Addams Family*, and *Havana*. In 1987 The Hunger Project held a meeting for potential high-level investors. The CEO had just flown in from Munich and spontaneously attended despite jetlag. There were presentations by scientists and policymakers, and frankly it was all a bit boring until Raul suddenly leapt out of his seat and boomed in his inimitable thick Puerto Rican accent, "In 1977, when The Hunger Project started, you asked me to give everything. I had no money, no acting work, no contract, nothing. I gave you everything: $500. Now you ask me again to give everything. I have no money, no job, no movie, no contract. I pledge to you $100,000." Raul sat down, and the room went electric. People cheered and jumped out of their seats. A group of a dozen people pledged several million dollars. The CEO was neither wealthy nor an official participant, but he grabbed a pledge form and wrote down what for him was as outrageous as Raul's investment: $25,000.

Raul's pledge embodied a principle of giving. You don't make a mere gesture, which is what most of us do when we drop some coins into the cup of a homeless man in the subway or into a collection box, or when we give charity from what's left over (companies or wealthy individuals might make $10,000 gestures that don't mean much to them). While these are all *mitzvot*, acts of goodness and kindness, they fall short of building a new future. The next level, tithing, is giving a delineated portion of your earnings; tithing is a much more thoughtful act that deserves the name investment. But at the highest level of *tzedakah*, you stand not in your financial circumstances but in your desired financial future; you foresee not your current but your *intended* wealth; and you commit yourself to giving a portion of the money you *will* have. The trick is that you have to make the bold pledge and start giving *before* you have the money.

When you make a sacred pledge, it is already real; it's as if you have already fulfilled it. A sacred pledge is like saying I love you and meaning it with all your heart. In order to keep Julia's pledge (which he and his wife Merel did; in fact, by the time of his death in 1994, they had given over $1 million), he had to realize a new future in his acting career. His pledge forced him to be a tough negotiator on Broadway and in Hollywood. Demanding compensation not just for himself but for the future of humanity added a new level of boldness to his bargaining power. And the deal Julia got for his role as Gomez Addams gave his family a whole new level of wealth, made him a star, and allowed him to invest in ending hunger, in the words of The Hunger Project, at his "highest appropriate level."[299]

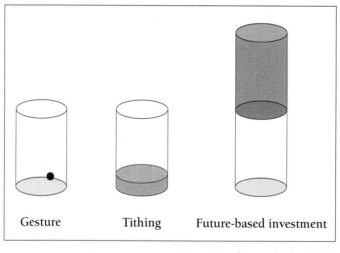

Figure 8.1: Three Levels of Tzedakah

Almost a millennium ago, Maimonides wrote in his *Laws of Contributions to the Poor* that it is important to give often, ideally on a daily basis into a charity box, because *tzedakah* is not only a matter of how much you give, but also how often; it is not merely about helping others, but also about transforming yourself. The Hunger Project's philosophy likens contributing to dancing: If you dance rarely and someone asks you to dance, you feel rusty and awkward, and may even offer a weak excuse for staying in your seat. But if you dance regularly, it is fluid and comes easy. The lesson: If you practice contributing frequently, it becomes easier to reallocate "your" money and make a difference with it, rather than getting an anxiety attack every time someone invites you to give.

The Hunger Project aims at yet another principle of *tzedakah*: by giving, you create a bridge between the poor person and yourself. You shouldn't remain two separate entities; there must be a human merger. The highest level of giving, Maimonides wrote, is not to give a person a few dollars, a one-time gift, and then say, Goodbye, I'll never see you again. Giving is partnership designed to set people on their own two feet, nourish them until they are ripe, and then wean them so that they never have to ask for money again, for example by putting them into business or giving them jobs.[300] This type of investment creates not passive recipients of aid, but self-reliant leaders. The results of this bottom-up approach are many multiples of traditional top-down development. As of late 2007, 3.5 million people in South Asia, Africa, and Latin America have participated in The Hunger Project's Vision, Commitment and Action Workshop in which they learn to take charge of their lives and communities; resource-poor people have built their own rural banking system used by 3 million people; the African Woman Food Farmer Initiative has issued more than 83,000 individual loans to women building their own businesses; and in perhaps the boldest leadership experiment of our time, more than 80,000 volunteer "animators" in Bangladesh alone—people working without any incentive other than their own personal commitment to realizing a hunger-free Bangladesh—have empowered millions of people to meet their needs. When The Hunger Project mobilized hungry people to end their own hunger, their first reflex was to ask for handouts; but the organization refused and gave them only enough seed capital for catalytic projects, projects that would put them on the path to self-sufficiency.

When the Patrick J. Smyth Foundation and Swiss Consulting Group collaborated in Haiti to train and mobilize some 150 emerging leaders to take charge of developing their country, many participants felt

trapped by a mindset that said they couldn't accomplish anything
without first getting money from the foundation. But once they
adopted a stance of self-reliance, 60 percent of them had enough
resourcefulness to deliver their own catalytic projects, from a clean-up
in a Port-au-Prince *bidonville* (slum) to computer trainings for women—
without a single handout. They found their own financing and equipment. They had turned from passive beneficiaries into agents of their
own development—in short, into leaders.

> **Tip:** The Talmud states that *tzedakah* will bring an end
> to war and disease and will speed the final redemption of
> the world.[301] That is why the Rabbi and his wife have dedi-
> cated their lives to outreach—helping underprivileged
> children get a Jewish education, bringing toys for tots
> in hospitals, fundraising, and dozens of other actions
> to inspire *yiddishkeit* (Yiddish for Jewishness) as well as
> teaching the Noahide Laws (see Appendix) to people of all
> nations. By committing countless acts of goodness and
> kindness, and requesting that others follow our lead, we
> can speed up the world's healing and unity. Place a charity
> box in your kitchen, children's bedrooms, or office. Every
> morning, put in a few coins or bills. When the box is full,
> give the money to your favorite charity or charities. It will
> enrich you.

Open Source in Business

Open source, contributing your intellectual property to the community, may well be what *tzedakah* looks like in business; and it can pay
rich dividends. Take Linus Torvalds, who was honored as one of the
top twenty-five IT executives of 2004, but is neither a chief executive
nor a chairman. Why? Because the then 34-year-old gave away the
source code of Linux, the operating system he had created with thou-

sands of other programmers. Torvalds believes in the idea that a code should not be proprietary but transparent for all to see so that users can see what software they have and can change it to fit their needs—instead of legal bullying or other forceful methods to guard intellectual property. The open-source approach makes commercial sense. It's profitable, since companies like Red Hat pay Torvalds and other developers based on their programming work for clients. In addition, it has forced companies like Microsoft, Apple, and Sun Microsystems to take notice and alter their own business models. Making the Linux code freely available is the best P.R. and smart business strategy; it builds the brand and serves as a standard-setter. China's adoption of Linux over Microsoft's Windows in the 1990s was only a start; more and more governments and multinational companies now use the open-source operating system.

Large companies may be following Torvalds' lead. Consider I.B.M. In 2004, the company registered more new patents than any other company—3,248, to be exact, almost ten a day, and earned $1 billion from licensing and selling its ideas that year alone. In early 2005, I.B.M. made a surprising move: It gave away five hundred patents and pledged that more would follow. Why would I.B.M. share its wealth for free? Had chief executive Samuel J. Palmisano lost it? No. It's called enlightened self-interest. Departing from conventional wisdom, the company calculated that sharing technology can sometimes be more profitable than jealously guarding its property rights on patents, copyrights, and trade secrets. "If you open up your technology and reveal quickly, people will build on your stuff," said Eric von Hippel, a professor and innovation expert at the Sloan School of Management at M.I.T. "It becomes more economically efficient to be open." I.B.M. is not doing this naïvely. "The layer of technology that is open is going to steadily increase, but in going through this transition we're not going to be crazy," said John E. Kelly, an I.B.M. senior vice president put in charge of the initiative in May 2004 by Palmisano himself. "This is like disarmament. You're not going to give away all your missiles as a first step." But I.B.M. understood that by contributing its intellectual property to the public domain, it could win over new markets and customers. So far, the gamble seems to have paid off: In January 2007, IBM reported an overall annual revenue growth of 7 percent, and its technology consulting business had grown by a whopping 55 percent in the same period.

Torvalds is by no means the first leader to believe in the power of open source. Half a century before him, Jonas Salk, the inventor of the vaccine that saved an entire generation from the scourge of polio, famously refused to patent his creation. In 1955, the TV broadcaster Edward J. Murrow interviewed Salk live on *See It Now* and asked him, "Who owns the patent on this vaccine?" Salk's response perfectly embodied the spirit of giving. "Well, the people, I would say. There is no patent. Could you patent the sun?"

The Bottom Line

- What you own is not really yours. Your resources have been entrusted to you for the time being to make a difference. Some cultures define wealth not by how much money you have (or even hoard), but by how much money flows through you.

- *Tzedakah* (righteous giving) is perhaps the highest commandment that integrates all others. It has the power to bring an end to war and disease and can speed the final redemption of the world. Through countless acts of goodness and kindness, and asking others to follow your lead, you can speed up the world's healing and unity.

- When you give, you break the myth of scarcity: you experience that you are, have, and do enough. By boldly committing to, and investing in, a cause greater than yourself, you can catalyze your future wealth.

- When you embed making a difference into your corporate strategy and culture, you boost customer loyalty and employee morale, which in turn boost productivity.

- Sharing your intellectual property, for example in an open-source approach, can be sound business strategy: you grow the pie and become a standard-setter in your industry.

CHAPTER NINE

Commandment IX
No False Witness:
Breakdown to Breakthrough

Perhaps all the dragons in our lives are princesses
who are only waiting to see us act, just once, with beauty and courage.
—Rainer Maria Rilke

Far better it is to dare mighty things, to win glorious triumphs,
even though checkered by failure, than to take rank with those poor
spirits who neither enjoy much nor suffer much,
because they live in the gray twilight that knows not victory nor defeat.
—Theodore Roosevelt

THE NINTH COMMANDMENT: *"You shall not bear false witness against your neighbor."* Leaders are not needed while things go smoothly; they prove their mettle when the going gets tough. But the moment things don't go as planned, we bear false witness: we tend to hide the breakdown, feel shame, blame others, or worst of all, reduce the challenge. In essence, instead of grabbing the bull by the horns and facing the facts, we want to make things (and not least ourselves) look better than they really are. Such false testimony is an entirely human response, and entirely counter-productive. Great leaders like Job or Churchill are unafraid of bad news. In this chapter you will learn the tool that distinguishes leaders from the pack and makes them invincible: Unlike others who are stymied by breakdowns, leaders cull the raw materials of those very same breakdowns and harness their power to create breakthroughs.

One night in the late 1960s, when Philip Anschutz was laying the groundwork for what was to become a multi-billion dollar fortune, he received a call in Denver. A drilling supervisor at one of his Wyoming oil rigs gave him bad news: the well was on fire, and if the fire kept burning, it would bankrupt him.

Common-sense crisis management in such a situation is to limit your exposure, sell off the bad investment, and get out of there quickly. Anschutz did the exact opposite. He immediately saw the bright side: the fire meant that he had finally struck oil. He rented a plane, flew to Wyoming, and by eight in the morning had gambled more money on his oil venture—a lot more. He bought as much land around the burning well as he could. He then hired Red Adair, a legendary oil-field firefighter, to put out the blaze, and invited a Hollywood studio to shoot the episode for the John Wayne thriller Hellfighters. When he recalled the fire some four decades later, Anschutz said, "There's always a point that if you go forward you win, sometimes you win it all, and if you go back you lose everything."[302]

When you lead, breakdowns like this happen all the time; the road of leaders is seldom smooth. In fact, managers who want to cruise along on the freeway and are not ready for bumpy dirt roads need not apply. Breakdowns come with the territory; without them leadership would not be needed—a manager or caretaker could do the job. But it goes beyond managing a few bumps: The best leaders feed on adversity. In fact, what leadership theorists ignore is that breakdowns are a great leader's most underrated allies; they are the very stuff that forges his or her resolve. If you analyze and harness breakdowns correctly, you can use them as raw material for breakthroughs. Take Ted Turner, whose many accomplishments—multibillionaire, founder of the most prominent global media company, owner of the Atlanta Braves, America's largest landowner, and $1 billion donor to the United Nations, to name but a few—are fueled not least by overcoming extraordinary adversity. He recalled that when he was a child, his father was prone to fits of rage and used to beat him with a coat hanger. Ted's younger sister died from an immune disease at the age of twelve and his father committed suicide when Ted was twenty-four.[303] Life dealt him several blows that could have easily done him in, and he could have used these catastrophes as reasons for being a loser. "All my life people have said I wasn't going to make it," he explained. Instead he used these experiences for good, and in that sense they *were* good. Because they made him stronger, they were blessings in disguise. Turner is famous for saying (though he might have borrowed it from legendary football coach Vince Lombardi), "You can never quit. Winners never quit, and quitters never win."

Winston Churchill exhibited the same kind of attitude in the hot May of 1940 when, bald and grey after forty years in and out of government, he became Prime Minister at last. Neither the king nor Neville Chamberlain, who had appeased Hitler two years earlier at Munich, was keen on Churchill as chief executive; it was only when the Labour party sent word that they would serve under no Conservative except Churchill that, at sixty-six, an age when most people retire, he got the top job.

Churchill faced his gravest challenge on his first day in office. Britain was on the brink of losing World War II to Germany. Half of Europe had been brought to its knees under the German boot. The British army, 220,000 Tommies, was trapped at Dunkirk, with their back against the sea; King George VI had been told they would be lucky to save 17,000. Hitler, close to being master of Europe, told his second-in-command and chief henchman Hermann Göring on June 18 with a gleeful glint in his eye: "The war is finished. I'll come to an understanding with England."[304] The situation seemed hopeless to everyone except Churchill. At that point he faced greater obstacles than many of us confront over a lifetime. His response was to gobble them up hungrily, saying (though he too might have borrowed, in his case from Abraham Lincoln), "A pessimist sees the difficulty in every opportunity; an optimist sees the opportunity in every difficulty." Leaders like Churchill are obviously of the latter, optimistic type. He summed up his philosophy in October 1941 when, still in the throes of the war, he visited Harrow to listen to the traditional songs he had sung there as a youth. He told the students: "Never give in. Never give in. Never, never, never, never—in nothing, great or small, large or petty—never give in, except to convictions of honor and good sense."[305]

Generations before Churchill, Benjamin Disraeli had become the first Jewish prime minister of any country. But few people today remember the failed attempts that preceded Disraeli's glory. As a young leader, he had run for British Parliament in three elections. He lost all three, probably because he came from a Jewish family. He went nearly bankrupt before finally winning his first seat, and then he proceeded to use these failures to hone his communication skills, refine his campaign strategy, and build a network of powerful supporters. Disraeli became one of the most revered prime ministers in Britain's history, as well as Queen Victoria's trusted adviser. Leaders from Disraeli and Churchill to Kennedy, from Intel's Andy Grove to CNN's Ted Turner, fed on the kind of difficult challenges that others would have seen as reasons to give up.

Disraeli was hardly the first Jewish leader in history to face adversity. In fact, few peoples throughout history did so more than the Jews. Perhaps what didn't kill them made them stronger; perhaps the very persecutions, pogroms, and injustices they faced over and over again made an indelible imprint on their leadership DNA. Going back to their source, the Torah is full of dramatic breakdowns. Adam and Eve were exiled from Eden, Noah faced the great flood, Sodom and Gomorrha lay in ashes, Israel succumbed to the golden calf, the people mutinied against Moses, Job was beset by endless calamities, and (as described in Chapter 6) Joseph found himself in a pit and in prison long before becoming Egypt's prime minister. A generation earlier, when Joseph's father Jacob was a young man himself, he fell head over heels in love with Rachel and asked her father Laban for her hand. Laban accepted on the condition that Jacob would first serve him for seven years. Jacob did. Finally, after seven long years, the wedding came. But on the wedding night, Laban secretly slipped in Rachel's older and comelier sister Leah. In the morning, when Jacob found he had been duped, he protested; but Laban's simple justification was that it was the custom to marry off the older sister first. He offered Jacob the opportunity to work for another seven years for Rachel, and proceeded to exploit his son-in-law like an indentured slave.[306] When you're at the receiving end of people or events that seem to work against you, what do you do? The first thing to know is what *not* to do.

The Four Pitfalls of Breakdowns

A captain of industry was once asked how he had become chairman of the board. He answered with his usual brevity: "Two words: right decisions." The interviewer insisted, "But how did you learn to make the right decisions?" The chairman's short retort: "One word: experience." "Yes, but how did you get experience?" "Two words," the chairman shot back, "Wrong decisions."

This chairman grasped the link between mistakes and successes— like Churchill, who used to quip that success consists of going from failure to failure without loss of enthusiasm. But most of us have a less than playful attitude toward breakdowns, even relatively minor ones. Imagine that ten minutes before you're scheduled to give a PowerPoint presentation to the board of directors of a big potential customer, the projector fails. In and of itself, a broken beamer is a minor nuisance; but given your commitment to sell the board on your multimillion-dollar project, it could be a major setback. When the going gets tough, our reaction is hard-wired into our brains: the amygdala responds to threats automatically, much as it does in apes. And our reactions tend to fall into four typical traps, which are only human and perfectly understandable. However, each of these traps is utterly counterproductive: shame, blame, hope, and hedge.

Pitfall #1: Shame. Thinking that a breakdown is something negative, even shameful, often causes us to react badly. We feel stressed, get upset, or panic. Whether the problem is about trouble with a co-worker or a deadline that can't be met, our instinct is to try to keep breakdowns secret and attempt to fix them before anybody finds out. We want to avoid bombing out or giving bad news to superiors or colleagues. We want to have it all under control before (or if ever) we go public.

But the costs of keeping breakdowns secret can be huge. In the mid-1980s Xerox executives had a rude awakening when a major new product, the 5046 mid-range copier, failed in the market because of serious reliability problems. How could this happen, given the company's focus on Leadership Through Quality (LTQ), a quality-assurance process that had been set up by the then CEO David Kearns himself? After investigating, Kearns found that Xerox managers at all levels had been all too aware of the problems but had conspired to keep them under the carpet. The cover-up had extended to the highest levels of management; the faulty copier would have never been brought to market but for this code of silence. What particularly distressed Kearns was that Xerox had set up the LTQ process precisely to prevent this kind of fiasco. But the process had failed because "the old culture of our people being afraid to deliver bad news was not yet rinsed from the company."[307] In all fairness, Kearns himself was not entirely innocent; some said he had failed to eliminate multiple management layers and had not taken down the walls between departments. Because of this twin problem, crucial information never reached the top. Whatever the cause, the bottom line is that managers did not make the breakdown public. It cost them their jobs and jeopardized Xerox's reputation and bottom line.

Pitfall #2: Blame. "I was never allowed to present to the board unless things were perfect," said a former Xerox executive. "You could only go in with good news."[308] Whoever gave bad news risked being blamed or booted out; the board would simply kill the messenger. And when directors finally forced managers to confront their poor performance, executives repeatedly blamed short-term factors, from currency fluctuations to trouble in Latin America. By the time the then president (and later CEO) Anne Mulcahy came out and spoke the truth—the company had an "unsustainable business model,"[309] she told analysts in 2000—it was too late; Xerox was already flirting with bankruptcy.

Unforeseen breakdowns, or dragons as the poet Rainer Maria Rilke called them, can make you want to rip your hair out, chew your nails, or curse everyone around you. Though a leader's ultimate test is how he or she copes in a crisis, many top managers have been known to throw temper tantrums when the world seemed to turn against them. Jeffrey Skilling, the disgraced former CEO of Enron, was so famous for his tongue-lashings, especially once Enron's implosion was imminent, that employees simply were too afraid to tell him the truth. Even whistleblower Sherron Watkins, one of Skilling's braver subordinates, chose to voice her concerns only in private rather than making them known until after Enron's collapse.

When breakdowns happen, casting blame on your colleagues, on yourself, or on the game as a whole is a major pitfall—*They're* wrong, *I'm* wrong, or *it's* wrong ("it" might be the task, the project, your job, the entire organization, or your life). A good example is Job, a fabulously rich man whose "possessions consisted of seven thousand sheep and goats, three thousand camels, five hundred pairs of cattle, five hundred she-donkeys, and very many enterprises. That man was the wealthiest man of all the people in the East."[310] But Job was not only loaded; he was also "wholesome and upright, he feared God and shunned evil. Seven sons and three daughters were born to him." Then, within hours, he lost it all.

It happened one day, when his sons and daughters were eating and drinking wine in the home of their eldest brother, that a messenger came to Job and said, "The oxen were plowing and the she-donkeys were grazing alongside them, when Sabeans befell and seized them. They struck down the servants by the edge of the sword. Only I, by myself, escaped to tell you!"

> This one was still speaking, when this [other] one came and said, "A fire of God fell from the heavens. It burned among the sheep and the servants and consumed them. Only I, by myself, escaped to tell you!"
>
> This one was still speaking, when this [other] one came and said, "The Chaldeans formed three divisions and deployed around the camels and seized them. They struck down the servants by the edge of the sword. Only I, by myself, escaped to tell you!"
>
> This one was still speaking, when this [other] one came and said, "Your sons and your daughters were eating and drinking wine in the home of their eldest brother, when behold, a great wind came from across the desert. It struck the four corners of the house, it collapsed upon the young men and killed them. Only I, by myself, escaped to tell you!"
>
> Job stood up and ripped his shirt, and he tore [the hair of] his head.[311]

Job was crushed. At first, he was able to discipline his mind. But then he finally broke down and blamed God in an unceasing stream of bile:

Job opened his mouth and cursed his day. "Why did I not die from the womb, [not] expire as I came forth from the belly? Why did the knees come to meet me? Why were breasts there for me to suckle?"[312]

It happens to the best of us, and Job was as good as they come. We may be able to tackle one breakdown, but when two- or threefold calamity strikes, we often cave in and curse our entire existence.

Pitfall #3: Hope. Too often we simply wait in the hope that the breakdown will somehow disappear if we just let it be. It won't. In the early 1930s, while banned from the British government, Churchill kept warning against Nazi aggression, but Chamberlain and many others had ridiculed him for crying wolf. Throughout the decade, they kept hoping that Hitler was not so bad after all, that the Anschluss of Austria in 1934 and the invasion of the Rhineland in 1936 were aberrations, and that Hitler's peace assurances at Munich were for real. But Churchill was not to be deterred. He had his own intelligence from reliable sources that Hitler was building a war economy. He declared a breakdown, a gap between the appeasers' inaction and the actions needed to preserve the future of democracy. Churchill shed a harsh light on reality and declared that complacency was unacceptable.

At first, his was a lone voice; but eventually he broke through the defeatism around him, built a worldwide alliance to stop the Axis powers, brought the United States into the war effort, and finally stopped Nazi aggression. This breakthrough would probably not have happened were it not for Churchill; often nothing happens, especially in organizations where people tend to pass the buck, unless someone—a leader—takes charge and cuts through business-as-usual.

A widespread example of the failure to address breakdowns head-on (on a much smaller scale, but still costly in business terms) is the custom of putting contingencies into cost estimates in capital development projects that range from buildings to bridges to oil pipelines. Say a general contractor is building a hotel and asks the client to deposit an additional $5 million in escrow as a cushion for unplanned expenses in case the project takes longer or goes over budget. But then costs spiral out of control. Even though the builders have exceeded their original estimate, nobody says anything and *nothing happens* as long as expenses stay within the higher contingency range. Since everybody hopes that somebody else will do something to avert a crisis, the unhappy customer is often left with the ballooning bill.

Losses like these are only the tip of the iceberg. A *Fortune* magazine survey of failed CEOs found a surprising commonality among them: Instead of facing breakdowns head-on, they tend to wait. "What is striking, as many CEOs told us, is that they usually know there's a problem; their inner voice is telling them, but they suppress it. Those around the CEO often recognize the problem first, but he isn't seeking information from multiple sources."[313] Worse, when CEOs feel threatened, "they focus even more on what brought them their success," adds leadership expert Warren Bennis. "They dismiss anything that clashes with their beliefs."[314] Such an attachment to old solutions is the exact opposite of what would help now. Former Mattel CEO Jill Barad's brilliant skills at public relations and promotion were what boomeranged to sabotage Mattel: Instead of giving investors the bad news, she told them twice that the toy company was doing just fine, only to see her announcements followed by immediate and huge drops in performance and shareholder value.

Pitfall #4: Hedge. Soon after their exodus from Egypt, the Jews came to the beautiful land of Canaan. Moses sent distinguished spies, one from each tribe, to reconnoiter the land and bring back strategic intelligence. He gave them a detailed checklist of questions:

> "See the Land—how is it? And the people that dwells in it—is it strong or weak? Is it few or numerous? And how is the Land in which it dwells—is it good or is it bad? And how are the cities in which it dwells—are they open or are they fortified? And how is the land—is it fertile or is it lean? Are there trees in it or not?" ... They returned from spying out the Land at the end of forty days ... They reported to him and said, "We arrived at the Land to which you sent us, and indeed it flows with milk and honey, and this is its fruit. But—the people that dwells in the Land is powerful, the cities are fortified and very great, and we also saw there the offspring of the giant. ... We cannot ascend to that people for it is too strong for us!"[315]

When the Jews heard the spies' frightening report, they questioned Moses' and Aaron's wisdom. Worse, just as they had done earlier at the Red Sea (see Chapter 2), they wavered in their commitment to the whole enterprise. "All the Children of Israel murmured against Moses and Aaron... they said to one another, 'Let us appoint a leader and let us return to Egypt!'"[316] It was open rebellion; everybody said the leaders should be fired. But the problem was not that they had committed to find the Promised Land. Quite the opposite was true: It was their hedging and equivocation. The commitment would have been the *solution*. Had the Jews stuck to their strategic intent and entered Canaan, they would not have been left wandering the desert for several more decades.

Backing off from your original objective instead of stretching to meet it can be the worst trap of all. When you are committed to something, there's bound to be a gap between your current situation and your future goal. In fact breakdowns cannot exist without prior commitments. If you're not committed to anything, you might have problems (as the Jewish saying goes, your pit might fill with snakes; you might turn into a vegetable, atrophy, or get sick), but you won't have breakdowns (or accomplishments) of size. Recall the broken projector: without the prior commitment of convincing your board to invest millions of dollars, there would be no gap, only the inconvenience of a broken machine. But lowering the bar is exactly the wrong thing to do.

Failure as Fuel

To avoid the four pitfalls of shame, blame, hope, and hedge we need a new way to look at *failure*. At first glance, failure is a bad thing that must be avoided at all costs. Old-economy giants boast of running zero-defects operations and avoiding failure altogether. The six-sigma total quality management method, with its implicit goal of producing failure levels of 3.4 defects per one million opportunities, aims for perfection; but the fewer failures you have, the fewer chances you have for learning or innovation. When the CEO coaches leaders, he uses a much different interpretation of failure, one that allows them to see—and harness—failures not as problems but as raw material for accomplishment.

The sixteenth-century kabbalist Rabbi Isaac Luria offered the insight that when God created the world, there was a malfunction. The ten vessels (*sefirot*) meant to contain the infinite light could not hold that much power, and they shattered. Because of this cosmic catastrophe, the archetypal values are out of sync, and the world as we know it is broken—full of chaos and injustice, war and terror, hunger and disease. (In the view of Luria and other kabbalists, not everything is lost though: they say that only seven of the ten vessels were fully crushed, or else the world would be in a state of *tohu vavohu*, the utter chaos that reigned before its creation.[317] This way we have at least some semblance of order and are not utterly adrift—a comforting fact, especially if you are an order-obsessed Swiss person.)[318] The breakdown of the vessels affords us an opportunity to be leaders: to fix the broken vessels and heal the world (*tikkun olam*).

Why did an omnipotent God put the tree of knowledge right in front of Adam and Eve? The Hasidic masters say that God planned the whole thing both to give them free choice and to force them to fail, and out of that original failure humanity would rise to greater heights. Ever since the original human beings, this cycle of descent and ascent has repeated throughout human history, and in fact with every leader. That is why Proverbs says, "For a *tzaddik* [righteous man, leader] falls down seven times and rises up again."[319] And Rabbi Schneur Zalman of Liadi adds, "Between one level and the next, before he can reach a higher one, he is in a state of decline from the previous level. Yet, it is written, 'Though he falls, he shall not be utterly cast down.'"[320] The bottom line: Every descent is for a higher ascent; every breakdown can turn into a breakthrough.

If you take the negativity out, a breakdown is simply a gap between the present and the future you want. This view is based on Allan Scherr's definition of breakdowns as "situations where the circumstances are inconsistent with and fall short of one's committed goals." Scherr analyzed sixteen different projects at IBM and found that breakdowns are far from bad. On the contrary, breakdowns are *necessary* for breakthroughs in productivity.[321]

Scherr was not the first to come up with this counterintuitive finding. A study of thirteen significant commercial advances in sixteen companies from 1966 to 1986 found that the one thing common to all of them was a leader's obsessive urge to solve "a problem."[322] Groundbreaking innovations common today, from the CAT scan to the microwave, from Nautilus machines to Fed-Ex, from Nike to Club Med, rose like proverbial phoenixes from the ashes of breakdowns during the original process.

A classic example of a breakthrough resulting from a breakdown is the Post-It. It all began in 1968 when Spence Silver, an inventor at 3M, found he had accidentally invented a type of glue that was tacky rather than adhesive. Silver visited every single division of 3M, but nobody could make use of his strange discovery. In fact he had to wage a battle even to get his new adhesive patented, which 3M did only with great reluctance. It was not until six years later when Silver's colleague Art Fry was on his way to a church choir rehearsal and accidentally dropped his hymn book on the ground. All the paper slips he had used to mark the pages fluttered out—and Fry had a eureka moment: He realized in a flash that he could use Silver's "bad" glue for something! Without Fry's breakdown—and Silver's having the smarts and persistence to use it as fuel for innovation—the Post-It might never have seen the light of day and would not have become one of the most popular office supplies of all time.

Or in what seems like ancient history in an age of i-Pods, take Sony, which added the small TC-D5 portable model to its series of portable stereo cassette recorders in 1978. Though popular among audiophiles, the new model was too heavy to be truly portable and too expensive at a cost of 100,000 yen. The then honorary chairman of Sony had a habit of taking a TC-D5 on overseas trips so he could listen to his music in stereo on long plane rides to Europe or North America. But he found it too bulky and heavy to schlep around airports. He could have opted to smile politely and say nothing, a response certainly not uncommon in Japan. Instead he chose to declare a breakdown to someone who could do something about it. He talked to Norio Ohga, who was executive deputy president at the time, and asked if Sony could build a smaller model with just a playback function. Out of a relatively small breakdown, harnessed to the max by Ohga, came a huge ripple effect: one of the most successful inventions in music history. Sony sold 330 million Walkmans. And Ohga, with his knack for leading from breakdown to commercial breakthrough, was on his way to becoming Sony's chairman.

Perhaps the most striking example of creating a breakthrough from a breakdown was Pfizer as it sought to develop a new heart medicine. Trial tests of the drug Sildenafil in 1994 showed unwelcome and huge (forgive the pun) side-effects: male patients who took the drug experienced increased blood flow to the penis. The drug acted by enhancing the smooth muscle relaxant effects of nitric oxide, a chemical that is normally released in response to sexual stimulation. If Pfizer managers had been ashamed, if they had conspired to keep the malfunctions a secret, if they had done nothing and waited, or if they had wavered in their commitment to make a blockbuster drug, nothing would have happened. They would have preserved the status quo and lost the company a lot of R&D money. But they made noise, and to make a long story short, out of a breakdown—a malfunctioning heart drug—a breakthrough was born. The new drug posted $1 billion in sales in its first year and became a household name: Viagra.

> **Tip:** The greater the breakdown—the gap—you can declare between where you are and where you intend to be, the greater the possible breakthrough.

Earlier innovations, too, were made by leaders who embraced failures as opportunities. The story goes that Thomas Edison made some one thousand attempts to invent the lightbulb. His contemporaries kept ridiculing his countless experiments, and even supporters counseled him to give up on his obviously quixotic quest. A young reporter came to interview him and asked him outright, "Mr. Edison, why do you persevere with this endeavor, after failing seven hundred times to make it work?" If Edison was discouraged, he didn't let it on. "Young man," he replied, "you have got it all wrong. I have not failed seven hundred times. I have not failed once. I have succeeded in proving that those seven hundred ways will not work. When I have eliminated the ways that will not work, I will find the way that will work."[323] Even when Edison triumphed in 1879 and found the incandescent light-bulb, the uphill battle was far from over—the lamp burned for only a few hours. Now Edison embarked on his next venture, testing no fewer than six thousand possible materials for the filament: carbonized filaments of every plant imaginable, including bay wood, box wood, hickory, cedar, flax, bamboo, and fibers from the tropics. Edison celebrated each time a trial failed; he insisted that each trial that did not work brought him one step closer to the trial that *would* work. He was right: Finally, in late 1880, he had produced a 16-watt bulb with a special carbonized cotton filament that could last 1,500 hours. The rest is well-lighted history, and we are indebted to his vision, persistence, and love of failure.

Today, one of the best companies at harnessing failures for innovation is Google. "Fundamentally, everything we do is experiment," said Douglas Merrill, a Google vice president for engineering. "The thing with experimentation is that you have to get data and then be brutally honest assessing it." When Google introduces new features, it has stayed true to a "fail fast" strategy: launch, listen, improve, launch again. When Google Answers, a four-year effort to build an expert answer service, failed and the company had to shut it down in late 2006, Merrill preferred to see even that failure as an experiment that yielded useful knowledge. "I don't think Answers was a failure, because we incorporated a lot of what we learned into our new custom search engine."[324] The only real disasters are the ones where you don't learn anything or where you give up.

With this new framework in mind, we need no longer be stopped by breakdowns. Instead, we can use them as jolts of energy to wake up (ourselves as well as others), to reallocate necessary resources (time, money, or relationships), and to take actions that turn the breakdown into a breakthrough.

Tool 9.1
From Lemons to Lemonade in Three Steps

How can you turn adversity into advantage in day-to-day management? Say your goal is to generate $250 million in sales this year. It's July and you're at only $80 million. You can keep the shortfall quiet, blame others, hope for the best, or lower the goal—or you can take the leadership route of declaring and managing the breakdown. If you choose the latter, apply the following three-step sequence.

Step One

Make the breakdown public in a way that interrupts business-as-usual, and tell the people who can do something about it. Your announcement of the breakdown forces you and your colleagues to confront the gulf between current and desired performance. A breakdown in this context is not a thing; it is a declaration, a call to action, an act of speech that puts you back in the driver's seat and focuses attention on the gap. That's why the rabbis counseled, "Discuss your cares with others." But not with just anyone; do so strategically, "with others who are 'others' only in the bodily sense but are completely united with him, for they empathize with him,"[325] wrote the Tzemach Tzedek (1789–1866), the Third Lubavitcher Rebbe. Above all, don't keep the breakdown secret. Unless you address it openly, it is bound to turn into a crisis that will come back to haunt you.

Sometimes a simple action speaks louder than many words, and some leaders declare breakdowns nonverbally. On a Thursday evening, December 1, 1955, after a long day as a seamstress in the Montgomery Fair department store, Rosa Parks took the usual bus home. Soon all thirty-six seats of the bus were filled, with twenty-two blacks seated from the rear and fourteen whites from the front. Driver J.P. Blake saw a white man standing in front of the bus and called out for the four "colored" passengers on the row just behind the whites to stand up and move to the back. Nothing happened: They did not move. Blake finally had to get out of the driver's seat and speak to the four: "You better make it light on yourselves and let me have those seats." Three of the four got up to stand in the back of the bus. The fourth was Parks. Many years later she told an interviewer that "one white man was left standing. When the driver noticed him standing, he spoke to us (the man and two women across the aisle) and told us to let the man have the seat. The other three all stood up."

We all know that Parks did not. She had finally had enough of being treated as a second-class citizen. As a black American, she had put up with discrimination on city buses, as well as in stores, restaurants, movie theaters, and other public places for years. She had been tired of it for a while, she and her husband had been activists for years, and yet on this cold winter evening, something within her shifted. Parks was not going to take it anymore. "The driver saw me still sitting there. He said would I stand up, and I said, 'No, I will not.'" He shouted at her to move; but now there was no way back. It was as if a switch had been thrown; she politely declined. The driver pulled the emergency brake, got out of his seat, and angrily marched over to Parks. He demanded that she move to the back of the bus; she still refused to get up—so softly that Blake would not have been able to make out her words above the drone of the bus, except that the entire bus was dead silent. "Then he said, 'I'll have you arrested.' And I told him he could do that." He left the bus and returned with a policeman. Parks was promptly taken into custody for violating segregation laws.

Instead of saying much or using big words, Rosa Parks mostly just sat there. But her simple action was one of the most effective declarations of a breakdown in history. The fact that she sat there quietly amounted to an outcry over the gap between the century-old status quo of accepted but unacceptable racial discrimination on the one hand, and a possible future of racial equality and respect on the other. She was unwilling to tolerate any longer what society had condoned for too long, and she was willing to go all the way. "Usually, if I have to face something, I do so no matter what the consequences might be. I never had any desire to give up. I did not feel that giving up would be a way to become a free person."[326] In your own life and work, ask yourself: what has become unacceptable once you think about it? Perhaps it is the insufficient partnership with a colleague or alliance partner, or the slow turnaround from sales to delivery and billing, or a new product's overblown development costs? Perhaps you are not satisfied with the way you listen to colleagues or family members, the way the board listens to you, or the lack of permission you have to challenge the head of a subsidiary? Such breakdowns are not bad in and of themselves. By declaring them as insufficient, you put them under the microscope, call on others to have a look, and make clear your intent to move to higher level, from good to great, or from great to extraordinary. In that way, you can use breakdowns for quality assurance; instead of complaining, you can declare them as gaps in quality, and call for moving them to a level of quality acceptable to you. As the nineteenth-century Rabbi Sholom DovBer Schneerson put it, "A single act is better than a thousand groans. ... Quit the groaning and work hard, and God will be gracious to you."[327] You may be surprised at the speed with which you can transcend issues.

Using the example of the $250 million sales breakdown, you might have to be a pain in the neck for a while. Set up a big flipchart right at your office entrance, and write in bold letters:

I DON'T CARE WHAT YOU THINK OF ME, BUT—
WE'RE AT $80 MILLION AND IT'S JULY.
WHAT ARE YOU GONNA DO ABOUT IT?

Step Two
Keep in mind your underlying goal, without which there would be no gap. By declaring the breakdown, you serve

public notice that something is unacceptable *in relation to a particular commitment*. It might not even be inherently bad; but relative to your commitment, it shows up as grossly inadequate. In our example, current sales by themselves are not a problem; they are just that, current sales. They are insufficient only against the background of a $250 million goal. Remember, and help others remember, why everyone committed themselves in the first place. Why did you and your team choose this game? What would be missing in your lives, in your organization, or in the world if you gave up or stuck with business-as-usual?

At this stage, you may have to be a "wall" for people's commitments so they "kill the alternative," as a former boss and mentor of the CEO used to put it when missing the goal was simply not an option. In many ways, your job as a leader is to remind your colleagues of their original commitment when they forget. Eighteen years ago the CEO led a global enrollment and education campaign in twenty-seven countries. The team in Mexico had set a challenging monthly campaign goal; the end of the month was fast approaching and they had been out of touch. So the CEO called the team leader and asked how it was going. She said, "They have revoked their goal for the month—they just can't see how they'll meet it." For a moment, he thought he should simply defer to her seniority and let it go. But then he told her it would make a real difference to morale worldwide if the Mexican team led the way, and asked her if they could all recommit to their goal. Whatever she ended up saying to them, it worked. They recommitted, delivered the goal, and boosted their confidence for all future campaign cycles.

Step Three

Call a meeting or teleconference with all relevant stakeholders, and brainstorm breakthrough options—extraordinary actions you could take to fill the gap between status quo and desired result. Ask your colleagues: if we don't change anything, where will we likely end the year (for example $150 million)? If we were on-target to meet our goal, what would the desired performance level look like right now? What in this breakdown is an opportunity in disguise? What new pathways could we take to get to the finish line? What resources or opportunities have we left untapped? Don't be afraid to wake people up and rattle them enough so they shift their focus, engage in new thinking, and consider openings they haven't seen before. Be sure to step back from your fixation on old pathways or solutions that may have worked in the past but are used up or too limited now.

Tip: Don't keep hitting your head against the wall; instead, transcend a breakdown by creating a *bigger* commitment. Instead of crying over a lost customer, see what whole new commercial breakthrough becomes available with the time and resources freed up from the loss. Or if you have a bad working relationship, co-create a vision that is so great that it encompasses even the agenda of your adversary and becomes the vessel for a whole new level of partnership.

Jack Welch defined leadership as "looking reality straight in the eye and then acting upon it with as much speed as you can."[328] Sounds simple, but few people have the guts to do it; and you cannot possibly take on every problem in your environment. So choose your battles carefully: Be strategic about which breakdowns you declare and manage, and let go of the other ones, at least for now. No matter what you do, remember this: A true leader sees the openings rather than the obstacles, the good in any challenge, the light at the end of every tunnel, the sweet lemonade in every sour lemon. It is an attitude switch that will make you unstoppable.

Tip: Until declaring and managing breakdowns becomes second nature, you may want to make that method a routine: every Wednesday, for example, declare three key breakdowns and turn them into breakthroughs in quality, speed, or money.

The Bottom Line

- The path of leaders–from Adam and Eve to Moses, from Joseph to Job, from Churchill to Rosa Parks, from Intel to Pfizer–is fraught with breakdowns. Without breakdowns, leadership would be unnecessary; a manager or even a caretaker would suffice.

- The best leaders feed on breakdowns to create breakthroughs. Those who can turn adversity into advantage are unstoppable.

- If things don't go your way, it's only human to fall into four traps: 1. Shame (you feel terrible, but hide the breakdown and pretend everything is fine so that nobody finds out); 2. Blame (you blame the game, others, or yourself); 3. Hope (you wait and hope for the best); and/or 4. Hedge (you set a less ambitious goal). These reactions are all perfectly understandable, but utterly counterproductive.

- We need a new understanding of failure, based on the reality that breakdowns are correlated to breakthroughs in productivity and innovation (or as the Hasidic saying goes, "for every descent a greater ascent").[329] Commercial breakthroughs, from the Post-It note to Viagra, were each a phoenix that arose from the ashes of a breakdown.

- Turning adversity to advantage happens in a three-step process: 1. You loudly declare the breakdown to the people who can do something about it, and make clear that inaction is unacceptable. 2. You revisit your underlying original commitment (for example, to find the Promised Land or invent the lightbulb) and rededicate yourself to it. 3. You brainstorm new pathways to meeting the commitment, declare the breakthrough, and above all, take extraordinary, immediate, and decisive action (for example, parting the Red Sea, vanquishing Nazi aggression, or turning the small print about side-effects of your cardiovascular drug into large print and rebranding the heart drug into a lifestyle drug called Viagra).

CHAPTER TEN

Commandment X
Don't Covet: In *Their* Shoes

*If you want to raise a man from mud and filth, do not think it is enough
to stay on top and reach a helping hand down to him.
You must go all the way down yourself, down into the mud and filth.
Then take hold of him with strong hands
And pull him and yourself out into the light.*
—Martin Buber

Staying aloof is not an option, but an act of cowardice.
—Eleanor Roosevelt

THE TENTH COMMANDMENT: *"You shall not covet your
neighbor's house. You shall not covet your neighbor's wife, nor
his manservant, nor his maidservant, nor his bull, nor his donkey, nor anything that is your neighbor's."* Envy is everywhere;
we look at other people's lives from the outside, and their
grass often looks greener. But instead of being jealous of the
possessions and successes of others, the most effective leaders are able to understand how people tick and see the world
from their vantage point. With the rise of global markets, outsourcing, offshoring, and virtual teams, your ability to stand
in the shoes of alliance partners, negotiating opponents, and
even competitors or enemies, has become an indispensable
strategic competence. In this final chapter you will learn the
pinnacle of leadership: How to decode the mindset of people
with different value systems and be a global citizen who gets
the job done in (or with) any culture.

King Solomon, one of the great leaders of all time, could make his proverbial Solomonic judgments because he stood in the shoes of those who came before him. In a famous case, two women, both innkeepers and both harlots, appeared in his Jerusalem court, each claiming the same baby boy as hers. They had given birth within a few days of each other; one of the two babies had died because of his mother's negligence (she had accidentally smothered him in her sleep). Now each woman accused the other of having switched the dead baby with the surviving one.

> One woman said: "Please, my lord, I and this woman dwell in one house, and I gave birth while with her in the house. On the third day after I gave birth, this woman gave birth as well. We [were] together; there was no outsider with us in the house; only the two of us were in the house. The son of this woman died during the night because she lay upon him. She arose during the night and took my son from my side while your maidservant was asleep, and laid him in her bosom, and her dead son she laid in my bosom. When I arose in the morning to nurse my son, behold, he was dead! When I studied him in the morning, I realized it was not the son to whom I had given birth."
>
> But the other woman said, "It is not so! My son is the live one, and your son is the dead one!"
>
> But this one said, "It is not so! Your son is the dead one, and my son is the live one!" And they went on speaking before the king.

Finally Solomon held up a hand, and the women fell silent.

> The king said, "this one claims, 'This is my son, who is alive, and your son is the dead one,' and this one claims, 'It is not so! Your son is the dead one, and my son is the live one.'" So the king said, "Fetch me a sword!" and they brought a sword before the king. The king said, "Cut the living child in two and give half to one and half to the other."
>
> The woman whose son was the live one spoke to the king—because her compassion was aroused for her son—and she said, "Please, my lord, give her the living newborn, and do not put it to death!"

> But the other one said, "Neither mine nor yours shall he be. Cut!"
> The king spoke up and said, "Give her [the first one] the living newborn and do not put it to death; she is his mother!"[330]

It was arguably the first major recorded decision in the history of legal jurisprudence. It was also an example of psychological insight. By threatening to cut the infant in half, King Solomon had forced the true mother to express her selfless love and come out with the truth. Only a mother would love her baby enough to give him up rather than see him killed.

(In a modern version of the story, two mothers-in-law came before Solomon, each claiming that the young man who was with them was her son-in-law. King Solomon said, "Cut him in half." The first mother-in-law cried, "Yes, do it, do it!" The other pleaded, "No, please don't!" Solomon ruled, "The first woman is the real mother-in-law.")

We now come full circle. Chapter 1 was about leading yourself and the courage to be you. Now, in this final chapter, we return to that original theme, but this time at a much higher level: Coveting your neighbor's possessions is one of the gravest and most pernicious sins. When you pit yourself, your accomplishments, or your material belongings against those of others, when you compare what you have to what they have, be it more money, or a more advanced educational degree, or a more attractive spouse, you lose your power because you are looking at others from the outside in. In truth you have no idea how life is for other people. Though it may sound paradoxical, instead of eyeing your neighbor's possessions, the highest competence is to stand in his or her shoes looking at the world from *that* point of view.

This notion is based on the Golden Rule, a universal tenet (all major religions have their own version) first stated in the Torah: "Do not seek revenge or bear a grudge against one of your people, but love your neighbor as yourself."[331] The Talmud says that two millennia ago, during the reign of Herod, a gentile came to the eminent Jewish scholar Shammai in Jerusalem and declared he was willing to become Jewish if someone could just teach him the whole knowledge of Torah while standing on one foot. Shammai flew into a rage. What insolence! He seized a builder's measuring stick and drove out the gentile, who promptly went to Shammai's chief rival, Hillel, for a second opinion. Hillel, one of the towering religious leaders in Jewish history who lived in Jerusalem during the reign of the Roman emperor Augustus and was associated with developing the Talmud, gave one of his trademark bottom-lines: "That which you despise do not not do unto others. That is the whole Torah; the rest is commentary; go and learn."[332] (In another pithy one-liner, Hillel summed up all of Jewish philosophy and leadership: "If I am not for myself, who will be? And when I am for myself, what am I? And if not now, when?")[333]

Standing With "Them"

The code word is empathy: the identification with and understanding of another's situation, feeling, and motives. Without empathy, you won't see all perspectives, you'll miss out on vital intelligence, your judgment will be impaired, and you'll likely make decisions that are not best for all concerned. You need not be as public about your empathy as former President Bill Clinton who was famous for saying "I feel your pain" (when Clinton went to India, many villagers said afterwards they had never been heard with such complete attention). But you must allow those who tell you about their trials and tribulations to have an effect on your heart. Rabbi Shmuel, the fourth Rebbe of Lubavitch, was once asked why he perspired so profusely whenever he counseled people who came to see him. He answered, "If I am to counsel each man well, I must experience his distress exactly as he himself experiences it; I must divest myself of my own garments and clothe myself in his. Afterwards, I put my own garments back on; and when the next person comes, I put on his garment, so for every person who comes in with a question, I have to dress and undress."[334] Rabbi Shmuel knew that to truly be helpful to people, he had to get into their skin. That's why he sweated so much and had to change his shirt each hour.

Rabbi Shmuel's son Shalom DovBer used to play a game with his older brother Zalman Aharon when they were both teenagers and long before they became famous rabbis. The game was called Rebbe and Hasid. Zalman played the role of a rabbi, and Shalom came to him as a

Hasid asking for advice: What was the best way to fix a mistake he had made? Zalman gave him objective advice. Shalom told him, "You are not a rebbe. A rebbe would hear the problem of his fellow man, and before doing anything else, would first *krechts* (Yiddish for an Italian-style sob) and sigh and say 'oy vey,' and feel the full pain of his neighbor's problem. You did not." Decades later, Rabbi Zalman Aharon did not become the rebbe (leader) of the Lubavitch movement; Rabbi Shalom DovBer did.

Even Jack Welch, a leader not exactly known for his compassion (he said about his merciless layoffs in the 1980s that earned him the nickname Neutron Jack, "we didn't fire the people...we fired the positions, and the people had to go"),[335] after his retirement softened a bit and came to remind business leaders that "any time you are managing people, your job is not about you, it's about them. ... It starts out about you as you go as an individual into a company. But once you get a leadership job, it moves very quickly to being about them. You have to hire great people who can excite, and make you look good and make the company win. It quickly goes from 'you' to 'them.' The higher you rise, the less it's about you. It's about them."[336] So you need to stand with "them" or you might lose your most valuable assets.

But while Welch was wont to dress people down in his office (as noted in chapter 6), just like an irate headmaster dealing with schoolboys, and was known for his hard-charging style, his successor Jeffrey Immelt, GE's chairman and CEO since 2001, brought a new, more diplomatic style to the table. It may be a more quiet style, but one more suited to the twenty-first century, a truly global business culture, and to sustainable high performance. One of Immelt's top ten management principles on his Things Leaders Do checklist is: "*LIKE PEOPLE*: Today it's employment at will. Nobody's here who doesn't want to be here. So it's critical to understand people, to always be fair, and to want the best of them."[337] It is this principle of pulling for the best, not pushing—of trusting, not thrusting—that generates long-term co-leaders who think and act like co-owners of the business.

Diplomatic leadership works much better if you are willing to check your ego at the door. A good example is Walter Shipley, who in his role as chairman and CEO quietly led two successful banking mergers in a row (a rare feat when two-thirds of all mergers fail) that eventually became Chase Manhattan Bank. What was Shipley's secret? "Some people's philosophy is I win, you lose," he said. "Our philosophy is that the best is when both sides feel they've come out winners." Though Shipley stands a towering six feet eight, he never enjoyed the star power of a Jack Welch or Sandy Weill. The key: he is modest and self-effacing to a fault, and willing to share power. "Walter has been able to do the deals he has because he has a very contained ego," said Larry Bossidy, the former head of Allied Signal. When Chemical Bank hitched up with Manufacturer's Hanover in 1991, Shipley, then Chemical's CEO, agreed to take a back seat as president of the joined company and let John McGillicuddy of Manufacturer's take the reins as CEO. His humility paid off: He succeeded McGillicuddy in 1994 and a year later produced his second blockbuster deal with Chase, which secured the new bank's place in the top tier of financial institutions. Even though Chemical clearly took over Chase, Shipley adopted the Chase name and bent over backward to make room for Chase's then CEO Thomas Labrecque, insisting the two should be considered equals.[338]

Lost in Translation

Contrast Immelt and Shipley with Jürgen Schrempp, the ousted head of the former DaimlerChrysler. Back in 1998 the German company Daimler, maker of luxury sedans and precision aircraft engines, had bought the U.S. car company Chrysler. Financially it seemed like a perfect idea and was hailed as a marriage made in heaven. Daimler's stock was then worth $48 billion, and it issued an additional $36 billion of its stock to complete the acquisition.

But trouble started soon. Without a hint of Schadenfreude, the CEO recalls his own prediction, in 1999, that the merger of Daimler and Chrysler would fall on its face. The writing was on the wall: Even before the deal, Schrempp had declined an invitation to meet with the Chrysler board. "We just wanted to feel more comfortable with the merger and ask some questions," former Chrysler director John Neff recalled. But inexplicably, "He thought he didn't have to do it. I saw it as an example of his arrogance."[339]

Just ten months after the companies combined, the American top executive in charge of integrating the operations in Stuttgart with those in Auburn Hills resigned. Chrysler's president Bob Lutz had revitalized Chrysler in the early 1990s with trendsetting designs on a tight budget. But in 1998, his boss, Chrysler chairman Bob Eaton, did not give Lutz a position in the combined company. Lutz quit and was followed by a dozen Chrysler executives—a major talent drain. "The guys who were the soul of Chrysler walked out the door," said veteran auto analyst Maryann Keller.[340]

Though hyping DaimlerChrysler as a "merger of equals," Europeans dominated the new entity from the start. Co-chairman Schrempp put himself firmly in charge, pushed all but two Americans from the management board of the combined company, and in 2000 installed his trusted German aide Dieter Zetsche at Chrysler's helm. Zetsche promptly fired three more Chrysler top executives.

What topped it off was that, in the words of *Newsweek*, "Schrempp, the multinationalist, seems to have confused German business culture with U.S. culture."[340] Schrempp was blind to a major cultural difference. In Germany, the only stockholder to fear was Daimler's biggest owner, Deutsche Bank. In the United States, companies need to worry about all big holders, especially takeover tycoon Kirk Kerkorian, who came all the way to Berlin to meet with Schrempp. But Schrempp blew off the meeting and went to his ranch in South Africa instead. Kerkorian sued for $2 billion.

The result: Schrempp's inability to stand in the shoes of the other side contributed to massive post-merger pains, layoffs of over 37,000 people, billions in sunk costs, a huge drop in shareholder value, and ultimately an ugly breakup. In a globalizing world of free agents and cross-border collaboration, a lack of empathy and diplomacy has become a deadly sin.

What is the truest definition of Globalization? Princess Diana's death. Why? An English princess with an Egyptian boyfriend crashes in a French tunnel, driving a German car with a Dutch engine, driven by a Belgian who was drunk on Scottish whiskey, followed closely by Italian paparazzi on Japanese motorcycles, treated by an American doctor using Brazilian medicines.

And this is sent to you by an American, using Bill Gates' technology which he enjoyed stealing from the Japanese. And you are probably reading this on one of the IBM clones that use Taiwanese-made chips and Korean-made monitors, assembled by Bangladeshi workers in a Singapore plant, transported by lorries driven by Indians, hijacked by Indonesians, unloaded by Sicilian longshoremen, trucked by Mexican illegal aliens, and finally sold to you.

That, my friend, is globalization.[342]

According to the Torah, there once was a time when "the whole earth was of one language and of common purpose" and everyone understood everyone else effortlessly. But then we coveted more and built the tower of Babel, and God's action came swiftly. He "confused the language of the whole earth, and from there scattered them over the face of the whole earth."[343] For several thousand years since then, we have had a hard time knowing how others felt. But when you deal with knowledge workers who often work remotely (in virtual teams, outsourcing or offshoring), you cannot simply tell them what to do; you need to understand their value-system to work with them effectively. Few are trained to do so. According to the ECA International study "Trends in Managing Mobility 2007," while more companies than ever send employees abroad, only 25 percent test "soft" factors like cross-cultural management skills.[344]

This goes not only for your employees, but also your customers. In a flattening world, how do you serve emboldened consumers who no longer passively accept your products but want to have a hand in their design? As a doctor, how do you interact with patients who reject your treatment plan because they have checked the Internet for a second, third, and fourth opinion? How do you know what matters to people in other parts of the world? How will prospects from China or India, Brazil or Russia (the four emerging markets with middle classes that vastly outnumber consumers in the United States or Europe) feel about your Web site when they visit online?

And finally, how do you deal with competitors, and even enemies? Say you are a Google executive and take on Microsoft, or a U.S. military officer fighting Al Qaeda. How do you foresee the strategic moves of your adversary?

"From My Enemies I Became Wise"

To answer questions like these, you need to build your cross-cultural savvy. Collaborating with people from other value-systems means, to "understand the differences, act on the commonalities," in the concise words of John Marks, founder of Search for Common Ground, a non-profit organization dedicated to conflict resolution that has brought cross-cultural understanding to war-torn places like Rwanda and the Middle East.[345] Modern-day global citizens need to have a mind-set like that of the biblical warrior Yiftach who had been thrown out by his brothers because his mother was a concubine, but who became Israel's army chief, a judge, and quite possibly the world's first diplomat. Why? Because of his openness of mind (his name comes from the word *poteach*, open), Yiftach did not go to war with his enemies until he had talked to them; and he started negotiations by first asking them questions about their perspective, for example, "What is there between you and me that you have come to me to make war in my land?" and only then stating his own people's interests.[346]

Isn't that going too far, though? How can we be empathic in today's world when terrorists are plotting to eliminate our way of life? Isn't that tantamount to appeasement, and didn't we see how British appeasement in the 1930s allowed Hitler to take over half of Europe? No; empathy with other people's world view does not mean moral relativism. Not everybody is right; there *is* right and wrong. Yet unless you stand not only in your friends', but also your adversaries' shoes, you will neither understand their values and thinking nor foresee their strategic moves, let alone defeat them. That is why King David, the slayer of the mighty Goliath, exclaimed: "From my enemies I became wise."[347]

Even the U.S. armed forces have learned the lesson. A few days after 9/11, the CEO received a call from the U.S. Military Academy at West

Point. The colonel on the phone, head of West Point's leadership program, was brief. "Tom, we need you over here. When can you come?"
The CEO arrived at West Point and was treated to a nice lunch with
several officers. Afterward, he thought the colonel and he would have a
quiet meeting on a potential collaboration. But the colonel announced,
"I have assembled the faculty so they can all hear your presentation."
Presentation? What presentation? The CEO had nothing prepared. In a
split second, he decided to wing it: he gave the professors a mini-work-
shop on cross-cultural management. Several points he made were quite
risqué, such as, "The U.S. administration had it coming to them" or
"Let's face it, our government was ethnocentric and blind!" Some faculty members sat there with their arms crossed, leaning way back in
their chairs; they obviously had a hard time listening to this kind of
wake-up call by a Swiss-American who was not even born in the United
States and had never served in the U.S. military. But the CEO thought,
"Better tell them the truth," and went for broke.

The gamble paid off. The highest brass of the U.S. Army had realized, it turned out, that military officers needed to be trained not only
as competent fighters, but also as skillful diplomats. It was not a question of playing nice with Al Qaeda; it was a strategic intelligence issue
of decoding how Islamist terrorists ticked in order to anticipate their
moves. The Army knew what many companies don't: empathy isn't
merely a people skill reserved for use by human resources departments—it's a strategic competence. The CEO pointed out to the faculty that to truly know Al Qaeda, its culture and ways of thinking, West
Point cadets needed to study things like the Qur'an, the history of
Islam, and world history from Islam's perspective. (One professor
asked: "What if the cadets like the Qur'an more than the U.S. Constitution?" The CEO shot back with a Jewish-style counter-question:
"How much confidence do you have in our Constitution?") Ultimately,
West Point asked the CEO to help integrate global skills with its cur-
riculum. Now all leadership courses have a cross-cultural component.

This skillset may take a generation to stick and make a difference in
the battlefield. It is a crucial skillset now that the U.S. must fight a new
enemy: networks instead of nation-states. In network warfare, or Net
War in military lingo, traditional armed forces, organized in a strict hier-

archy from generals down to privates, are pitted against networks that have flat command structures and are widely dispersed, self-reliant, highly agile, and able to improvise. To foresee their strategic moves and fight them effectively, Western militaries must put themselves in their minds and hearts to truly understand what they think, how they think, and where they think *from*.

If this is true for defense, it is just as true in business competition. To anticipate Google's moves, Microsoft strategists must put themselves in Google's shoes. The Rabbi asked the business leader Joseph Steinberg, president and chief operating officer of Leucadia, the holding company known as the Mini Berkshire Hathaway, what his worst failures had been. Steinberg said with a wry smile, "I cannot tell you those." What he did say was that his company had lost a lot of money because it could not sell Pepsi in Russia. Leucadia had bought a license to distribute Pepsi-Cola in the former Soviet Union, but it grasped a trivial reality too late: you could not sell Russians cold drinks at the time. Steinberg said it was like the proverbial task of selling ice to Eskimos: "You have to teach people to make ice-cubes before you can teach them to drink Pepsi." Leucadia was forced to sell the license back to Pepsi, at a loss of $60 million. The point of the story: get into the shoes of your customer.

The prophet Ezekiel saw a four-faced angel who moved simultaneously east and west, north and south. This is the skillset needed by both international and diversity managers. They must see the world (including competitors, customers, suppliers, or problems, as the case may be) from several points of view at the same time. During World War II, Chinue Sugihara (likely a relative of SelectBooks publisher Kenzi Sugihara) was stationed in Lithuania as Japan's consul-general. When the Germans advanced on Vilnius in July 1940, only Sugihara and a Dutch consul remained. Getting visas to leave the country was almost impossible, so in desperation Lithuanian Jews turned to the Japanese consul general, whose government, they knew, was allied with the Nazis. Skeptical about their plea, Sugihara asked his Jewish visitors, "Why do the Germans hate you so much?" Their answer was brilliant: *"Because we are Asians."* With one simple sentence, the Jewish leaders had put themselves both in the shoes of the Germans *and* of Japan's consul general, and saved themselves by seeing the agenda of the other side and knowing just what to say to push the buttons of a Japanese. The result: Defying the strict regulations of his own superiors in Tokyo, the consul general and his wife spent four long weeks writing thousands of visas by hand. According to witnesses, after the consulate closed and he had to leave his post, he was still writing visas in his hotel room, and after boarding the train, throwing visas out of the train window into the crowd of desperate refugees as the train pulled out. Of some six thousand Jews armed with Sugihara visas, almost all were saved and ended up living in Japan until after the war—including several of the Rabbi's teachers who settled in Japanese-held Shanghai until after the war. Sugihara's humility kept him from discussing his courageous deeds even after the war was long over; though Israel bestowed the Righteous Among the Nations award on him in 1985, the year before he died, it was only after his death that his heroism came to light.

Tool 10.1
Theater—Acting Out the Other Side

A less dramatic but equally effective example of standing in the other side's shoes is evidenced in a workshop held outside London with railroad suppliers for the Chunnel, the tunnel connecting Britain and France. The suppliers were charged with building an integrated rail system on both the French and the English side. Naturally, there was quite a culture clash. The British side didn't communicate as directly as the French side, and they thought the French unreliable; the French couldn't understand why the Brits avoided clear-cut deadlines and agreements, while the Brits thought the French were overly legalistic and impatient, to name but a few mutual opinions. The workshop facilitators had the French and British firms split into breakout groups, whose assignment was to answer three simple questions on flipcharts: What are your concerns (or complaints) about the other side; what are your expectations of them; and what are your promises to them?

The answers the two groups came up with gave them some clarity. But then came the clincher—they had to turn the tables and put themselves in the shoes of the other side. On a different flipchart, they had to answer the same questions but from the other side's perspective, as if this view were their own. Looking through the eyes of their alliance partners, what were their concerns, expectations, and promises? It was as if a veil had been lifted. They came back into the plenary session and said, "Now I see why the other guys always teased us about shoddy quality, about being on time, about being too rigid," etc.

The process is like that of actors, who have to *become* the character they play. Imagine how you would see the world if you were a murderer, a baker, or a general. In a global bank that was having trouble integrating its private banking and investment banking operations after multiple mergers, the private bankers (although they would not admit this) tended to be more conservative, straight-laced, hierarchical, and risk-averse; the investment banking culture on the other side was much more freewheeling, testosterone-driven, participatory, and ad-hoc. Once the senior managers from each side embodied the other side, however, they were able to come up with operating rules—what to do or not to do—that worked in interacting with the other side. The result was that joint productivity of the units improved dramatically within months.

This technique works with multiple groups, too. The Australian subsidiary of a global pharmaceutical company wanted to improve its dealings with Asian cultures, from India to China to Korea; but more importantly, the Australians suffered from cultural clashes with Swiss headquarters, whose senior managers had never checked their assumptions (for example, about Australia being a stagnant market, or about Australians being notoriously lazy and on permanent vacation). No company CEO or chairman had ever come to Australia. The managing director of the Australian subsidiary (who was actually British) first gave the Australian perspective on the Swiss. Then he acted out the Swiss perspective, saying things like, "We make the rules; you must play by the rules ..." The other participants laughed so hard at his dour face and his bureaucratic tone of voice that they almost fell off their chairs. It was a revelation; putting themselves in the shoes of the other side gave the company vital intelligence for its strategy. The results: Within nine months the Australian subsidiary was recognized as a champion performer within the global firm.

Unfortunately, most of us loathe seeing the world from the point of view of another person or culture. This is most apparent in negotiations, where the biggest cause of failure is the negotiator's fixation on his or her own viewpoint. Say you want to buy a company, and the seller has just told you through an attorney that your first offer is far below the property's market value. Most of us get so attached to getting the deal done that we cannot coolly see the negotiation from the seller's point of view. Enter what is known as the Onion Model, first developed by the Dutch cultural anthropologist Geert Hofstede, which allows us to decode the mindset of another person or culture.

Tool 10.2
Decoding Another Mindset: The Onion Model[348]

How can you peer into another person's mindset? The more mastery you have in decoding, and ultimately influencing, a person's world view, the more power you have vis-à-vis his or her actions and results. The simplest tool for understanding another person comes from cultural anthropology. Using the Onion Model, you can distinguish three layers of culture:

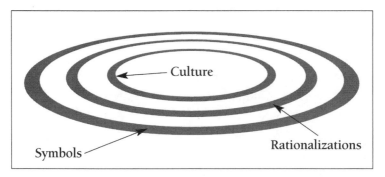

Figure 10.1: The Onion Model (adapted from Vijay Sathe 1985)

The outermost and most apparent layer, Symbols, is made up of what you can readily observe. It could be something historic or trivial: a specific event or behavior, a company's logo, a dress code, how people talk, or how they eat. For example, let's say you observe that Swiss people tend to refrain from taking sides in conflicts; and indeed, Switzerland stayed neutral in World War II. The second layer, Rationalizations, is how people rationalize or justify the first layer: "The way we do things around here is … because …" For example, the Swiss might say that neutrality, which was guaranteed by the Great Powers at the Vienna Congress in 1815, is good for a small country with powerful neighbors, and has made for good business with anybody, regardless of the trading partner's political bent.

The third and innermost layer, Culture, consists of fundamental attitudes, behaviors, or past decisions—in short, a world view—that have become so automatic that they are invisible, and perhaps even unconscious. What is it that people don't even know they don't know? These blind spots are what we call culture (based on the Latin *colere*, to plow or cultivate), and this basic world view is the source of all the actions, events and behaviors you have observed at the Symbol level of the onion. For example, if you happen to be near a computer, look at the keyboard. Is the position of the letter A really the most efficient position, given how often we type that letter? No. But somehow QWERTY has become the standard,

and most people never question where its design came from.
Answer: The QWERTY keyboard was deliberately designed to
slow down the typing so that the keys would not jam in early
mechanical typewriters. When the design was patented in
1874, it was a sensible idea. But with the advent of electrical
typewriters and computers, the QWERTY keyboard makes no
sense anymore. And yet, despite proposals for a change of the
keyboard design, there is no change. We all plow ahead on our
keyboards. That is a perfect example of culture in the context
of the onion model. How can you decode this innermost,
invisible mindset? An elegant way involves four facets: the
founders, heroes, villains, and defining moments.

Who were the founders?

A group of farmers from the center of Switzerland met at the
Rütli (a meadow at Lake Lucerne) in 1291 and made a collective oath, known as the *Rütlischwur*, to get rid of their foreign
oppressors and fight for independence. They fiercely valued
their autonomy; they believed in sharing power (which may be
what later led the Swiss to establish a seven-member executive,
the Federal Council, instead of a single head of state); and they
were stubborn.

To understand U.S. culture, you would want to study the
country's founding fathers, who enshrined their values of life,
liberty and the pursuit of happiness in their Declaration of
Independence. (By contrast, no European founding document,
least of all the Swiss, offers such a fundamental right to pursue
happiness. As a Swiss, you do your duty, and then you die;
that's it.)

Who are the heroes?

The myth of William Tell, who ambushed the Hapsburg vassal
Hermann Gessler and catalyzed a movement to throw out the
Hapsburgs and found Switzerland, is basic to understanding
why Switzerland fiercely guards its independence, so much so
that it waited more than fifty years before joining the United
Nations, and has thus far steadfastly refused European Union

membership. A modern-day Swiss hero is Roger Federer, who embodies Swiss neutrality and diplomacy (he has never had a bad word to say about his opponents, while quietly obliterating them), top quality and precision (his game is like clockwork), perseverance and long-term commitment (Switzerland has been around for more than seven hundred years).

Modern American heroes might include business leaders like Steve Jobs (who stands for pioneering new ground, cutting-edge innovation, creativity, entrepreneurialism, and brazen confidence) and Warren Buffett (who embodies business savvy, hard work, philanthropy, a down-to-earth folksy attitude, and making lots of money). Both are highly successful self-made men. (Interestingly, in other cultures business leaders are less revered; they might even be mistrusted, which might explain why the European Union, for example, has tougher standards than the United States for what constitutes a monopoly.[349])

Who are the villains?

When decoding a culture, it is important to also see the anti-heroes. Who are the villains or outcasts? What behaviors are not permissible, even taboo, in the dominant culture? In Switzerland, outsiders who might upset the apple cart tend to be mistrusted. In Cuba, the Latin machismo culture, including the state, oppresses and ridicules homosexuals. In the United States, the villains might include communists or smokers. Atheism is permissible, but atheists find themselves clearly outside the mainstream, even suspect. For example, Rep. Pete Stark of California came out as the first openly atheist member of Congress in March 2007; if there are any other atheists in the 435-member House or the 100-member Senate, they surely are not coming out. It is rare for U.S. politicians to win political office unless they vociferously affirm their belief in God—not usually a requirement for politicians in other countries.

What were the defining moments?

Wars and other (e.g., economic) crises can be defining

moments in shaping a culture, when an entire collectivity makes a fundamental decision like "Never again ..." (as Germany and Japan did after World War II when they decided never again to attack other countries militarily). The defining moment that led to the fundamental decision for Swiss neutrality was probably the Thirty-Years War (1618–48), when the Swiss realized that they were not able to compete with Europe's great powers, above all France and its absolutist king, Louis XIV.

In U.S. culture, World Wars I and II helped shape a self-image of America as the good guy fighting against the bad guys in order to save the world. President Wilson declared that the United States was fighting World War I to "make the world safe for democracy." U.S. participation in World War II prevented Nazi Germany's world dominance. Both wars ended the previous U.S. policy of isolationism and neutrality in the affairs of Europe which had been the norm since the 1823 Monroe Doctrine. By entering World War II, the United States actively embraced a new role: that of saving the world—first from Nazism, then from Communism and most recently from Islamic terrorism. Since the end of World War II, the U.S. has seen itself as a benevolent hegemon, imposing democracy in Germany and Japan, going to war in Korea, Vietnam, and the Persian Gulf, underwriting much of the UN system, and monitoring elections in Zambia, among other pursuits.

This noble stance had many beneficial effects. Examples can be seen in the Marshall Plan, in which the United States sponsored the reconstruction of Europe after World War II, or the fact that the United States still underwrites about one-quarter of the regular UN budget. But at the same time, its commitment to help the world has at times turned the United States into a global policeman and has pitted it against those who have felt that the U.S. was exerting undue influence in the internal affairs of other countries. For better or for worse, the attitude of "We know what's good for you" has become an unquestioned cultural assumption not only of U.S. foreign policy, but also of U.S. multinationals.

Life Is Plural

Have you ever been rubbed the wrong way, say, by a flight attendant? Welcome to the club. As a beginner's exercise in embracing another - person's mindset, put yourself in the shoes of a flight attendant for just a moment (believe it or not, airline personnel must take their shoes off at the screening machines just like the rest of us). "Often we arrive with our beverage carts, obviously ready to take their drink order," said Robert Ward, a flight attendant based in San Francisco, "but the customer will wait until we have asked once or twice before removing their headphones and saying, 'What?' They're civil under duress. It's feeling that 'I am being nice because I have to be nice, and I'm not going to be any nicer than I have to be.'" Alan Boswell, a US Airways flight attendant, has experienced the same cold shoulder. On a typical flight, "I got to row four before I heard a single 'please' or 'thank you.' I had gone through thirteen people."[350]

That is peanuts compared to Mary Sutphen's story. On a flight from New York to Amsterdam, a passenger first cursed her for refusing to serve him another whiskey, then kicked her in the knee, and finally decided to get her attention by urinating on her jump seat. On arrival, he was met by the local authorities at the aircraft door. "I will never understand what happens to people when they get on an airplane," said Sutphen. "Some people check their brains with their bags."[351]

When you are in a plane or another enclosed space, it is easy to see only your own point of view, feel that you must fend for yourself, and guard your space in a world that's reduced to you-or-me thinking. In fact, since on aircraft we are all interdependent, they are great laboratories for developing cross-cultural empathy. On a plane, you constantly fight for limited resources and against encroaching elbows, crying babies, overstuffed overhead bins, or coffee spilling on your open laptop (especially if you fly coach). Life on a plane is a microcosm of life on the planet.

In moments like this, Jewish philosophy comes as a godsend (quite literally). The very word for life in Hebrew, *chayim*, is a plural term (the *-im* ending indicates the masculine plural). Jewish tradition holds that without a *minyan* (a quorum of ten Jews) you cannot pray *kaddish* (the mourner's prayer) or read the Torah scroll in public; no Jew, no matter how great elsewhere in life, can do so unless a *minyan* is present. This age-old rule promotes a collective spirit, akin to the Jewish adage that two people sitting together are better than the best person sitting alone. Life does not transpire within an individual existence; as even the brilliant individual Albert Einstein recognized:

> A human being is part of the whole called by us "Universe," a part limited in time and space. He experiences himself, his thoughts and feelings as something separated from the rest—a kind of optical delusion of consciousness. This delusion is a kind of prison for us, restricting us to our personal desires and to affection for a few persons nearest us. Our task must be to free ourselves from this prison by widening our circle of compassion to embrace all living creatures and the whole nature in its beauty.
>
> A hundred times everyday I remind myself that my inner and outer life depend on the labors of other men, living and dead, and that I must exert myself in order to give in the measure as I have received and am still receiving.[352]

Take a moment to reflect on how your life, in fact your every activity, relies on others. Try to think of one object that you could acquire without anybody's help. It is impossible to be 100 percent autonomous: your clothes, the chair on which you sit, the mobile phone next to you, the lamp or glasses you use for reading this book—you would have none of them if you were totally isolated and left to fend for yourself. Perhaps you would not even exist. There is no "I" without a "Thou," for in our lives we are profoundly dependent on each other. When the CEO's high school friend Eva Staehelin and her late husband Gary Ellis decided to leave civilization and move into the Australian bush, they built their own farmhouse with their own hands, lived from livestock and subsistence farming, collected rainwater in their cistern, and home-schooled their two daughters. They were as close as possible to being truly self-sufficient. But even they relied on their fellow humans for a minimal level of comfort: a jeep to get into town, a nail-clipper and soap, matches for candles and the fire.

The recognition of the "I" in individual has brought us far; it has freed us from being mere subjects of tyranny, turned us into people with rights and liberties, and led to universal human rights. But at the same time, it has given us the illusion that you and I are separate. In the business world, it has led to CEOs who protect themselves jealously from their people and use armies of secretaries to wall themselves off. At one company in Germany, some middle managers had worked on the first and second floors for ten years without ever being invited inside the president's third-floor office. By isolating themselves, leaders deprive themselves of strategic intelligence from the front lines. And since the way to be a leader, by definition, is to be with the people (you cannot lead without co-leaders or at least followers), such separation can be costly for productivity, loyalty, and morale.

In the extreme, individualism has led to 45-year-olds driving alone in SUVs and guzzling away the United States' energy independence, and to Bud Light commercials, shown during the 2007 Super Bowl, of a game of rock, paper, scissors in which one fellow bashes his chum with an actual rock to get the last bottle of beer while the others step over the loser, who is sprawled lifeless on the lawn. This showed the sort of callousness associated with heroin junkies; though meant to be humorous, it was pretty dark. This type of individualism is founded on the principle that ours is a you-or-me world, that life is a zero-sum game in which you have to fight to prevent me from getting what I want, because the more I get what I want, the less you will get. The idea of separate individuals may well have become the greatest obstacle we have put in our own paths. It may keep us from being the leaders we can truly be. And it may cost us our common future.

Amazing things happen when people recognize that they are interconnected. Five months into World War I, on Christmas Day 1914 in Armentières, France, Major Kenneth Henderson of the British Expeditionary Corps saw what amounted to any officer's nightmare: "I found the entire nowhere land occupied by a mass of people: our men and the Germans, all mixed up, in friendly conversation."[353] Day after endless day, since early November, British and German soldiers had fought each other bitterly, inch by inch in mud and snow, in battles of attrition. But now the unimaginable had occurred. A few days before Christmas, Saxon soldiers had lobbed an unusual bomb in a high arc: instead of hand grenades, a tightly wrapped chocolate cake. When the British soldiers opened the package, they found a note inserted in the cake: Would it not be feasible to have a truce that evening from 7:30 p.m. to 8:30 p.m.? The British accepted. English soldiers stood up from their trenches, listened to imperial German music, and even applauded.

On Christmas Eve, Lieutenant Kurt Zehnisch, in civilian life a high school teacher, gave orders to his German soldiers that "today on Christmas Eve and during the Christmas holidays, no shot shall be fired if it can be avoided." And the British were just as quiet that evening. Zehnisch, who spoke a little English, opened communication with the enemy who was dug in barely a hundred meters away. "Soldier Möckel from my brigade, who had been in England several years, and I call the English in English, and soon quite a funny conversation developed between us," Zehnisch explained. The two enemies agreed to meet halfway between their trenches. Two soldiers from the German side climbed out of their cover and crawled through the barbed wire. It was a frightening moment. Barely breathing, on both sides the other soldiers waited. Finally, one Englishman came out of his trench "and held up both hands. In one hand he held a cap filled with English cigarettes and tobacco." He shook the Germans' hands and wished them "Merry Christmas." They both wished him a "Merry Christmas." Then the British and German soldiers applauded from their trenches, and enthusiastic screams of joy came from both sides.

Enemy soldiers came out of their trenches, smoked and ate together, played soccer, and even cut each other's hair. Soon, like a pleasant dream, it was all over. But it did happen. Josef Wenzl wrote home to his parents on December 28, 1914: "What I will now report to you sounds barely believable, but it is the pure truth. ...Christmas 1914 will be unforgettable to me." On May 6, 1917, Wenzl fell in battle.[354]

> **Tip:** Whenever you don't know which of two actions to take at any given moment, take the more generous action.

Team, Unity, Alignment

Phil Jackson (see Chapter 6) has taken this spirit of interconnectedness to the basketball court. His own example comes from the American Indians: To the Lakota Sioux warriors, even the enemy was sacred. If you and your opponent are part of the same interdependent system, then your connection with your own teammates can go that much deeper; and it is this unity that allows you to beat impossible odds. Jackson knew that standing in your colleagues' shoes is the essence of teamwork—in the tradition of Gandhi, who knew that "A small body of determined spirits fired by an unquenchable faith in their mission can alter the course of history." A team's interconnectedness indeed makes for great accomplishments; but how do you build such strong alignment?

In a rare non-sport interview, Jackson charged that "most leaders tend to view teamwork as a social engineering problem: take X group, add Y motivational technique, and get Z result. In reality the most effective way to forge a winning team is to call on the players' need to connect with something larger than themselves." Jackson believes that the power of "we" is stronger than the power of "me"; to achieve victory the "me" must become the servant of the "we."

> I knew the only way to win consistently was to give everybody—from the starters to the No. 12 player on the bench—a vital role on the team and inspire them to be acutely aware of what was happening, even when the spotlight was on somebody else. In my work as a coach, I've discovered that by approaching team problems like injured players from a compassionate perspective—trying to empathize with the player and looking at the situation from his point of view—can have a transformative effect on the team. Not only does

it reduce the player's anxiety and make him feel as if someone understands what he's going through—it also inspires the other players to respond in kind and be more conscious of each other's needs.

In 1990 came a dramatic example of what such collective empathy can achieve. Scottie Pippen's father died while the Bulls were in the middle of a tough playoff series against the Philadelphia 76ers. Pippen skipped Game 4 to attend his father's funeral. He was still in a solemn mood before the start of the next game. "I thought it was important for the team to acknowledge what was going on with Scottie and give him support," recalled Jackson. "I asked the players to form a circle around him in the locker room and recite the Lord's Prayer. 'We may not be Scottie's family,' I said, 'but we're as close to him as anyone in his life. This is a critical time for him. We should tell him how much we love him and show compassion for his loss.'"[355]

In the rough world of the NBA—not unlike in business—it takes guts to talk about, let alone show, compassion and love. Jackson's gamble paid off: Pippen was visibly moved. That night, buoyed by his teammates, he went on a 29-point romp, and the Bulls finished off the 76ers.[356] When people achieve such unity, the whole is larger than the sum of its parts. They are no longer a group of individuals working together; they are a new entity, a united force, one hand with many fingers. Such unity does not negate the individuality and brilliance of each team member, since every individual possesses a divine spark, a unique quality that he or she contributes to the whole, and these sparks combine to light a fire that in turn illuminates and reveals each participant's hidden potential.

For the Sake of Peace You May Bend the Truth

Moses's brother Aaron had the love and compassion to see both sides in a conflict. If for example two businessmen had a quarrel, Aaron would go to each party to the dispute in an instance of ancient shuttle diplomacy. The importance of honesty cannot be undermined, as discussed in Chapter 7, but for the sake of conflict resolution, Aaron would allow himself to stretch the truth just a little bit, just enough to bring about peace. He assured businessman A that businessman B had expressed words of appreciation and eagerness to resolve their dispute. Once businessman A agreed to sit down with businessman B, Aaron immediately went to B and told him that A was ready to make peace. The sages later backed Aaron up: "For the sake of peace one is allowed to change [the truth]."[357] (Aaron never lied, which is always forbidden in Jewish thought; he merely left out some of the truth.) Aaron was beloved for his diplomacy as well as for his marriage counseling. Just as he resolved business disputes in the boardroom, he brought peace between husbands and wives in the bedroom. That is why it is said that half the people of Israel, i.e., the men who had studied with Moses, wept when he died, but when Aaron died, the men *and* the women grieved. (To be fair, Moses, as intermediary between God and the Jews, had to be a bridge and integrator too; he could not afford the illusion that his was the only perspective.)

In 1919, an Arab leader and a Jewish leader practiced the principle of being in the other side's shoes for the sake of peace, and did so in perhaps the toughest place: the Middle East. Emir Feisal, whose father Sherif Hussein of Mecca had led the Arab world in World War I, and who represented the Arab Kingdom of Hedjaz at the Paris peace conference after World War I, met with Chaim Weizmann, the representative of the Zionist organization. Meeting first in Aqaba, Jordan and then in Paris, they signed an agreement calling for all necessary measures to "encourage and stimulate immigration of Jews into Palestine on a large scale."[358] In a follow-up letter to Weizmann, Feisal wrote:

> We feel that Arabs and Jews are cousins in race, having suffered similar oppressions at the hands of powers stronger than themselves, and by a happy coincidence have been able to take the first step towards the attainment of their national ideals together. ... We Arabs, especially the educated among us, look with the deepest sympathy on the Zionist movement ... we will wish the Jews a most hearty welcome home. ... We are working together for a reformed and revised Near East, and our two movements complete one another. The Jewish movement is national and not imperialist. Our movement is

national and not imperialist, and there is room in Syria for us both. Indeed I think that neither can be a real success without the other.[359]

Although this took place less than one hundred years ago, such empathy or partnership between Muslims and Jews has become virtually unthinkable. Few people in the region say even as much as "I'm sorry" now. Imagine what would be possible if people had the guts—and the skill—to stand in each other's shoes. This is as true for the Middle East as it is for mergers between the Daimlers and the Chryslers of this world.

And it is possible. André Azoulay, the Jewish senior advisor to the king of Morocco, likes to joke that he's a member of a very elite club of Jewish advisors to Muslim rulers. That club has precisely one member—him—and so far, he is the only Jew to hold such a position in any Arab country. On a more serious note, Azoulay acknowledges that "it is very frustrating to be in the only Arab and Muslim country where a Jew can be in my position." Azoulay has given his life for peace between Arabs and Jews, and he feels equally Jewish and Arab. "I'm an Arab because I was born in an Arab country, and I'm an Arab because I absorb Arab culture, and I'm an Arab because I live in an Arab environment," Azoulay said in an interview before receiving an honorary doctorate from Ben-Gurion University of the Negev in Beer Sheva, Israel. "If I could only make peace between Jews and Muslims, I would feel that I had fulfilled my life's ambition."[360]

What is *your* life's ambition? We say, Do it. As W.H. Murray, the first man to conquer Mount Everest, which he could accomplish only by joining forces with his colleague, Sherpa Tenzing, put it:

> Until one is committed, there is hesitancy, the chance to draw back, always ineffectiveness. Concerning all acts of initiative (and creation), there is one elementary truth the ignorance of which kills countless ideas and splendid plans: that the moment one definitely commits oneself, the providence moves too. A whole stream of events issues from the decision, raising in one's favor all manner of unforeseen incidents, meetings and material assistance, which no man could have dreamt would have come his way.[361]

Are you willing to make this world a better place? Are you willing to live now as if a glorious future were the reality today? As God asks Adam at the start of the Torah, "Where are you?"

The Bottom Line

- The best leaders in a globalized world have the competence to put themselves in the shoes of another person or culture and see issues from the other side's point of view—even (and especially) if the other side is an enemy or competitor.

- The Hebrew word for life is *chayim*, a plural term. Each person is an individual, but life is not individual; it happens only together, with other participants. We are all interdependent. Nothing you have done is your accomplishment alone.

- Our built-in ethnocentrism keeps us from seeing the world from another person's or culture's perspective. The inability to stand in the shoes of the other side is the most frequent mistake in negotiations.

- Adopting the vantage point of another person or culture means you need to be like an actor. How would the world look to you if you were a murderer, a baker, a general?

- Decoding a culture (including your own) is like peeling off an onion: first, what you can see, hear, and touch (the symbols); second, how the culture explains its behaviors (the rationalizations); and finally, what the culture does not know it does not know (the blind spots). To get to this inner core, identify the founders, heroes, villains, and defining moments of the culture.

- Empathy and compassion are key ingredients in building championship teams. As Gandhi put it, "A small body of determined spirits fired by an unquenchable faith in their mission can alter the course of history." Under coach Phil Jackson, the Bulls used collective unity, and even love, to beat the 49ers. With alignment, virtually any accomplishment is possible.

Endnotes

[1] Thomas D. Zweifel, *International Organizations and Democracy: Accountability, Politics, and Power*. (Boulder, CO: Lynne Rienner Publishers, 2005), 59-60, 74.

[2] "Just Making an Honest Buck?" *Business Week*, online edition, September 19, 2005. http://www.businessweek.com/magazine/content/05_38/b3951020.htm.

[3] Lynn Zinser, "Drug Testing: Pound Builds And Badgers In His Battle Against Doping," *New York Times*, August 8, 2006.

[4] Peter Drucker, "Managing Oneself," *Harvard Business Review*, March-April 1999: 65-74.

[5] Bruce Nussbaum, "Are Designers the Enemy of Design?" *Business Week*, March 18, 2007. http://www.businessweek.com/innovate/NussbaumOnDesign/archives/2007/03/are_designers_t.html.

[6] Eric von Hippel. *Democratizing Innovation*. (Cambridge, MA: MIT Press, 2005), 1-3. http://web.mit.edu/evhippel/www/.

. [7] Burson-Marsteller, "Who Wants to Be CEO? Understanding CEO Capital," 2005. http://www.ceogo.com/documents/2005CEOCapitalBrochure.pdf.

Asia/Pacific executives (51 percent) were divided on whether they wanted the top job; only 27 percent of Latin Americans did not covet it.

[8] Emily Brandon, "Talk About a Hard Act to Follow," *U.S. News & World Report*, July 29, 2007.

[9] Remarks by Herb Kelleher, World Business Forum, October 2007, New York City.

[10] The *shofar* is a ram's horn used as a musical instrument on the Jewish High Holidays (Rosh Hashana and Yom Kippur); the *tefillin* are phylacteries—two black leather boxes that contain scrolls of parchment inscribed with biblical verses—that observant Jews don during weekday morning prayers to symbolize their connection with God and their liberation from Egypt.

[11] "Fasse ich den Baseler Congress in ein Wort zusammen—das ich mich hüten werde öffentlich auszusprechen—so ist es dieses: In Basel habe ich den Judenstaat gegründet." Theodor Herzl's diary, entry September 3, 1897.

Chapter 1

[12] *Hashem*, literally "the Name," is one of the terms for God. Spelled "Yud-Hei-Vav-Hei", or the tetragrammaton, God's name is ineffable and pronounced in prayer only. Pronounc-

ing "God" would turn the infinite divinity into a person or thing and would be tantamount to idolatry; hence many Jews prefer to say *Hashem* (the Name) or *eyn sof* (meaning without end, or infinite).

[13] Tim Boyle, as told to Eve Tahmincioglu, "Executive Life: The Boss; The Reality Classroom," *New York Times*, January 18, 2004.

[14] Patricia Bellew Gray, "Don't Mess With Gert," *Your Company*, June-July 1998: 29-38.

Tim Boyle, "Executive Life: The Boss," as told to Eve Tahmincioglu, *New York Times*, January 18, 2004.

[15] According to the Greek historian Strabo (63 BCE - 24 CE), Moses was an Egyptian priest who became critical of the Egyptians' "representing the Divine Being by images of beasts and cattle"; the first-century Roman Jewish historian Flavius Josephus wrote that Moses led an Egyptian campaign against Ethiopia.

[16] Rainer Maria Rilke, "Aufzeichnung über Kunst," in *Rainer Maria Rilke: Sämtliche Werke*, Bd. 12 (Frankfurt a.M., Rilke-Archiv, 1899/1975, ed. Ernst Zinn), 1161.

[17] Yitzchak Ginsburgh, *Awakening the Spark Within* (Jerusalem: Linda Pinsky Publications), 152.

[18] Exodus 3:11, 4:1, 4:10, 4:13.

[19] Exodus 6:6-7.

[20] Kotsk (today Kock) is a Polish town 120 kilometers southeast of Warsaw. The word Rebbe stems from rabbi; it means master, teacher, or mentor and often refers to the leader of a Hasidic community. The Kotsker Rebbe (1787-1859) was a Hasidic rabbi who established the Kotsk dynasty; was known for his sharp-witted sayings and down-to-earth philosophy, and seems to have had little patience for false piety or stupidity. In the last twenty years of his life he lived in seclusion.

[21] Martin Buber, *The Way of Man: According to the Teachings of Hasidism*. (Secaucus, NJ: The Citadel Press, 1963), 17.

[22] Martin Buber, *The Way of Man: According to the Teachings of Hasidism*. (Secaucus, NJ: The Citadel Press, 1963), 16.

[23] *Bob Dylan – No Direction Home*, directed by Martin Scorsese (Paramount, 2005).

[24] Dylan flirted at least briefly with becoming observant. One religious holiday in the 1980s, Michael Behrman, a friend of the authors, went to another friend's house and knocked. The door opened, the host stuck his head out, glanced left and right furtively, and whispered, "Come in, quick!" Behrman was escorted to the living room—and there was Bob Dylan sitting among a group of excited Lubavitchers. And as recently as 2007, Dylan participated in a Yom Kippur service in Atlanta, Georgia. Arriving in a ski cap and tallit, he stayed for the duration of the morning services, during which he was called up by his Jewish name Zushe ben Avraham. The legendary singer/songwriter said the blessings in Hebrew without stumbling, like a pro, reported Rabbi Yossi Lew. http://www.chabad.org/news/article_cdo/aid/573406/jewish/SingerSongwriter-Bob-Dylan-Joins-Yom-Kippur-Services-in-Atlanta.htm.

[25] *Bob Dylan – No Direction Home,* directed by Martin Scorsese (Paramount, 2005).

[26] Tana Devei Eliahu, ch. 14; Bereshit Raba, 1:4.

[27] Herb Kelleher, "Building a People-Focused Culture," (keynote, World Business Forum, New York City, October 10-11, 2007).

[28] George Bernard Shaw, *Mrs. Warren's Profession* (Bel Air, CA: Dodo Press, [1893] 2007), Preface.

[29] Brachot 17a; Shemoneh Esrei, "Peace," *The Complete Artscroll Siddur*, trans. and ed. Nosson Sherman (Brooklyn, NY: Mesorah Publications, 1984), 118.

[30] Arnie Gotfryd, "A Tanya for Professor Wheeler," http://www.chabad.org/library/article_cdo/aid/81944/jewish/A-Tanya-for-Professor-Wheeler.htm.

[31] Genesis 18:27-30.

[32] At other times God could be equally brutal in his response. For example, just before Moses came down from Mount Sinai with the two tablets on which were written the Ten Commandments, God informed him that while he had gone up Mount Sinai, the people down below had begun worshipping the golden calf: "I have seen this people and behold they are a stiff-necked people. Now leave me alone and my wrath will blaze against them and destroy them. I will then make you into a great nation." Exodus 32:9-10.

[33] *Pirkei Avot* 2:16.

[34] Rabbi Shneur of Liadi (1745-1812), also called the Alter Rebbe, was the founder and first leader of Chabad, a branch of Hasidic Judaism. A prolific writer, he was the author of many works and is best known for his seminal work *Likkutei Amarim*, or *Tanya*, first published in 1797, and the *Shulchan Aruch HaRav*, a code of Jewish law. A translated version with commentary is at http://www.chabad.org/library/article_cdo/aid/6237/jewish/Lessons-in-Tanya.htm.

[35] A righteous person; in the Hasidic tradition, a leader.

[36] Rabbi Shlomo Yosef Zevin, *A Treasury of Chasidic Tales on the Torah*, trans. Uri Kaploun (Jerusalem: Mesorah Publications, 1980), 30. For commentary on this story, see Buber, *The Way of Man*, 9-14.

[37] Fritz J. Roethlisberger and William J. Dickson, *Management and the Worker* (Cambridge, MA: Harvard University Press, 1939), 14-18.

[38] Baba Shiv, Hilke Plassmann, Antonio Rangel and John O'Doherty, "Marketing Actions Can Modulate Neural Representations of Experienced Pleasantness," published online, January 14, 2008, Proceedings of the National Academy of Sciences. http://www.gsb.stanford.edu/news/research/baba_wine.html.

[39] Reply to a criticism during the Great Depression of having changed his position on monetary policy, quoted in Alfred L. Malabre, *Lost Prophets: An Insider's History of the Modern Eonomists* (Cambridge MA: Harvard Business School Press, 1994), 220

[40] Richard P. Feynman, *The Meaning of It All: Thoughts of a Citizen-Scientist*. (Reading, MA: Perseus Books, 1987), 28.

[41] Quoted by Michael J. Mahoney, *Scientist as Subject: The Psychological Imperative* (Cambridge MA: Ballinger, 1976), 168.

[42] Richard Paul and Linda Elder, "The Miniature Guide to Critical Thinking: Concepts and Tools" (Dillon Beach CA: The Foundation for Critical Thinking, 2006): 9.

[43] Tom Leonard, "Leona Helmsley," *Telegraph (UK)*, August 24, 2007.

[44] Joseph B. Treaster, "Polar Opposites? Not Where It Counts; Warren Buffett Gets All the Attention, But Hank Greenberg Is Posting Better Returns," *New York Times*, July 23, 2000.

[45] Ibid.

[46] Joseph B. Treaster, "Broker Accused of Rigging Bids for Insurance," *New York Times*, October 15, 2004.

[47] *Webster's New Universal Unabridged Dictionary*, New York: Barnes & Noble Books, 1989.

[48] Exodus 19:6.

[49] Morris Mandel, ed., *Stories for Public Speakers* (New York: Jonathan David Publishers, 1996), 236.

[50] Likutei Sichot, Vol. 13:30; Vol. 17:1.

[51] Proverbs 25:6.

[52] Yitzchak Ginsburgh, "Kabbalah" keynote, Chabad, New York City, December 16, 2003.

[53] *Bob Dylan – No Direction Home*, directed by Martin Scorsese (Paramount, 2005).

[54] Ecclesiastes 3:20.

[55] Numbers 12:3.

[56] Numbers 27:15-18.

[57] Dennis Overbye, "Ideas & Trends; Unbreakable: He's Still Ready for His Close-Up," *New York Times*, May 12, 2002.

[58] Brian Greene, "One Hundred Years of Uncertainty," *New York Times*, April 8, 2005.

[59] Ben Ratliff, "Listening to CD's With: Sonny Rollins; Free Spirit Steeped in Legends," *New York Times*, September 30, 2005.

[60] Ron Grossman, "Lesson in Decency from an Age of Shame: How a Gentle Man Clung to His Values and His Children Amid the Horrors of the Holocaust," *Chicago Tribune*, April 30, 2000.

[61] Suzanne Daley, "Beloved Country Repays Mandela in Kind," *New York Times*, March 23, 1999.

[62] John Markoff, "Bill Gates's Brain Cells, Dressed Down for Action; Pressed to Innovate, Microsoft Relies Again on an Inner Circle," *New York Times*, March 25, 2001.

[63] Justin Fox, "Nokia's Secret Code," *Fortune*, May 1, 2000, 164.

[64] R.F. Vancil, *Passing the Baton: Managing the Process of CEO Succession*. (Boston: Harvard Business School Press, 1987).

[65] Barry A. Macy and Hiroaki Izumi, "Organizational Change, Design, and Work Innovation: A Meta-Analysis of 131 North American Field Studies – 1961-91," in *Research in Organizational Design and Development*, vol.7, eds. R. Woodman and W. Pasmore (Greenwich, CT: JAI Press, 1993), 235-313.

Chapter 2

[66] The word for God, *YHWH*, means "present," for God constantly creates the present, similar to the word "essence" that comes from the Latin word *esse* (to be).

[67] Deuteronomy 34:10, 12.

[68] Jean M. Twenge, S. Konrath, J.D. Foster, W.K. Campbell and B.J. Bushman, "Egos Inflating Over Time," San Diego State University, 2007.

[69] Gene I. Maeroff, "Study Finds Fewer Freshmen in College Look Into Teaching," *New York Times*, January 29, 1983.

[70] Warren Bennis and Burt Nanus, *Leaders: The Strategies for Taking Charge* (New York: HarperCollins, 1985), 89-91.

[71] The 24 books that begin with the Torah. (The Five Books of Moses are Vol. 1; Vol. 2 is Prophets, and Vol. 3 is Writings.)

[72] Isaiah 3:12.

[73] Isaiah 2:4.

[74] Talmud, Megillah, 14a. According to the Midrash Rabba, Song of Songs 4:11, for every male prophet there was one female prophetess.

[75] Numbers 11:29.

[76] Kenneth Labich and Charles A. Riley II, "The Big Comeback at British Airways," *Fortune*, December 5, 1988.

[77] William Bridges, "Getting Them Through the Wilderness: A Leader's Guide to Transition," *New Management*, 1987: 50-55.

[78] Proverbs 29:18.

[79] David Brooks, *On Paradise Drive: How We Live Now (and Always Have) in the Future Tense* (New York: Simon & Schuster, 2004), 42-43.

[80] "Bush to invoke Vietnam in arguing against Iraq Pullout," CNN.com, August 22, 2007. http://www.cnn.com/2007/POLITICS/08/21/bush.iraq.speech/.

[81] Yitzchak Ginsburgh, *Awakening the Spark Within: Five Dynamics of Leadership That Can Change the World* (Jerusalem: Linda Pinsky Publications, 2001), 138.
Another one thousand year before Rabbi Saadia Gaon, Rabbi Eliezer recommended in *Pirkei Avot*: "Repent one day before your death." (Pirkei Avot 2:10) The Talmud asked: "Does a person know when he will die?" Rabbi Eliezer responded, "Surely you should start today, because you may die tomorrow, and therefore all your days will be with *teshuva* [repentance]." Shabat 153a.

[82] Quoted by Joan Holmes, President and CEO of The Hunger Project from 1977 to 2008 and member of the Africa Prize for Leadership international jury, comment in meeting with the CEO, 1988.

[83] Bureau of Land Management, "The South Canyon Fire Investigation, Executive Summary," U.S. Department of the Interior, September 1998. http://www.blm.gov/co/st/en/fo/gsfo/fire_and_fuels/south_canyon.html.

[84] U.S. Forest Service, *Mann Gulch Transcript*, Appendix 5 (Washington DC 1994).
U.S. Forest Service, *Report of the South Canyon Fire Accident Investigation Team*, August

17, 1994, (Washington, DC, 1994), cited in Karl E. Weick, "Drop Your Tools: An Allegory for Organizational Studies," *Administrative Science Quarterly*, 41(1996): 301-313.

[85] Alice Calaprice, ed. The Expanded Quotable Einstein (Princeton NJ: Princeton University Press, 2000).

[86] Exodus 3:3.

[87] See I Samuel 17:38-39.

[88] H.W. Brands, *Masters of Enterprise: Giants of American Business from John Jacob Astor and J.P. Morgan to Bill Gates and Oprah Winfrey* (New York: The Free Press, 1999), 308.

[89] Moses Maimonides, *Mishneh Torah*, approx. 1170-1180, Chapter 9, Law 3.

[90] Devaki Jain, "Panchayat Raj: Women Changing Governance," UN Development Programme, Gender in Development, September 1996. http://www.sdnp.undp.org/gender/resources/mono5.html.
    Mani Shankar Aiyar, India's minister for panchayati raj, interview by Rashme Segal, Infochange, July 2004. http://www.infochangeindia.org/analysis29.jsp.

[91] Geraldine Fabrikant, "The Deal for MCA," *New York Times*, November 27, 1990.

[92] Arun Gandhi quoting Mohandas Gandhi, in Michel W. Potts, "Arun Gandhi Shares the Mahatma's Message," in *India—West* (San Leandro, CA, February 1, 2002), Vol. XXVII, No. 13: A34.

[93] Tamid 32A.

[94] George Santayana, "Ultimate Religion," in *The Works of George Santayana*, Triton Edition, vol. X. (New York: Charles Scribner Sons, 1937), 245.

[95] Exodus 14:21.

[96] Martin Luther King, Jr., "I've Been to the Mountaintop," speech delivered at Mason Temple (Church of God in Christ Headquarters), Memphis, Tennessee, April 3, 1968.

[97] Walter Mischel, Yuichi Shoda, and Monica L. Rodriguez. "Delay of Gratification in Children," *Science* 244 (1989): 933-938.

[98] Proverbs 29:18.

Chapter 3

[99] Yitzchak Ginsburgh, *Awakening the Spark Within: Five Dynamics of Leadership That Can Change the World* (Jerusalem: Linda Pinsky Publications, 2001), 22.

[100] Exodus 12:37, 14:11-12.

[101] "Time to Cut Out Your 'Management Speak'?" *Investors in People*, Issue 18, February 2007: 7. http://64.233.169.104/search?q=cache:IaeKLtoBJBAJ:www.investorsinpeople.co.uk/Documents/Raising%2520The%2520Standard/RTS18.pdf+yougov+survey+ducks+in+a+row&hl=en&ct=clnk&cd=5&gl=us.

[102] George Orwell, "Politics and the English Language," *Horizon*, April 1946. http://www.mtholyoke.edu/acad/intrel/orwell46.htm.http://www.mtholyoke.edu/acad/intrel/orwel146.htm.

[103] Thomas D. Zweifel, *Communicate or Die: Getting Results Through Speaking and Listening*. (New York: SelectBooks, 2003), 64-71.

[104] Ken Auletta. *World War 3.0: Microsoft and Its Enemies.* (New York: Random House, 2001). John Heilemann, *Pride Before the Fall: The Trials of Bill Gates and the End of the Microsoft Era.* (New York: HarperCollins Publishers, 2001).

[105] John Heilemann, The Truth, The Whole Truth, and Nothing But The Truth," *Wired*, Issue 8.11, November 2000.

[106] *United States of America vs. Microsoft Corporation*, Transcript of Proceedings, Washington D.C., December 15, 1998.

[107] Eric Pfanner, "Europeans Threaten More Fines For Microsoft," *New York Times*, March 2, 2007.

[108] Meredith Levine, "Tell the Doctor All Your Problems, But Keep It to Less Than a Minute," *New York Times*, June 1, 2004.
Benedict Carey, "New Therapy On Depression Finds Phone Is Effective," *New York Times*, August 25, 2004.

[109] Ibid.

[110] Lawrence Dyche and Deborah Swiderski, "The Effect of Physician Solicitation Approaches on Ability to Identify Patient Concerns," *Journal of General Internal Medicine*, 20: 3, March 2005: 267–270.

[111] Gina Kolata, "When the Doctor Is In, but You Wish He Wasn't," *New York Times*, November 30, 2005.

[112] Ibid.

[113] Ibid.

[114] Genesis 1:26.

[115] Daily morning liturgy, Baruch She'amar, *The Complete Artscroll Siddur*, trans. and ed. Nosson Sherman (Brooklyn, NY: Mesorah Publications, 1984), 58.

[116] Sa'adiah ben Yosef Gaon, *Sefer Yetzirah* [Book of Creation], 10th Century C.E., ed. by Arieh Kaplan (Newburyport, MA: Weiser, 1997).

[117] Rabbi Menachem M. Schneerson, *Hayom Yom* (Brooklyn, NY: Kehot Publications Society, 1988), Tishrei 29.

[118] Zweifel, *Communicate or Die*, 12-13

[119] George Bernard Shaw, *The Doctor's Dilemma*, (Teddington, Middlesex: Echo Library, [1906] 2006), preface.

[120] Interview, *MarketWatch*, September 27, 2006.

[121] Leslie A. Perlow, *When You Say Yes But Mean No: How Silencing Conflict Wrecks Relationships and Companies ... and What You Can Do About It.* (New York: Crown Business, 2003).

[122] Claudia H. Deutsch, "At Lunch With: Leslie A. Perlow; Corporate Silence Has a Vocal Opponent," *New York Times*, August 3, 2003.

[123] Rabbi Schneur Zalman, *Tanya* (Brooklyn, NY: Kehot Publications Society), Chapter 32, citing *Sefer Haredim*.

[124] Rabbi Menachem M. Schneerson, *Hayom Yom* (Brooklyn, NY: Kehot Publications Society, 1988), Elul 22.

[125] Rabbeinu Tam, *Sefer Hayashar*, Gate 13, Question 69A.

[126] Rabbi Menachem M. Schneerson, *Hayom Yom* (Brooklyn, NY: Kehot Publications Society, 1988), Sivan 12.

[127] Gary Rivlin, "Keeping Your Enemies Close," *New York Times*, November 12, 2006.

[128] Psalms 119:98.

[129] Alison Maitland, "Stakeholders: Listening puts you on fast track to credibility," *Financial Times*, November 25, 2005.

[130] Nigel Nicholson, "How Hardwired Is Human Behavior?" *Harvard Business Review*, July-August 1998, 134-147.

[131] Don Cohen and Laurence Prusak, *In Good Company: How Social Capital Makes Organizations Work* (Cambridge, MA: Harvard Business School Press, 2001), 104.

[132] Erchin 15b; see also Rabbi Menachem M. Schneerson,, *Hayom Yom* (Brooklyn, NY: Kehot Publications Society, 1988), Cheshvan 16.

[133] Sotah 42a.

[134] Numbers 16.

[135] Erchin 15b.

[136] "Russian mayor bans excuse making," BBC News, International Version, September 1, 2007; http://news.bbc.co.uk/2/hi/6974216.stm.

[137] Michael Wex, *Born to Kvetch: Yiddish Language and Culture in All of Its Moods.* (New York: St. Martin's Press, 2005).

[138] Exodus 14:15.

[139] Martin Buber, *Das Problem des Menschen [The Problem of Man].* (Heidelberg: Verlag Lambert Schneider, 1982), 65.

[140] Thomas D. Zweifel, interview by Felix Müller, "Den Leuten die Angst Nehmen [Taking People's Fear Away]," *Tages-Anzeiger*, October 13, 2004.
Felix Müller, "ZKB legt Messlatte höher [ZKB Raises the Bar"], *Tages-Anzeiger*, October 15, 2004.

[141] Numbers 3:30.

[142] Zweifel, *Communicate or Die*, 33-41.

[143] Schulz von Thun, Friedemann, *Miteinander Reden: Störungen und Klärungen: Psychologie der zwischenmenschlichen Kommunikation [Talking With One Another: Disturbances and Clarifications: Psychology of Interpersonal Communication].* (Hamburg: Rowohlt, 1981).

Chapter 4

[144] Matt Richtel, "Tethered; It Don't Mean a Thing if You Ain't Got That Ping," *New York Times*, April 22, 2007.

[145] Richard Waters, "Blackberry addiction cure is in your hands," *Financial Times*, December 3, 2005.

[146] Tina Kelley, "Only Disconnect (For a While, Anyway)," *New York Times*, June 25, 1998.

[147] Lee Rainie and Deborah Fallows, "The CAN-SPAM Act has not helped most email users so far: A PIP Data Memo," Pew Internet & American Life Project, April 10, 2005.

The Harris Poll #75, "The Many Sources of Stress and the Hassles of Daily Life," Harris Interactive, October 6, 2006.

[148] For many more examples of the nonstop life, see James Gleick, *Faster: The Acceleration of Just About Everything.* (New York: Vintage Books, 1999).

[149] Quoted in Sol Stein, *Stein on Writing: A Master Editor of Some of the Most Successful Writers of Our Century Shares His Craft, Techniques and Strategies.* (London: Macmillan, 1995), 46.

[150] Glenn H. Snyder and Paul Diesing, *Conflict Among Nations.* (Princeton, NJ: Princeton University Press, 1977).

[151] Lesya Y. Ganushchak and Niels O. Schiller, "Effects of Time Pressure on Verbal Self-Monitoring: An ERP Study," Brain Research, vol. 1125, issue 1, December 13, 2006: 104-115.

George Usdansky and Loren J. Chapman, "Schizophrenic-like Response in Normal Subjects under Time Pressures," *Journal of Abnormal and Social Psychology* 60 (January 1960): 143-146.

[152] Larry Collins and Dominique Lapierre, Freedom at Midnight (New York: Avon Books, 1975), 60-61.

[153] Marcia Barinaga, "Buddhism and Neuroscience: Studying the Well-Trained Mind," *Science*, vol. 302, no. 5642: 44-46.

[154] Sari Botton, "God help us: If you think He can keep you will, you may be right," *Time Out New York*, October 16-23, 2003, 65-66.

[155] Peter Spang, *Zennis* (New York: Perigee, 1998), 31.

[156] Interview with the Omega Institute, "Coach Phil Jackson on Meditation," *Conscious Choice*, April 2004. http://consciouschoice.com/2004/cc1704/ch_philjackson1704.html.

[157] Tina Kelley, "Only Disconnect (For a While, Anyway)," New York Times, June 25, 1998.

[158] Jim White, "Do nothing, save the world: it's the only option," *Telegraph (UK)*, November 13, 2006.

[159] II Samuel 11:1-2.

[160] Yitzchak Ginsburgh, *Awakening the Spark Within* (Jerusalem: Linda Pinsky Publications, 2001), 86.

[161] Abraham Joshua Heschel, *The Sabbath* (New York: Farrar Straus Giroux, 2005), 10.

[162] Exodus 23:10-11; Leviticus 25:1-7; Deuteronomy 31:10-13; Nehemiah 10:32.

[163] Claudia Dreifus, "The Dalai Lama," *New York Times Magazine*, November 28, 1993, 52-55.

[164] *Zohar*, vol. II, 49a.

[165] Søren Kierkegaard, "A Discourse for an Occasion," March 1847: 27. In *Purity of Hearth*, transl. Douglas V. Steere (New York: Harper Perennial, 1956), 53.

[166] Andrew Carnegie, "Business Negotiations." Chapter XII in *The Autobiography of Andrew Carnegie*. (Boston: Houghton-Mifflin, 1920).

[167] Taylor Branch, *Parting the Waters: America in the King Years, 1954-63* (New York: Simon & Schuster, 1989), 195.

[168] Exodus 18:17-23.

[169] Timothy Ferriss, "The 4-Hour Workweek," *Fortune Small Business*, May 2007, 47-48.

[170] Larry Collins and Dominique Lapierre, *Freedom at Midnight* (New York: Avon, 1975), 61-62.

[171] Interview with Jörn Donner, *Ingmar Bergman on Life and Work*, documentary, Criterion, 1998.

[172] Patricia Cohen, "An Eye for Patterns In the Social Fabric; Patriarch of Sociology Sees His Insights Become Just What Everyone Knows," *New York Times*, October 31, 1998.

[173] The sixth Lubavitcher Rebbe (1880-1950), aslo known as the Frierdiker (Yiddish for Previous) Rebbe.

Chapter 5

[174] Martin Heidegger, *What Is Called Thinking?* trans. J. Glenn Gray (New York: Harper & Row, 1968), 139.

[175] Talmud, Brachot 60b.

[176] The protagonist of Jonathan Safran Foer's novel *Everything Is Illuminated* (New York: Houghton Mifflin, 2002), 60, mentions even four hundred synonyms for *schmuck*, but that is probably hyperbole.

[177] Siddur, (daily prayerbook), Tehillat Hashem.

[178] *Scorsese on Scorsese*, directed by Richard Schickel (Turner Classic Movies, 2004).

[179] Rabbi Menachem M. Schneerson, *Hayom Yom* (Brooklyn, NY: Kehot Publications Society, 1988), 2, Adar 1.

[180] Talmud, Baba Batra 110a.

[181] *Kuntres Acharon*, Essay 6, 160A,B.

[182] Warren Commission Hearings, March 10, 1964.

[183] Atul Gawande, "Annals of Medicine: The Checklist," *The New Yorker*, December 10, 2007.

[184] Peter Pronovost et al., "An Intervention to Decrease Catheter-Related Bloodstream Infections in the ICU," *New England Journal of Medicine*, vol. 355, no. 26: 2725-2732.

[185] Jane E. Brody, "A Basic Hospital To-Do List Saves Lives," *New York Times*, January 22, 2008.

[186] H.W. Brands, *Masters of Enterprise* (New York: Free Press, 1999), 322.

[187] Peter Lauria, "Yahoo! Blues: Big-Picture Semel Faces Season of Discontent," *New York Post*, October 2, 2006.

[188] Paul R. La Monica, "Despite Yahoo's down year, Semel gets a big bonus," *CNNMoney.com*, March 2, 2007.

[189] Harry Maurer, "By Terry, Hi Jerry," *BusinessWeek*, July 2, 2007.

[190] Robert Lowenstein, "Alone At the Top," *The New York Times Magazine*, August 27, 2000.

[191] Ibid.

[192] Ibid.

[193] Shemot Rabba 2:2.

[194] Numbers 1:1-1:4.

[195] J.W. Elphinstone, "Monday water cooler: The Gatekeeper, Office runway, Life's rewards," *Pittsburgh Post-Gazette*, September 18, 2006.

[196] Bereishit Rabbah 61:3. Yevamos 62b.

[197] Hyman Goldin, ed., *Ethics of the Fathers* (New York: Hebrew Publishing Company, 1962).
Talmud, Shabbat 97a, 127b.

[198] Proverbs 26:24-25.

[199] Pirkei Avot 4:1b.

[200] David Barboza, "Enron's Many Strands: Fallen Star; From Enron Fast Track To Total Derailment," *New York Times*, October 3, 2002.

[201] Alan Feuer, "The Former Don As a Pen Pal: Sweet and Kind; Somehow, a Michigan Woman and John Gotti Just Got Along," *New York Times*, June 15, 2002.

Chapter 6

[202] Michael Bonsignore, op-ed, *Financial Times*, October 17, 2001.

[203] Jovi Tañada Yam, "Enter: 'Super Mario'," *Business World Online*, November 15, 2001. http://itmatters.com.ph/column/yam_11222001.html.

[204] Jim Collins, *Good to Great* (New York: HarperBusiness, 2001), 130-133.

[205] Peter Sanders, "Anger Management in the News." February 29, 2004. http://www.andersonservices.com/resourcesnews-2.html.

[206] Rebecca Speer, "Can Workplace Violence Be Prevented?" *Occupational Hazards*, August 1998.

[207] Partnership for Prevention, *Domestic Violence and the Workplace Study* (Washington, DC: Partnership for Prevention, 2002).

[208] Exodus 2:11-16.

[209] Exodus 16:20, 24:12-15; Midrash Rabbah, Shemot 25:10.

[210] Exodus 24:12-15, 24:25; Midrash Tanchuma, Korah 3.

[211] Lizette Alvarez, "Helsinki Journal; A Word to Finns: 'For Your Own Good, Blow Your Top,'" *New York Times*, March 11, 2004.

[212] "Angry voicemail from Baldwin goes public," *Associated Press*, April 20, 2007. www.youtube.com/watch?v=oZf2D57o8Kg

[213] "Fighting surgeons leave patient in the lurch," *Reuters*, February 21, 2007.

[214] Rabbi Schneur Zalman, *Tanya*, (Brooklyn, NY: Kehot Publications Society), Chapter 2, Iggeret Hatshuva.

[215] Del Jones, "Helping bring corporate jets to the masses," *USA Today*, March 8, 2004.

[216] H.W. Brands, *Masters of Enterprise*. (New York: Free Press, 1999), 321.

[217] Joseph Nocera and Alynda Wheat, "I Remember Microsoft," *Fortune*, July 10, 2000.

[218] Ina Fried, "Court docs: Ballmer vowed to 'kill' Google," *CNET News.com*, September 2, 2005.

[219] Margaret Kemeny, "Healing and the Mind: Emotions and the Immune System," The Mann Family Resource Center, UCLA, 2000.

[220] Seth Mnookin, "How Harvey Weinstein Survived His Midlife Crisis (For Now)," *New York*, October 4, 2004.

[221] Edward O. Welles, "Phil Jackson: Inc. talks to the world-champion coach of the Chicago Bulls about the abuse of anger and the handling of key employees," *Inc.*, September 1996. http://www.inc.com/magazine/19960901/1799.html.

[222] Nicholas Bakalar, "Ugly Children May Get Parental Short Thrift," *New York Times*, May 3, 2005.

[223] Genesis 37:5-20.

[224] Genesis 39:1-23; 41:1-41.

[225] Samuel J. Mann, "Joseph and His Brothers: A Biblical Paradigm for the Optimal Handling of Traumatic Stress," *Journal of Religion and Health* 40:3 (Fall, 2001): 335-342.

[226] Genesis 45:5-7.

[227] Genesis 50:20.

[228] Rabbi Menachem M. Schneerson, *Hayom Yom* (Brooklyn, NY: Kehot Publications Society, 1988), Sivan 12.

[229] Nelson Mandela, interview by Bill Moyers, *Beyond Hate* (PBS/Mystic Fire video, 1991).

[230] Rabbi Dovid Shraga Polter, *Chassidic Soul Remedies: Inspirational Insights for Life's Daily Challenges*. (Brooklyn, NY: Sichot in English, 2004), 20.

[231] Adapted from Stanley Bing, "Bing!" *Fortune*, January 12, 1998: 57-58.

[232] Erich Fromm, *The Anatomy of Human Destructiveness* (New York: Holt, Rinehart and Winston, 1973), 4.

[233] Baal Shem Tov, *Kesser Shem Tov. Hotafot* #119 and #127. (Brooklyn, NY: Kehot Publications Society, [1794]1998).

The notion of *Hashgacha Protis*, popularized by Rabbi Yisrael Baal Shem-Tov in the early 18th century, means that God directs and causes everything in the world to happen according to a universal plan – even when a blade of grass bends right or left.

[234] Rabbi Eliyahu Touger, trans., *Maimonides's Laws of Daos* (New York/New Jersey: Moznaim Publications, 1989), Chapter 2, Law 3.

[235] For some Jewish theologians, there is a contradiction between a fate predetermined

by God on the one hand and human free will on the other; but—and therein lies the paradoxical beauty of Jewish thought—they can coexist in the same sentence: "Everything is predetermined but freedom of will is given." Pirkei Avot 3:14.

[236] Rabbi Shneur Zalman, "Iggeret Hakodesh," *Tanya* ("A Holy Letter"), transl. Sholom and Levi Wineberg (Brooklyn, NY: Kehot Publications Society, 1998), Epistle 25.

[237] Stefan Klein, "Die Macht des Zufalls [The Power of Chance],"*Der Spiegel*, August 9, 2004, 104.

[238] Albert Einstein, letter to Max Born, December 4, 1926.
Anatole France, *Le Jardin d'Epicure* [The Garden of Epicurus] (Paris: CODA, [1895]2004).

[239] Harold Kushner, *When Bad Things Happen to Good People* (New York: Avon,1983), 52.

[240] Rabbi Joseph Ginsburg and Herman Branover, eds. *Mind Over Matter: Teachings of the Lubavitcher Rebbe, Rabbi Menachem Mendel Schneerson, on Science, Technology and Medicine.* (Jerusalem: Shamir, 2003.), 15.

[241] Marc Gunther, "God and Business," *Fortune*, July 9, 2001.

[242] Moses Maimonides, *Mishneh Torah*, approx. 1170-1180, Chapter 7, Law 5.

[243] Mickey Meece, "Management; The Very Model of Conciliation," *New York Times*, September 6, 2000.

Chapter 7

[244] Deuteronomy 25:5-10.
The practice, still practiced by some Orthodox Jews today, is called *yibum* or Levirite marriage.

[245] Genesis 38:9-26.

[246] Sukah 52a.
In Jewish thought, God created the evil inclination, but also the Torah to smoke it out.

[247] II Samuel 11:2-15.

[248] Taylor Branch, *Parting the Waters: America in the King Years, 1954-63.* (New York: Simon & Schuster, 1989); Seymour Hersch, *The Dark Side of Camelot* (Boston: Little, Brown, 1997).

[249] Chris Newmarker, "Toll Records Trip Up Philanderers," *ABC News*, August 10, 2007.

[250] Phil Stewart, "Lying about your lover is 'self-defense' in Italy," *Reuters*, March 7, 2008.

[251] Catherine Price, "Having an affair? New you've got an alibi," *Salon*, September 14, 2007. http://www.alibila.com.

[252] David Margolick, "His Last Name Is Scheme," *New York Times Book Review*, April 10, 2005.
Michael Zuckoff, *Ponzi's Scheme: The True Story of a Financial Legend* (New York: Random House, 2005).

[253] Amanda Lenhart and Mary Madden, "Teens, Privacy and Online Social Networks," Pew Internet and American Life Project, Pew Charitable Trusts, April 18, 2007: 18.

[254] Po Bronson, "Learning to Lie," New York, February 10, 2008.

[255] "Sharon son jailed for corruption," *BBC News*, February 14, 2006

[256] David Barboza, "A Chineses Reformer Betrays His Cause, and Pays," *New York Times*, July 13, 2007.

[257] Abraham J. Heschel, "No Time for Neutrality," in Susannah Heschel, ed., *Moral Grandeur and Spiritual Audacity: Essays* (New York: Farrar, Straus & Giroux. 1997), 131.

[258] Ibid.

[259] Hazel Rowley, *Tête-à-Tête: Simone de Beauvoir and Jean-Paul Sartre*. (New York : Harper-Collins, 2005).

[260] Abraham J. Heschel, "No Time for Neutrality," in in Susannah Heschel, ed., *Moral Grandeur and Spiritual Audacity: Essays* (New York: Farrar, Straus & Giroux. 1997), 140. 131.

[261] Martin Buber, *The Way of Man: According to the Teachings of Hasidism*, (Secaucus, NJ: Citadel Press, 1963), 29.
In the Torah, God's punishment for transgressions is always immediate: He sends the plague or destroys entire cities—now, not later.

[262] "Spitzer Resigns," NY1 News, March 12, 2008.

[263] Ralph Blumenthal, "A Zealous Prosecutor of Drug Criminals Becomes One Himself," *New York Times*, February 15, 2005.

[264] Rick Lyman, "A Tobacco Whistle-Blower's Mind Is Transformed," *New York Times*, October 15, 1999.

[265] Rabbi Moshe Chaim Luzzatto (the RaMChaL), "Concerning the Divisions of Watchfulness," *Path of the Just* (Jerusalem: Feldheim, [1740]2004), Chapter III.

[266] Martha Sherrill, "The Buddha Of Detroit," *New York Times Magazine*, November 26, 2000. *New York Times*, March 28, 2002.

[267] Danny Hakim, "Talking Green vs. Making Green," *New York Times*, March 28, 2002.

[268] Mark Bowden, "The Dark Art of Interrogation," *Atlantic Monthly*, October 2003.

[269] Adam Cohen, "What Google Should Roll Out Next: A Privacy Upgrade," *New York Times*, November 28, 2005.

[270] Peter Fleischer, privacy counsel-Europe, and Nicole Wong, deputy general counsel, "Taking steps to further improve our privacy practices," March 14, 2007. http://googleblog.blogspot.com/2007/03/taking-steps-to-further-improve-our.html.

[271] Warren Buffett, "An Owner's Manual," Berkshire Hathaway, June 1996; principle 12.

[272] Timothy L. O'Brien, "The Oracle of Omaha's Latest Riddle," *New York Times*, April 10, 2005.

[273] The full Credo can be found at: http://www.jnj.com/our_company/our_credo/.

[274] Stephen J. Greyser, "Johnson & Johnson: The Tylenol Tragedy," Harvard Business School Case 583043, 1982.
Francis J. Aguilar and Arvind Bhambri, "Johnson & Johnson (A)," Harvard Business School Case 384053, 1983.

[275] "Johnson & Johnson and Tylenol," *Economist*, September 28, 2002.

[276] Alan Riding, "Perrier Widens Recall After New Finding," *New York Times*, February 15, 1990.

[277] Jeffrey L. Seglin, "The Right Thing; Corporate Values Trickle Down From the Top," *New York Times*, July 21, 2002.

[278] Martin Buber, *The Way of Man*, 31-32.

Chapter 8

[279] "La propriété, c'est le vol!" (usually translated as "Property is theft"), Pierre-Joseph Proudhon, *What Is Property? Or, an Inquiry into the Principle of Right and Government* (New York: Cosimo Classics, [1840]2007).

[280] Genesis 18:19.

[281] Genesis 18:2,8.

[282] Rabbi Menachem M. Schneerson, *Hayom Yom* (Brooklyn, NY: Kehot Publications Society, 1988), Iyar 6. See also Cheshvan 22.

[283] Genesis 26:12, 28:22; Deuteronomy 14:22, 28-29.

[284] Andrew Carnegie, *The Gospel of Wealth and Other Timely Essays* (New York: Century Company, 1901), 19.

[285] Rabbi Moshe Bogomilsky, *Vedibarta Bam: And You Shall Speak of Them*, vol. II—Shemot (Brooklyn NY: Moshe Bogomilsky, 2003), 209.

[286] Howard Jonas, *On a Roll: From Hot-Dog Buns to High-Tech Billions* (New York: Viking Adult, 1998), 1.

[287] Pirkei Avot 2:7.

[288] Chanah Zuber Scharfstein, "The Mirror," Chabad.org Stories, http://www.chabad.org/library/article_cdo/aid/3252/jewish/The-Mirror.htm.

[289] Proverbs 19:17.

[290] Ruth Rabbah 2:14.

[291] Bava Batra 9A; see also *Tanya*, 178.

[292] Deuteronomy 24:19-22.

[293] Rick Bragg, "Oseola McCarty, a Washerwoman Who Gave All She Had to Help Others, Dies at 91," *New York Times*, September 28, 1999.

[294] Jeffrey Swartz, "The Moral Responsibility of Corporations," *The United Synagogue Review*, Spring 2000: 20-21.

[295] Jennifer Reingold, "Walking the Walk," *Fast Company*, November 2005: 80.

[296] Stephanie Strom, "Make Money, Save the World," *New York Times*, May 6, 2007.

[297] Ibid.

[298] Pirkei Avot 5:13.

[299] The Hunger Project, "What Does It Mean to Be an Investor?" June 1999 Investor Newsletter.

300 Moses Maimonides, "Laws of Contributions to the Poor," *Mishneh Torah*, approx. 1170–1180, Chapter 10:7.

301 Bava Batra 10a.

Chapter 9

302 Graham Bowley, "Goal! He Spends It on Beckham," *New York Times*, April 22, 2007.

303 Oliver Burkeman, "Ted's Tears," *The Guardian*, June 18, 2002.

304 William Manchester, *The Last Lion: Winston Spencer Churchill. Visions of Glory, 1874–1932.* (New York: Dell, 1983), 3-5.

305 Keynote, Harrow (United Kingdom), October 29, 1941.

306 Genesis 29:21.

307 David Kearns and David Nadler, *Profits in the Dark.* (New York: Harper Business Books, 1992). 249-250.

308 Ibid.

309 Daniel Eisenberg, "An Image Problem At Xerox," *Time*, October 30, 2000.

310 Job 1:2-3.

311 Job 1:13-20.
Job was punished so severely because when the pharaoh asked his advisors how to deal with the Jews, Job had remained silent and had said nothing, good or bad. Yitro, by contrast, had spoken up on behalf of the Jews, and his daughter had married Moses.

312 Job 3:10-11.

313 Ram Charan and Geoffrey Colvin, "Why CEOs Fail," *Fortune*, June 21, 1999.

314 Ibid.

315 Numbers 13:18-31.

316 Numbers 14:1-4.

317 Genesis 1:2.

318 Jacob Immanuel Schochet, *Mystical Concepts in Chassidism* (Brooklyn, NY: Kehot Publication Society, 1988), Chapter 7.

319 Proverbs 24:16.

320 Psalms 37:24.
Rabbi Schneur Zalman, Shaar Hayichud, Chinuch Katan. *Likutei Amarim Tanya*, Part 2.

321 Allan L. Scherr, "Managing for Breakthroughs in Productivity," *Human Resource Management* 28:3 (Fall 1989): 403-424.

322 P. Ranganath Nayak and John M. Ketteringham, *Breakthroughs!* (New York: Rawson Associates, 1986), 347.

323 Association of American Railroads, Car Service Division, "Proceedings of the Regular Meeting," 1924: 23.

324 Tom McNichol, "A Startup's Best Friend? Failure," *Fortune Small Business*, April 2007.

[325] Rabbi Menachem M. Schneerson, *Hayom Yom* (Brooklyn, NY: Kehot Publications Society, 1988), Sivan 25.

[326] Rosa Parks, answers to students' written questions, Scholastic, January-February 1997. http://teacher.scholastic.com/rosa/arrested.htm.

[327] Rabbi Menachem M. Schneerson, *Hayom Yom* (Brooklyn, NY: Kehot Publications Society, 1988), Adar Sheni 8.

[328] Carol Loomis, "Dinosaurs?" *Fortune*, May 3, 1993.

[329] Rabbi Menachem M. Schneerson, *Likutei Sichot* (Brooklyn, NY: Kehot Publications Society, 1962), vol. 20, 528.

Chapter 10

[330] Kings 3:16-27.

[331] Leviticus 19:18.

[332] Shabbat 31a.

[333] Pirkei Avot 1:14.

[334] Rabbi S.Y. Zevin, *A Treasury of Chassidic Tales* (Brooklyn: Mesorah Publications, 1980), 322.

[335] Welch, John F., *Jack: Straight from the Gut.* (New York: Warner Books, 2001), 128.

[336] William J. Holstein, "The View's Still Great From the Corner Office," *New York Times*, May 8, 2005.

[337] Final Earnings Report, General Electric Corp., 2001.

[338] Timothy O'Brien, "The Friendly Merger Banker," *New York Times*, June 23, 1999.

[339] "A Mess of a Merger," *Newsweek*, January 25, 2008.

[340] Ibid.

[341] "A Deal for the History Books," *Newsweek*, December 11, 2000.

[342] http://forum.ebaumsworld.com/showthread.php?t=227972.

[343] Genesis 11:1-9.

[344] ECA International, *Trends in Managing Mobility 2007*, January 2007: http://www.eca-international.com.

[345] http://www.sfcg.org.

[346] Judges 11:1-33.

[347] Psalms 119:98.

[348] Geert Hofstede, *Cultures and Organizations.*

[349] Thomas D. Zweifel, *Democratic Deficit? Intitutions and Regulation in the European Union, Switzerland and the United States.* (Lanham, MD: Lexington Books, 2002).

[350] Francine Parnes, "For Flight Attendants, Stress Comes With the Job," *New York Times*, August 12, 2003.

[351] Ibid.

[352] Thomas Burke, ed., *Einstein: A Portrait* (Des Moines IA: Oxmoor House, 1984), 44.

[353] Michael Jürgs, "Singen mit dem Feind [Singing With the Enemy]", *Der Spiegel*, November 3, 2003; based on Michael Jürgs, *Der Kleine Frieden im Grossen Krieg [The Small Peace in the Great War]* (Munich: Bertelsmann, 2003).

[354] Ibid.

[355] Brian S. Moskal, "Running With the Bulls," *Industry Week*, January 8, 1996.

[356] Ibid.

[357] Yevamot 65B; See also Avot D'Rab Natan 12:4 and Rashi on Moshe Rabbeinu 20:29. See also Menachem M. Schneerson, *Mind Over Matter: Teachings of the Lubavitcher Rebbe on Science, Technology and Medicine,* ed. Joseph Ginsburg and Herman Branover (Jerusalem: Shamir 2003), lvi.

[358] Feisal Hussein and Chaim Weitzmann, Joint Arab-Jewish agreement on Jewish Home-land, January 3, 1919.

[359] Walter Laqueur and Barry Rubin, *The Israel-Arab Reader* (New York: Penguin, 2001), 19.

[360] Orly Halpern, "Moroccon king's Jewish advisor fights for the Palestinian cause. 'It makes me a full Jew'," *Jerusalem Post*, May 31, 2006.

[361] W.H. Murray, *The Scottish Himalayan Expedition* (London: J.M. Dent & Sons Ltd., 1951), 206.

Appendix

[362] Encyclopedia Talmudit. Ed. Rabbi Shlomo Yosef Zevin (Jerusalem: Talmudic Ency-clopedia Publ. Ltd.) Vol. 3, 357.

Appendix

The Ten Commandments
(Exodus 20:1-14)

God spoke all these commandments, saying: [1] I am Hashem, your God, Who delivered you from the land of Egypt, from the house of slavery. [2] You shall not recognize the gods of others before My presence. You shall not make yourself a carved image nor any likeness of that which is in the heavens above, or of that which is on the earth below, or of that which is in the water beneath the earth. You shall not prostrate yourself to them nor shall you worship them; for I am Hashem, your God—a jealous God, remembering the sins of fathers upon children, to the third and fourth generations of My enemies, but showing kindness for thousands of generations to those who love Me and who keep My commandments. [3] You shall not take the Name of Hashem, your God, in a vain oath. [4] Remember the Sabbath day to sanctify it. Six days you are to work and accomplish all your tasks. But the seventh day is Sabbath to Hashem, your God; you may not do any work – you, your son, your daughter, your manservant, your maidservant, your animal, and the convert within your gates—for in six days Hashem made the heavens, the earth, the sea and all that is in them, and He rested on the seventh day. Therefore, Hashem blessed the Sabbath day and sanctified it. [5] Honor your father and mother so that your days may be lengthened upon the land which Hashem, your God, gives you. [6] You shall not kill. [7] You shall not commit adultery. [8] You shall not steal. [9] You shall not bear false witness against your neighbor. [10] You shall not covet your neighbor's house. You shall not covet your neighbor's wife, nor his manservant, nor his maidservant, nor his bull, nor his donkey, nor anything that is your neighbor's.

The Seven Universal Laws of Noah

The Laws of Noah, also known as the Noahide Laws, are seven moral imperatives which, according to the Talmud, were given by God to Noah as a binding moral code for all humankind (Genesis 9:4-6). According to Judaism, any non-Jew who lives according to these laws is regarded as a Gentile who has a place in the world to come.

1. Prohibition of idolatry: You shall not make for yourself an idol.
2. Prohibition of murder: You shall not murder.
3. Prohibition of theft: You shall not steal.
4. Prohibition of promiscuity: You shall not commit adultery.
5. Prohibition of blasphemy: You shall not blaspheme.
6. Prohibition of cruelty to animals: Do not eat the flesh of a living animal.
7. Requirement to have just laws: You shall set up an effective government to police the preceding six laws.

In addition, "there are those who say that the sons of Noah are also commanded to give to charity."[362]

The Thirteen Principles of Faith

When the twelfth-century rabbi, physician, philosopher, and global citizen Maimonides proposed the thirteen principles of faith, they at first stirred controversy and then were ignored for several centuries. But eventually they became Judaism's most widely accepted statement of belief:

1. I believe with perfect faith that God is the Creator and Ruler of all things. He alone has made, does make, and will make all things.
2. I believe with perfect faith that God is One. There is no unity that is in any way like His. He alone is our God. He was, He is, and He will be.

3. I believe with perfect faith that God does not have a body. Physical concepts do not apply to Him. There is nothing whatsoever that resembles Him at all.

4. I believe with perfect faith that God is first and last.

5. I believe with perfect faith that it is only proper to pray to God. One may not pray to anyone or anything else.

6. I believe with perfect faith that all the words of the prophets are true.

7. I believe with perfect faith that the prophecy of Moses is absolutely true. He was the chief of all prophets, both before and after Him.

8. I believe with perfect faith that the entire Torah that we now have is that which was given to Moses.

9. I believe with perfect faith that this Torah will not be changed, and that there will never be another given by God.

10. I believe with perfect faith that God knows all of man's deeds and thoughts. It is thus written (Psalm 33:15), "He has molded every heart together, He understands what each one does."

11. I believe with perfect faith that God rewards those who keep His commandments, and punishes those who transgress Him.

12. I believe with perfect faith in the coming of the Messiah. How long it takes, I will await His coming every day.

13. I believe with perfect faith that the dead will be brought back to life when God wills it to happen.

Further Reading

Alter, Robert. 2004. *The Five Books of Moses*. New York: W.W. Norton.

Argyris, Chris. 1991. Teaching Smart People How to Learn. *Harvard Business Review*, May-June: 99-109.

Bennis, Warren G. and Burt Nanus. 1985. *Leaders: The Strategies for Taking Charge*. New York: Harper & Row.

Berne, Eric. [1964] 2004. *Games People Play: The Basic Handbook of Transactional Analysis*. New York: Random House.

Bonder, Nilton. 1999. *Yiddishe Kop: Creative Problem Solving in Jewish Learning, Lore and Humor*. Halifax (Canada): Shambhala.

Branch, Taylor. 1989. *Parting the Waters: America in the King Years, 1954-63*. New York: Simon & Schuster.

Brands, H.W. 1999. *Masters of Enterprise: Giants of American Business from John Jacob Astor and J.P. Morgan to Bill Gates and Oprah Winfrey*. New York: Free Press.

Buber, Martin. [1957] 1970. *I and Thou*. New York: Charles Scribner's Sons.

_____. 1963. *The Way of Man: According to the Teachings of Hadisism*. Secaucus NJ: The Citadel Press.

_____. 1982. *Das Problem des Menschen*. Heidelberg: Lambert Schneider.

Collins, Jim. 2001. *Good to Great*. New York: HarperBusiness.

Covey, Stephen R. 1991. *Principle-Centered Leadership*. New York: Summit Books.

Drucker, Peter F. 1988. The Coming of the New Organization. *Harvard Business Review*, January-February: 45-53.

_____. 1999. Managing Oneself. *Harvard Business Review*, March-April: 65-74.

_____. 2001. *The Essential Drucker*. New York: HarperBusiness.

Erhard, Werner, Michael C. Jensen and Steve Zaffron. 2007. Integrity: a Positive Model that Incorporates the Normative Phenomena of Morality, Ethics and Legality. Harvard NOM Working Paper No. 06-11.

Flaherty, James. 1999. *Coaching: Evoking Excellence in Others*. Boston: Butterworth-Heinemann.

Flores, Fernando and Terry Winograd. 1986. Understanding Computers and Cognition. Norwood, NJ: Ablex Publishing Corporation.

Gandhi, Mohandas K. [1927] 1992. *An Autobiography, Or The Story of My Experiments with Truth*. Ahmedabad (India): The Navajivan Trust.

Ginsburgh, Yitzchak. 1995. *The Dynamic Corporation: Involvement, Quality, and Flow*. Rechovot, Israel: Gal Einai Publications.

_____. 2001. *Awakening the Spark Within*. Jerusalem: Linda Pinsky Publications.

Goldberg, Florian and Michael Haensch. 2004. *Auf Welche Gipfel Wollen Sie?* Berlin: Lardon Media AG.

Goldin, Hyman, ed. and trans. 1962. *Ethics of the Fathers*. New York: Hebrew Publishing Company.

Goleman, Daniel. 1995. *Emotional Intelligence*. New York: Bantam Books.

_____. 2004. What Makes a Leader? *Harvard Business Review*, January: 82-91.

Goodwin, Doris Kearns. 2006. *Team of Rivals: The Political Genius of Abraham Lincoln*. New York: Simon & Schuster.

Goss, Tracy, Richard Pascale and Anthony Athos. 1993. The Reinvention Roller Coaster: Risking the Present for a Powerful Future. *Harvard Business Review* Reprint #93603.

HaLevi, Aharon. [13th c. C.E.] 1958. *Sefer ha-Chinuch* [Book of Education]. Berlin: Eshkol Publishing.

Hamel, Gary. 1996. Strategy as Revolution. *Harvard Business Review*, July-August: 69-82.

_____ and C.K. Prahalad. 1989. Strategic Intent. *Harvard Business Review*, May-June: 63-76.

Handy, Charles. 1995. Trust and the Virtual Organization. *Harvard Business Review*, May-June: 40-50.

Hargrove, Robert. 2002. *Masterful Coaching*. San Francisco: Jossey-Bass/Pfeiffer.

Heidegger, Martin. 1968. *What Is Called Thinking?* J. Glenn Gray, trans. New York: Harper & Row.

Heschel, Abraham J. [1951] 2005. *The Sabbath*. New York: Farrar Straus Giroux.

Hofstede, Geert. 2001. *Culture's Consequences: Comparing Values, Behaviors, Institutions and Organizations Across Nations* (2nd ed.). Thousand Oaks, CA: Sage Publications.

Jackson, Phil. 1995. *Sacred Hoops: Spiritual Lessons of a Hardwood Warrior*. New York: Hyperion.

Jacobson, Simon. 2004. *Toward a Meaningful Life, New Edition: The Wisdom of the Rebbe Menachem Mendel Schneerson*. New York: Harper Paperbacks.

Kabat-Zinn, Jon. 2005. *Wherever You Go, There You Are: Mindfulness Meditation in Everyday Life*. New York: Hyperion.

Katzenbach, J.R. and D.K. Smith. 1993. *The Wisdom of Teams: Creating the High-Performance Organization*. Cambridge, MA: Harvard Business School Press.

Kotter, John P. 1990. *A Force for Change: How Leadership Differs from Management*. New York: Free Press.

_____ and James K. Leahy. 1993. Changing the Culture at British Airways. Harvard Business School Case #9-419-009.

Liadi, Schneur Zalman. 2000. *Tanya*. Brooklyn, NY: Kehot Publication Society.

Machiavelli, Niccoló. 1961. *The Prince*. Luigi Ricci, trans. London: Penguin Classics.

Manchester, William. 1983. *The Last Lion: Winston Spencer Churchill, Visions of Glory 1874–1932*. New York: Dell Publishing.

_____. 1989. *The Last Lion: Winston Spencer Churchill, Alone 1932-1940*. New York: Dell Publishing.

Mandela, Nelson R. 1994. *Long Walk to Freedom*. Boston: Little, Brown and Company.

Matt, Daniel Chanan, ed. 2002. *Zohar: Annotated & Explained*. Woodstock, VT: Skylight Paths Publishing.

_____ trans. 2003/2005. *The Zohar: Pritzker Edition*, vols. 1, 2, 3. Palo Alto, CA: Stanford University Press.

Maturana, Humberto and Francisco Varela. 1987. *The Tree of Knowledge: The Biological Roots of Human Understanding*. Boston: Shambhala.

Messick, David M. and Max H. Bazerman. 1996. Ethical Leadership and the Psychology of Decision Making. *Sloan Management Review*, Winter: 9-22.

Northouse, Peter G. 1997. *Leadership: Theory and Practice*. Thousand Oaks, CA: Sage.

Orwell, George. 1946. Politics and the English Language. *Horizon*. .

Perlow, Leslie A. 2003. *When You Say Yes But Mean No: How Silencing Conflict Wrecks Relationships and Companies...and What You Can Do About It*. New York: Crown Business.

Prahalad, C.K. 2004. *The Fortune at the Bottom of the Pyramid*. Philadelphia: Wharton School Publishing.

_____ and Kenneth Lieberthal. 1998. The End of Corporate Imperialism. *Harvard Business Review*, July-August: 69-79.

Rahman, Anisur. 1993. *People's Self-Development: Perspectives on Participatory Action Research*. London: Zed Books.

Raskin, Aaron. 2003. *Letters of Light: A Mystical Journey Through the Hebrew Alphabet*. Brooklyn, NY: Sichot in English.

Sathe, Vijay. 1985. How to Decipher and Change Organizational Culture. In Ralph H. Kilman, Mary J. Saxton, and Roy Serpa, eds., *Gaining Control of the Corporate Culture* (pp. 230-261). San Francisco: Jossey-Bass.

Scherman, Nosson (ed.). 1998. *The Chumash*, Stone Edition. Brooklyn, NY: Mesorah Publications.

_____ 2001. *The Tanach,* Stone Edition. Brooklyn, NY: Mesorah Publications.

Scherr, Allan L. 2005. Managing for Breakthroughs in Productivity. Barbados Group Working Paper No. 1-05.

Schneerson, Menachem M. 1995. *Hayom Yom*. Brooklyn, NY: Kehot Publication Society.

_____ 1964. *Likutei Sichot. An Anthology of Talks*. New York: Kehot Publication Society.

Schochet, Jacob Immanuel. 1988. *Mystical Concepts in Chassidism*. Brooklyn: Kehot Publication Society.

Schulz von Thun, Friedemann. 1981. *Miteinander Reden: Störungen und Klärungen: Psychologie der zwischenmenschlichen Kommunikation*. Hamburg: Rowohlt.

Senge, Peter. 1990. The Leader's New Work: Building Learning Organizations. *Sloan Management Review*, Fall: Reprint #3211.

Solomon, Robert C. and Fernando Flores. 2001. *Building Trust: In Business, Politics, Relationships, and Life*. Oxford, England: Oxford University Press.

Spang, Peter. 1998. *Zennis: An Innovative Approach to Changing Your Mind, Your Play, and Your Entire Tennis Experience*. New York: Perigee Trade.

Steinsaltz, Adin. 2006. *Essential Talmud*. New York: Basic Books.

Stogdill, R.M. 1974. *Handbook of Leadership: A Survey of Theory and Research*. New York: Free Press.

Sun Tzu. [500 BCE] 1963. *The Art of War*. Samuel B. Griffith, trans. London: Oxford University Press.

The Hunger Project. 1996. Unleashing the Human Spirit: Principles and Methodology of The Hunger Project.

Tichy, Noel M., Ram Charan and Lawrence A. Bossidy. 1995. The CEO As Coach: An Interview with AlliedSignal's Lawrence A. Bossidy. *Harvard Business Review*, April: 69-78.

Twist, Lynne. 2003. *The Soul of Money: Transforming Your Relationship with Money and Life*. New York: W.W. Norton.

Varela, Francisco. 1999. *Ethical Know-How: Action, Wisdom and Cognition*. Palo Alto, CA: Stanford University Press.

Von Foerster, Heinz. 2003. *Understanding Understanding: Essays on Cybernetics and Cognition*. New York: Springer Verlag.

Watzlawick, Paul. 1984. *Invented Reality: How Do We Know What We Believe We Know? (Contributions to constructivism)*. New York: W.W. Norton.

Weber, Max. 1946, 1958. Bureaucracy. In H. H. Gerth and C. Wright Mills, eds. *From Max Weber: Essays in Sociology* (pp. 196-244). Oxford, England: Oxford University Press.

Weinstein, Simcha. 2006. *Up, Up, and Oy Vey! How Jewish History, Culture and Values Shaped the Comic Book Superhero*. Baltimore MD: Leviathan Press.

Wineberg, Yosef, Sholom Wineberg and Levi Wineberg. 1998. *Lessons in Tanya*. Brooklyn, NY: Merkos L'Inyonei Chinuch.

Wouk, Herman. 1992. *This Is My God*. Lebanon, IN: Back Bay Books.

Zaleznik, Abraham. 1992. Managers and Leaders, Are They Different? *Harvard Business Review*, March-April: 126-138.

Zweifel, Thomas D. 2002. *Democratic Deficit? Institutions and Regulation in the European Union, Switzerland and the United States*. Lanham, MD: Lexington Books.

_____. 2003. *Communicate or Die: Getting Results Through Speaking and Listening*. New York: SelectBooks.

_____. 2003. *Culture Clash: Managing the Global High-Performance Team*. New York: SelectBooks.

_____. 2005. *International Organizations and Democracy: Accountability, Politics, and Power*. Boulder, CO: Lynne Rienner Publishers.

Index

The Authors

Thomas D. Zweifel has been coaching senior managers in Fortune 500 companies and startups, governments and UN agencies, NGOs and the military since 1984, helping them to build leadership competencies in the action of producing breakthrough results. He is the CEO of Swiss Consulting Group, which was awarded the 1998 "Fast Company" title by Fast Company magazine, and has taught leadership at Columbia University and business schools in Australia, Israel, Switzerland, and the United States since 2000. He is the author of five books, including *Communicate or Die* (SelectBooks, 2003), *Culture Clash* (SelectBooks, 2003), and *International Organizations: Accountability, Politics, and Power* (Lynne Rienner, 2005).

Born in Paris, Dr. Zweifel was educated in Switzerland, Germany, and the United States. His parents named him Thomas and wanted to baptize him, but his great-grandmother's threat to disinherit them if they went ahead and if the boy didn't get at least a Jewish middle name made them change their minds. He received the middle name David, after his great-grandfather, Dr. David Strauss, a Zurich rabbi who had attended the first Zionist Congress in 1897 in Basel.

Dr. Zweifel and his books have been featured on ABC, CNN, NY1 and Bloomberg TV. As a Vistage Speaker and a member of the International Speakers Bureau (www.internationalspeakers.com), he frequently gives global leadership keynotes to CEOs and senior managers, and serves on the boards of several companies and organizations. In 1996 he realized his dream of breaking three hours in the New York City marathon and in 1997 was cited as "first finisher among CEOs who ran the New York City marathon" in the Wall Street Journal.

Aaron L. Raskin comes from a long lineage of rabbis and community leaders. All his uncles are rabbis; his grandfather Rabbi Jacob J.

Hecht, the official interpreter for the Lubavitcher Rebbe Menachem M. Schneerson, served on the Ethics Committees in the administrations of President George H.W. Bush and New York Governor Mario Cuomo.

Born in Brooklyn, New York, Rabbi Raskin was educated at the United Lubavitcher Yeshiva and the Rabbinical College of America and received his ordination at Tomchie Timimim Lubavitch in Brooklyn. While serving as *shliach* (emissary) of the Lubavitcher Rebbe in Great Britain, he visited the House of Lords as a representative on Jewish leadership. As the *shliach* of the Lubavitcher Rebbe to Downtown Brooklyn, and as founder and spiritual leader of Congregation B'nai Avraham, the only Orthodox synagogue in Brooklyn Heights, he inspires his constituents, many of whom are prominent business and/or community leaders, with ethics and spiritual guidance.

Rabbi Raskin has published a series of 200 audiotapes on topics ranging from the Kabbalah to anger management, stress, women in Judaism, and medical ethics. His work has been covered by *The New York Times*, *Daily News*, *Jewish Week*, *Jewish Press*, *Jerusalem Post*, 1010 WINS, NY1, ABC and CBS. Through his 1990s radio talk show *The Spirit of the Law* (on the *Forward*'s radio station WEVD, now ESPN) about secular and Jewish law, he became known as The Judges' Rabbi. He is the author of *Letters of Light* (Sichot In English, 2003) on the essence of the Hebrew alphabet. He, his wife Shternie (who initiated the first Brooklyn Heights mikvah and founded a Jewish preschool program), and their five children live in Brooklyn Heights.

Other Books

Letters of Light: A Mystical Journey Through the Hebrew Alphabet
By Rabbi Aaron L. Raskin. (Sichot in English)

"I warmly recommend Rabbi Raskin's book on the Hebrew alphabet; it reflects our people's passion for learning."
—ELIE WIESEL

Communicate or Die: Getting Results Through Speaking and Listening
By Thomas D. Zweifel. (SelectBooks)

"Everybody should read this book. You can substitute one evening of entertainment and make a difference in your life and work for years to come."
—ALI VELSHI, Anchor, CNN

Culture Clash: Managing the Global High-Performance Team
By Thomas D. Zweifel. (SelectBooks)

"I just wish *Culture Clash* had been available at the start of my personal globalisation, it would have saved me a lot of time and pain. I would recommend this book as essential reading for any international manager."
—DR. MARTIN CROSS, CEO, Novartis-Australia

Democratic Deficit? Institutions and Regulation in the European Union, Switzerland and the United States
By Thomas D. Zweifel. (Lexington Books)

"Thomas Zweifel's pathbreaking book delivers a compelling empirical analysis of transparency and accountability in the European Union. A must-read."
—ANDREW MORAVCSIK, Princeton University and *Newsweek*

International Organizations and Democracy: Accountability,
Politics and Power
By Thomas D. Zweifel. (Lynne Rienner Publishers)

"Zweifel's accessible book sets the stage for an informed debate on
the place of 'We, The People' in global governance."
—SHEPARD FORMAN, Center on International Cooperation,
New York University

Forthcoming:

Written by the Hand of God
By Rabbi Aaron L. Raskin. (Sichot in English)

Coaching Leaders to Meet the Future:
12 Steps to Unleash People Power and Performance
By Thomas D. Zweifel. (SelectBooks)

Strategy-In-Action: Marrying People, Planning and Performance
By Thomas D. Zweifel and Edward J. Borey. (SelectBooks)

Resources For Leaders

If you are interested in applying *The Rabbi and the CEO* to your organization, contact Rabbi Aaron Raskin (ravraskin@aol.com) or Thomas D. Zweifel (tdz@swissconsultinggroup.com or tdz2@columbia.edu), and/or visit www.swissconsultinggroup.com for leadership books, tools, workshops, and custom-designed processes that help leaders produce breakthroughs results.

The 10 Commandments for 21st-Century Leaders

An action-packed, multi-disciplinary half-day or one-day workshop that puts into practice the timeless and cutting-edge leadership principles and practices from *The Rabbi and the CEO*. Participants get winning insights and tools for lasting success.

Leadership-In-Action

A two-day workshop/process that systematically develops high-potential leaders and fills leadership gaps in your organization. Challenges participants to live the future in the day-to-day and to meet breakthrough goals using 100-day leadership projects.

Strategy-In-Action

A seven-step dynamic strategy process. Interviews lead to a "whitepaper" and a shared understanding; a two-day workshop aligns your management team around a bold business challenge and an elegant vision/strategy framework; and low-risk/low-cost pilots integrate the future with the present, provide feedback to the strategy, and yield quick wins.

Coaching-In-Action

A six-to-twelve month process tailored to executives (or leadership teams) that fosters breakthroughs in leadership ability by meeting a business and/or leadership challenge.

Communicate or Die

A two-day workshop that gives leaders tools for effective speaking and masterful listening that make the difference between good and great teams and/or organizations.

Culture Clash

A two-day workshop that prepares leaders to avoid costly mistakes when working with or in other cultures (e.g., in virtual teams and/or outsourcing), enabling them to get the job done while respecting local values and customs.